Acknowledgements

My thanks go to those senior executives and their teams who worked with me and took the bold step to adopt this system as the means to direct their operations to world class performance. In no small way they contributed to the content of this guide book.

Also to those who patiently reviewed drafts of this guide and provided improvements, especially a good friend, Ted Richman, who was instrumental in the use of "Gems" for clearly identifying key learning areas; to my wife Mary Anne for patiently reading each chapter over and over again and providing suggested improvements in simplicity and clarity, to Lea Pavente who proofed all the chapters without compensation just because she is good at it and wanted to help; and to the countless clients and leaders who, through the years openly shared their issues, challenges, and views. Finally, my heartfelt thanks go to my best friend and brother, Peter Palermo II, for all his advice and counsel through the consulting years and the many years before that.

Copyright © 2003 The Strategic Triangle, Inc.
Cover design and illustration copyright © 2003 Bob Wright Creative Group, Inc.
International Standard Book Number (ISBN) 0-9744508-0-4
Printed in the U.S.A.
1st Printing

Do The <u>Right</u> Things ... Right!

It Is That Simple!

Warning: This is not a "feel good" book laced with pithy slogans or vague ideas! Rather, it is a full system that provides a practical guide, a tool kit, and a direct means of performance improvement that current leaders, aspiring leaders, board members, investors and open-minded individuals in <u>any</u> type of organization can put into profitable practice.

This system will provide a comfortable return to proven, simple, logical basics, and provides a road map to leadership that can deliver world class performance. It will be invaluable to emerging, new, and/or open-minded veteran managers who accept that:

"It is what you learn after you know it all, that counts."

In many ways, adoption of this full system is to adopt a new culture where facts and measures are all important. Where:

- Customers, employees, and stakeholders are listened to, and are treated with equal respect.
- Identified: "Vital Few" areas for improvement are given appropriate focused attention.
- Adherence to values and mission is respected.
- Over and over again, factual understanding of the current state is sought.
- Bold desired states are committed to.
- Closing the gap to move toward a bold, defined vision of the future is all important.

Applying the concepts in this book will be akin to your first time on a bicycle. You may wobble and even fall. Support by a veteran coach, or a seasoned practitioner will be like having training wheels and as such is most desirable. The system can be learned and put into use without coaching as long as a page-by-page discipline is applied to the elements in each of the chapters in this guidebook. Practice and perseverance are necessary with or without a coach.

Guidebook Objectives:

Until now, the benefits of this system and its elements have only been available through a personal consulting agreement with experts in the Strategic Triangle Inc. The single, overarching objective of this book is to put the system within reach of all who aspire to greatness and world-class performance. Succinctly stated, the intent is to inform all who seek success, who face daily challenges, who dare to be great, that there is a way…a rather simple, effective, and proven way through the swamp that now threatens all action-oriented leaders.

About The Organization of This Text:

The book is organized in a manner that allows reading from cover to cover, diving into a specific topic, or using it as a reference as specific challenges arise. In order to have each chapter stand-alone, there is some minimal, but necessary repetition. Graphics and symbols are liberally used in an attempt to both make the concepts and approaches clear, and to assist in fixing them in the reader's memory. All of the symbols used in the text have specific meanings. The "how-to" forms are intended to encourage the reader to jump in and try the approach being featured. The following is a description of some of the symbols used early in the text:

The gemstones identify an earned piece of wisdom that is worth pondering and internalizing. This facilitates skimming to find or return to important points.

 The bulls-eye is the symbol for a Directive Mission

The owl is the symbol for a guiding set of Organizational Shared Values

The tree diagram is the symbol for a complex subject broken into bite-sized pieces

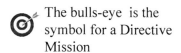 The crystal ball is the symbol for a Prescriptive Vision

 The star is the symbol for an element in which the organization should take pride

 The ball is the symbol for a "vital few" key drivers needing improvement

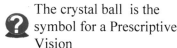

The fully decorated tree is a symbol for the Success Tree® System. Note on and around tree are the symbols for the Directive Mission The Prescriptive Vision Organizational Shared Values and the Key Drivers of Customer Satisfaction, Employee Motivation and Financial Performance

Table of Contents

Continued on next page

Table of Contents (Continued)

Continued on next page

Table of Contents (Continued)

Chapter 12. High Performance Assessment™

Appendix A. The Gem Collection

Appendix B . A List of Exhibits

Introduction

The Success Tree® System

A Leader's Guide for Doing the <u>Right</u> Things...Right

"Experience after experience indicates that there is a great need for a simple, logical, structured, balanced management system. The customers benefit from it, the employees want it, and the financial health of an organization depends on it."

R.C. Palermo

Introduction

During a successful 30-year corporate career and a 10-year consulting and executive coaching career, I have been fortunate to come in contact with many talented, and some not-so-talented organizational leaders. Valuable lessons were acquired from intense interactions with public, private, non-profit, academic, and other diverse organizations. Early on in my career, I studied my own managers, primarily to determine how to accelerate my advance up the corporate ladder. Later, as I interacted with, and ultimately coached other executives, experiences reinforced my belief that most successful leaders evidence some sort of style or philosophy that is, in effect, a management system. Although most did not recognize this as a system, it basically drove how they made decisions, set priorities, allocated resources, established goals, attacked problems, interacted with customers, employees, financial advisors, and managed to guide an organization.

Some of these management systems are most appropriately labeled "financial/reactive." Here, the leader single-mindedly drives for financial results and only reacts to issues that might impact financial results. The focus here is always to get back on the desired financial track.

Likewise, other leaders seem to employ a management system that might be called "obsessive/reactive." These leaders concentrate almost exclusively on a specific obsession like market share, cost reduction, or technology superiority. In the legal, medical, accounting, and other professions, the maintenance of core competencies are naturally obsessive focal points. In a scholastic setting, the obsession might be academic reputation or ranking. In each obsessive case, all other facets, factors, issues, or topics are subservient to the obsession. Other matters are dealt with only if they seemed to interfere with or negatively impact the selected obsession. Otherwise, non-obsessive issues are sacrificed, given sub-optimal attention or ignored altogether.

Most often, it appeared that the management system in question was stored in the mind of the leader, who administers it piecemeal and periodically from on high. No leader ever volunteered, "This is my management system. These are the steps I use to develop and lead a world-class organization."

In some cases, it was difficult to discern if there was <u>any</u> management system consistently applied by its leaders. It was clear from the poor results they achieved that they really would benefit from having a system, but the "fire-drill" chaos that was a daily happening showed that an effective system was missing. In truth, the "fire-drill" chaos <u>was</u> the management system in these cases!

Note that, throughout this book, for convenience I use the term "organization" to mean any entity for which a leader is accountable. It can be a company, a university, an agency, a department, a team, etc. When the term "leader" is used, it can mean a Chief Executive Officer, Chief Operating Officer, Chief Financial Officer, Director, Dean, President, or General Manager. It can apply to those holding such titles as Department Head, Business Unit Head, or Project Manager. This guide book will be useful to all these leaders or aspiring leaders:

- Senior leaders who understand that "it is what you learn after you know it all that counts" and have a mind open to new approaches and a disposition willing to entertain change.
- New leaders who eventually aspire to senior positions
- Emerging leaders who are making the transition from individual contributors

 If you are comfortable being a manager who does not have an effective, defined high performance management system in place, and you are satisfied with the status quo, put this guide down, but keep it handy. When unacceptable performance surfaces and it inevitably will, you will hopefully come to realize that you and your organization need such a system.

With some risk of reader alienation, the term "customer" is often used in the text to connote those who use, or are served by, the outputs of an organization. This referenced risk has manifested itself in the past by a few semantically correct clients who have stated, "We don't have customers, we have clients." In some organizations those who are served are called clients, consumers, students, voters, citizens, or patients. You get the point. Customers can be outside the enterprise, or they can also be inside the organization in groups that are served by the organization in question. For example, the Human Resource department's customers are the managers and people within the organization.

Likewise, the term "employee" is used to refer to the people in the organization who do the work. Here too, some would object to having their people referred to as "employees." For a few managers, the term "employees" seems to connote "those who are used." In some organizations, those who do the work are called workers, professors, teachers, individual contributors, associates, people, board members, associates, staff, et al. I have to pick a generally applicable term and I settled on "employee."

Finally, I use the term "stakeholder" to depict people who are financially impacted by, are interested in, or have an investment in the subject organization. These could be donors, grantors, stockholders, investors, or the leaders of a parent organization.

All within an organization, and all constituencies served by the organization, will benefit from the application of a system that ensures that <u>everyone</u> in the organization can comfortably and regularly select the "right things to do" and then "do them right."

An often asked question is: "Yes, but which one of these three constituencies is the most important? Surely it's the financial constituent!"

The three constituencies (customers, employees, financials) are as the legs of a three-legged stool. If you are standing on it, and the three legs are supporting you, which leg is the most important? If one is damaged, do you not have to fix it? Do you not ensure that the other two are not damaged by your fix? No! All are <u>equally</u> vital to the success of an operation!

Doing the Right Things

The first half of the Success Tree® System involves selecting the "right things to do." It requires:

- Prioritizing issues or opportunities that are totally consistent with an agreed, descriptive mission and a prescriptive vision for the organization. (Are we efficiently and effectively on course?)
- Focusing on the fact-based, prioritized needs of the customers, the employees, and the stakeholders who finance or fund the organization. (Are we working on improvements that our three constituencies are telling us are vital to their satisfaction or interests?)
- Allocating, arranging or acquiring needed resources (Are we sure that we have got the means to get needed results?).
- Above all, always behaving in a manner that is consistent with agreed organizational values.

Ultimately, "doing the right things" must include checking an organization's overall performance by measuring it against agreed standards that define "world-classness." This must be accomplished by utilizing an easy-to-use "organizational report card" that assesses the state of the organization and identifies areas that are most in need of improvement. This must include an assessment of customer, employee and financial performance. With this assessment in hand, selected "vital few" issue areas can be isolated for outstanding performance improvement.

Doing Things Right

The second half of the comprehensive Success Tree® System referred to in the prior page is termed "doing things right." This means clearly assigning selected "right things" to empowered individuals and/or teams for concentrated effort and efficient, effective action. Simply put it means:

- Developing measures so facts can dominate current status discussions. Other than in dire emergencies, opinions won't do. (How will we know we are making progress is being made if the challenge is not measured?)

- Achieving better results, by changing the way things are done. Merely hoping for better results in the future won't cut it. All results, good and bad, are the outcomes of the way things are done. (If we do things in the same way as in the past, why should anyone expect better results?)

- Advocating and implementing changes in how things must be done in the future must first start with a clear understanding of how things are really done today. Only then will the "good" be preserved and the "bad" replaced. (How can a path to a desired destination be plotted without knowing where the starting point of the journey is?)

- Detailed planning is needed. Improvement efforts must be adequately staffed and supported. Under-resourced teams are not acceptable. If we run out of resources, we have to adjust to continue our focus on the "vital few."

- Monitoring to determine if the desired change in process actually occurred, and that the needed results have been achieved. If not, we learn from the experience and go at it again.

Without the "doing things right" part of the management system, time and precious resources can be wasted, and sub-optimal performance is achieved. A wonderful former Xerox CEO, board chair, and personal mentor, David T. Kearns, galvanized me into action when he advised me that:

 "Anyone can manage with a bag of gold. It takes a good leader to manage with limited resources. Remember that <u>doing the wrong things right is as bad as doing the right things wrong</u>." History shows, over and over again, that without leaders who employ and deploy a system for "finding the right things and then doing them right," the long term future–and even survival–of any organization is continually in jeopardy!

The overall messages are very clear:

- If you, as an investor discover that an organization in which you have a vested interest is led by individuals who do not demonstrate by their words <u>and</u> deeds that they have a disciplined approach for selecting the right things to do, and then for insuring that these things are done right, you should immediately take action to change the leadership of the organization. Being unable to do so, or failing to do so, you should divest and move to a new interest area! It will avoid the pain of inevitable failure.

- If you are a manager in such an organization, you are well advised to work with a sense of urgency to change the organization. Failing to do so, you would do well to find a different career opportunity!

Over time, an organization that is managed in a haphazard way will find itself in an organizational death spiral characterized by:

- **Customers who are not delighted go elsewhere and readily share their negative perceptions and experiences with all who will listen.**
- **Sooner or later, financial results suffer greatly.**
- **Then, employees lose heart as they have to endure compensation constraints and or downsizing. The most talented employees seek and find more satisfying work environments elsewhere.**

This inevitable "death spiral" outcome has been demonstrated over and over in experiences in the marketplace. Consider your own experiences: Think of a failed enterprise or organization that you are familiar with. Consider which constituency or constituencies were ignored or alienated, thus precipitating the downfall. I am confident that the satisfaction of one or more of the organizational constituencies (customer, employee, financial) will have been sacrificed to emphasize another of the three constituency's interests. A great leader cannot and will not let this happen. All must be constantly assessed and strengthened.

Think of an organization that you believe delights its customers, has motivated employees, and that has very healthy financial returns. What is the name of that organization? – Notice how few readily come to mind. – Did you name your own organization? – Why not? If you adopt, execute, and internalize the Success Tree® System, it will be your organization that is so honored, by you, your employees, your customers, your alliance partners, and the marketplace.

What is needed to avoid this "death spiral" outcome is a simple, logical, easy-to-execute system that:

- Simultaneously <u>and</u> efficiently addresses the factually determined interests of each of the three constituencies (those who are served, those who do the serving and the financial backers).
- Rigorously sifts through challenges and opportunities to find the "right things to do." These are the ones that are not only aligned to missions, visions, and values, but also will have the maximum positive impact on customer satisfaction, employee motivation, and financial returns.
- Incorporates a simple, universally applicable approach for "doing these right things right."

Further, given the pressures that leaders are under today, a leadership system also has to be capable of dynamic adoption (changing the wheel on a moving car comes to mind). It must be easy-to-monitor, readily deployable throughout an organization, and one that will require only low on-going maintenance. The Success Tree® System is exactly such a system!

The Development of the Success Tree® System

During my 30 year tenure at Xerox Corporation, I was blessed to experience the Xerox boom of the 60's, the corporation's fall during the '70s, the rebirth during the '80s, and the ascension to recognized world-class levels of performance in 1989 with the receipt of the prestigious United States National Quality Award.

While at Xerox in the '70s, I was exposed to and became intrigued by the principles of Dr. W. Edwards Deming and Dr. J. M. Juran. I was only marginally interested in the application of these principles to repeatable manufacturing or other such continuous processes. This was not my area of responsibility or interest. My executive work was concentrated in strategic planning, marketing, and other senior-level executive challenges that were more event-oriented as opposed to the continuous processes that seemed so well fitted to the Deming and Juran approaches. For similar reasons, the recently popular Six Sigma, or Lean Six Sigma intensive quality approaches are not readily applicable to work in the executive suite. What is needed to serve organizational leaders well is a simple, powerful system addressing the specific challenges that all leaders face everywhere, every day.

I was however intrigued by the possibility that an effective <u>Executive</u> Management system might be developed. As an aside, you will note that in this book classic TQM and Six Sigma are not featured, or even mentioned (other than in this section) for two common sense reasons:

- First, too many leaders have wasted too many dollars trying to get a quick, organization wide cookie-cutter "TQM" fix for the challenges of leadership, thus leaving a very bad taste in the leaders' mouths. It was feared that these bad experiences would be erroneously considered synonymous with the Strategic Triangle's Success Tree® System.
- Second, the simple, logical, Success Tree® System is long-lasting and must not be confused with the complex, burdensome, organization-wide revolutions that formal quality or statistical approaches require. These requirements often give such initiative "fad status."

Unique Leadership Challenges

I have always perceived a leader to be akin to a juggler. This term, "juggler," is one that is used in the most positive sense. I consider juggling to be a desirable and necessary leadership skill. A leader must juggle many priorities and issues. Continuing with the juggling metaphor, the following observations are important:

- **The rewards for developing and exhibiting good juggling skills are more balls to juggle. As an individual moves up the career ladder, heavier and bigger balls are added to the challenge.**
- **It seems that few, if any, balls are ever taken away. Eventually, even the best jugglers drop a ball or two. When a major ball is fumbled, the juggler reaches for it, and thus drops a few more.**
- **When this stage is reached, the leader goes from directing to reacting and from initiating to merely coping. Serenity, security, and the comfort of a job well-done become distant memories. A good day is a day that is merely survived.**

Surely there had to be an approach or system that would serve leaders in their executive world of rapid decisions, seemingly endless problems, and multiple opportunities. Surely there had to be a way to make the critical resource allocations that follow each critical organizational decision in a logical and productive manner. There had to be a way to ensure that the resulting decisions were appropriately executed.

By the '80s, I had become a master juggler at Xerox Corporation. Every promotion had entailed additional, serious challenges for this juggler. By the late '80s my Senior Vice President and Corporate Officer level assignments positioned me as a juggler supreme. The loss of control, the need to react daily—if not hourly—to major crises made leadership more and more of a burden. The fun of leading was disappearing.

Therefore, I set about acquiring a complete management system that would allow me to efficiently and effectively regain control by confidently isolating only the "right things" for focused efforts. This had to be a system that would insure that these identified right things were "done right." All other activities and demands of the job would be delayed, deployed to others, or abandoned. The search for a simple, effective management system became an obsession. A literature search revealed that none of the existing systems touted in periodicals and books filled the bill. It soon became clear that I would have to develop my own system.

An initial, rudimentary approach that I developed, tuned, and put to the test in 1985 produced encouraging results even though it really wasn't a complete system. My teams became highly motivated. Internal customers moved from dissatisfaction and approached delight. Employees responded much more positively in simple annual surveys. Major, measurable contributions of the groups to the success of the Firm were logged and openly recognized. Largely as a result of this management approach, the Chief Executive of the firm honored me as the Role Model Manager of the year in 1990. This was the only time the award has ever been given. The award might have more appropriately been given to my system. As an aside, it was disappointing to see that this successful leadership approach was never fully adopted and deployed as a standard by Xerox management. I learned that old habits are difficult to overcome, leading to the development of a simple, effective change management system as will be discussed later in this book.

In March 1993, the urge to take on the new and different challenge of formalizing this executive system for wide-spread sharing became compelling. This led to the commencement of an enjoyable, energizing, and enlightening consulting and executive coaching career that continues to this day.

The primitive approach that had intrigued me in my late years at Xerox has been greatly improved over the ensuing years as I interacted with diverse clients around the world. The Success Tree® System is now tested, widely executed and mature. Its elements have been tested and tuned on the firing line in a multitude of organizations, large and small, legacy and startup, in Europe and in the U.S., public and private, government and non-profit entities have found the system's elements to be clear and logical. More importantly, they are proven to produce remarkably rewarding results in very short time frames.

A salient and underlying feature of the system is its simplicity. This enables the elements of the system to be understood, adopted and executed with remarkable speed. It is especially rewarding to note that many of the time-pressed leaders who had been exposed to the Success Tree® System elements in prior companies, have continued to apply the Success® System approach when they moved on to new, very different companies with new, very different challenges. This is an especially rewarding testimonial to the flexibility and value of the system.

Even now, after all these years and diverse engagements, I still find it exhilarating to share the details of this powerful system with challenged "jugglers" around the world and then see the outstanding results that it delivers. The system is simple, and because of this simplicity it is really tough to pull off. Sounds contradictory, but managers have come to respect elegance and complexity.

I wish that I could sit across the table from each of you, and go back and forth about the system and its application to your specific situation. I wish that we could develop a coaching relationship such that together we could fully apply the system, and have you gain the proficiency and confidence that will make it a basic part of your leadership philosophy and instincts. Alas, that is not possible.

Yet, I feel a strong need to share this system with thousands, not hundreds. So, through the pages of this book, all who seek success, who face the daily challenges of increasing size and complexity, all those who dare to be great, can become aware that there is a way…a simple, effective, and proven way through the maze.

This book is intended to guide each of you current and emerging "jugglers," to efficiently and effectively find the "right things" for your area of responsibility, and see that they are "done right."

 With this simple system in place, control will be regained and retained, allowing a leader to appropriately serve customers, motivate employees, and achieve needed financial performance, all in a most efficient and effective manner! This, after all, can be the only true definition of success no matter what the endeavor!

An emphasis has been placed on simplicity and logic throughout this book. Yet, no powerful or needed idea, process, or approach has been compromised. In our challenging, complex and dynamic world, simplicity is an absolute necessity.

Note this pitch for simplicity from a most respected business guru.

"An overload of information, that is, anything much beyond what is truly needed, leads to information blackout. It does not enrich, but impoverishes. The fewer data needed, the better the information."
                                                                                    Peter F. Drucker

Do The <u>Right</u> Things ... Right!

It <u>Is</u> That Simple!

Chapter 1

The Success Tree® System

Chapter Objectives:

To share the origins and make-up of the Success Tree ® System.

To set the stage for more in-depth learning by positioning the elements of the system and relating them to subsequent chapters.

© 2003 The Strategic Triangle Inc.

Do The <u>Right</u> Things ... Right!

It <u>Is</u> That Simple!

Chapter 1

The Success Tree® System

"Many things which cannot be overcome when they are together yield themselves up when taken little by little."   Plutarch

Positioning. The Success Tree® System is an efficient and effective high performance management system. Its disciplined application consistently results in remarkable improvements in all important measures of performance. Better yet, it does so while consuming less than normal time and fewer than the usual amount of resources. It accomplishes this by rapidly determining the fact-based, vital few areas or activities that will have the most significant effect on the success of an organization. It goes on to provide step-by-step guidance for acting on that priority information to produce desired results.

The Success Tree ® System name comes from its use of a management tool, the tree diagram. The tree diagram is an approach that takes a complex idea or challenge and breaks it into bite-sized, digestible pieces that can be prioritized for serial action. The old saw, "Q. How do you eat an elephant? A. One spoonful at a time" applies here. In this way, even the most daunting organizational challenges can be comfortably and successfully addressed.

As depicted in the introduction, and as shown in Figure 1-1, <u>The Juggler</u>, any leadership role requires juggling of priorities, issues, and opportunities, thus positioning the leader as a juggler. Intelligent juggling is a desirable and necessary leadership skill. As the leader progresses up the organization, more and bigger balls are added. Eventually even the best juggler drops some balls. When this stage is reached, the situation goes from leading to reacting and from initiating to coping. The serenity and comfort of a job well done become a distant memory. A good day becomes a day that is merely survived.

*The solution **is** really simple*

Merely, find the Right Things...

...and then do them Right

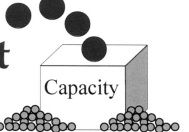

Capacity

Figure 1-1, The Juggler

This is an opportune point to explain a powerful concept called "closing the gap." It is a fundamental aspect of this high performance system, and is applied to every element of the system. The reader will see this "gap-closing" phrase repeated over and over again. The next paragraph summarizes this important concept:

The gap-closing concept basically involves these steps:

Step 1. **Factually determine the current state (as things are today), both the measured level of results, and the processes that delivers them.**

Step 2. **Determine the desired state levels (how we want or need things to be) including the processes that will be needed to put in place to deliver the desired state.**

Step 3. **Assess which drivers makes up this gap between the current and desired states.**

Step 4. **Determine which of the many gap drivers are best attacked first.**

Step 5. **Judge how much of the gap closed.**

Step 6. **Repeat until satisfied with the amount of gap closed, and go on to the next gap.**

See Figure 1-2, <u>Gap Closing</u>, below for a graphic portrayal of this concept.

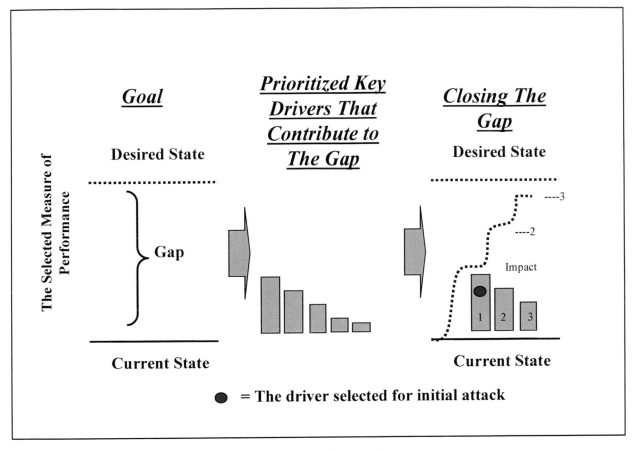

Figure 1-2, Gap Closing

Doing the Right Things

A critical first half of the Success Tree® System involves determining which of the many candidates the "right things are" and which of these should be addressed on a priority basis. These "right things" are necessarily aligned to an organization's Directive Mission, Prescriptive Vision, and a set of Shared Values. The priority issues or opportunities as prioritized by the Customers, Employees and Financial constituency input are key candidates. Each of these elements is described in the ensuing paragraphs of this chapter.

 There is a profound and unique benefit that is gleaned from the Success Tree® System. We know of no other approach other than the Success Tree® System that actually displays the strategic foundation (mission/vision/values), the goals, key drivers and selected "vital few" needed actions, on a single sheet of 8 ½ X 11 inch sheet of paper. This feature facilitates important communication and deployment throughout an organization.

See Figure 1-3, <u>The Right Things</u>, for a high-level portrayal of the valuable strategy page contents:

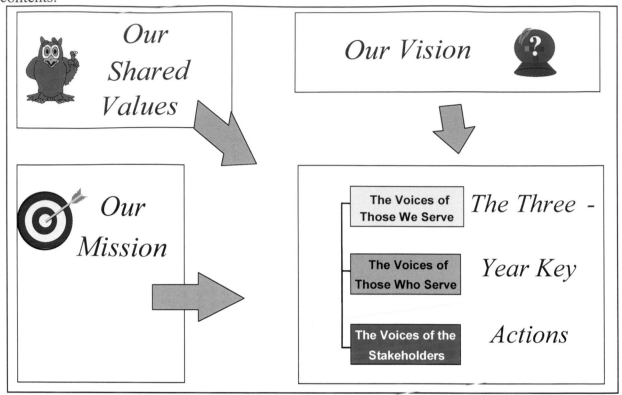

Figure 1-3, The Right Things

The Directive Mission

The wise words of Peter Drucker, the father of modern management, serve as a fitting introduction to the importance of an organization's mission. ***"Mission and philosophy [values] are the key starting points in business. It is defined by the business mission. Only a clear definition of the mission and purpose of the organization makes possible clear and realistic business objectives."***

The missions of organizations can take many forms. Some are as short as one sentence. Some seem to go on and on. Neither really gives the clear, bounding direction that is needed. In order to have a mission give specific guidance for decisions that continually have to be made, the mission needs to be clear, explicit and provide a boundary for the work of the organization. To do this, we have found that it is best to develop what we call a Directive Mission.

A Directive Mission gives specific guidance and sets organizational boundaries by delineating:

<u>What</u> the organization produces or provides.
<u>For Whom</u> the goods and/or services are provided.
<u>How</u> the goods or services are acquired or developed and delivered by the organizations.
<u>Why</u> the "business" of the organization is fundamentally conducted.

In this way, important decisions and accompanying resource allocations can easily be examined for consistency in light of a directive mission. See Figure 1-4, <u>The Directive Mission</u>, for a snapshot, and Chapter 2, The Directive Mission, for more "how-to" detail.

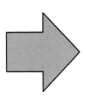

Directive Mission:
the reason for our existence

- **What** we do
- **For whom** we do it
- **How** we do it and our
behavior in doing so
- **Why** we do it

*Helps us stick to
our knitting and
keeps us from
"meddling" and/or
"dabbling"*

Figure 1-4, The Directive Mission

The Prescriptive Vision

When all organizational and resource allocation decisions are focused laser-like on taking the organization to new levels of defined success, amazing advancements are possible. Each group and each individual should be encouraged and enabled to make decisions that are consistent with progress toward a clear destination that the organization desires. As such, it is essential that a clear vision, covering exactly where the organization wants to be, must be developed, approved, and then thoroughly and continuously communicated throughout the organization.

 For simple logical reasons, a three-year time frame for the Prescriptive Vision is favored. Major advances and breakthrough improvements cannot generally be achieved in less than three years. Focused leadership for more than three years has proven to be quite unlikely. In fact, promotions, changes and turnover of key players combine to make sustained very long term efforts impossible.

Ordinarily, no one looks forward to a classical visioning exercise. In fact, one client indicated that she would as soon have a root canal as go through another visioning session! The Success Tree® System incorporates a unique, simple, four-column visioning approach that has proven to be not only rapid and effective, but painless as well.

See Figure 1-5 below, <u>The Prescriptive Vision Process</u> for an overview, and Chapter 3, Vision, for more information on the process.

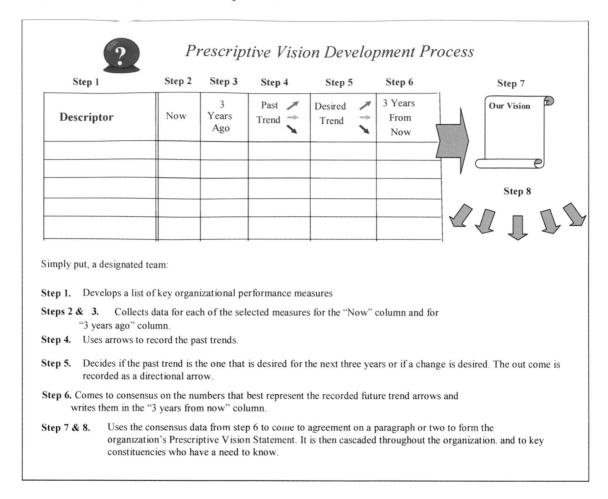

Figure 1-5, The Prescriptive Vision Process

The Organization's Set of Shared Values

Today, it is more important than ever that an organization come to consensus on what it values. With a set of Shared Values in hand, leaders can communicate behavior that is expected to the following groups or individuals:

- All members of the organization
- Its suppliers
- Its alliance partners

- Its customers
- Its stakeholders
- The public

At the same time, these same individuals or groups should be considered to be "assessors" who regularly determine whether or not the organization is actually adhering to its published values via interviews or surveys, e.g. "Walking the Talk."

The years 2000-2002 have given us painful examples of unethical and even illegal behavior by once-respected leaders of major organizations. It is not enough to agree on, and profess adherence to organizational values. It is <u>essential</u> to constantly assess the levels of actual conformance in practice. "Trust but verify" is the right thinking.

See Figure 1-6, <u>Organizational Shared Values</u>, for an example and Chapter 4, Organizational Shared Values, for more detail.

 Our organizational shared values...

Examples:

...help guide us as we strive to behave in a manner expected of all in the organization and all who interact with the organization.

- *Integrity*
- *Customer Delight*
- *Motivated Workers*
- *Financial Health*

Figure 1-6, Organizational Shared Values

Customer Satisfaction

The words of those who are served should give strong direction to an organization's improvement efforts. In order to capture this vital input in actionable form, current customers must be regularly surveyed and/or interviewed. Experience has shown that most of the customer satisfaction surveys that are done today are either useless or, at best sub-optimal. A careful critique of hundreds of professionally done surveys has shown that each consistently fails to provide explicit answers to critical leadership questions.

What leaders really should want to know about Customer Satisfaction are the answers to these simple questions:

- **What percent of the people we serve are delighted as characterized by such measures as: "Would willingly recommend the organization to others?"**
- **Of those who respond in the negative, we need to know what the prioritized reasons are for dissatisfaction. In essence we need to know, "If the organization could just improve one or two things, what would the customers recommend? In your opinion what should we be working on?"**
- **Finally, we need to know what the things these customers perceive to be that the organization is doing very well? We can publicize and brag about these.**

By focusing on these "vital few," the gap between the current satisfaction levels and the desired levels can be most efficiently and effectively identified and then attacked. Those areas noted by customers as being exceptionally well done can be used in "advertising" the value and benefits of the organization as well as for recognizing appropriate employee teams and individuals.

Here, it is important to recall that the tree diagram is a leadership tool that can be effectively used to reduce a large, complex, amorphous challenge to bite-sized attackable pieces that are labeled "branches." Thus, the Customer Branch displays actionable customer-related challenges.

Again, it has been our experience that very few, if any, customer research studies provide information in this needed, actionable form. See Figure 1-7, <u>The Customer Satisfaction Branch</u>, and Chapter 5, Customer Satisfaction, for more details.

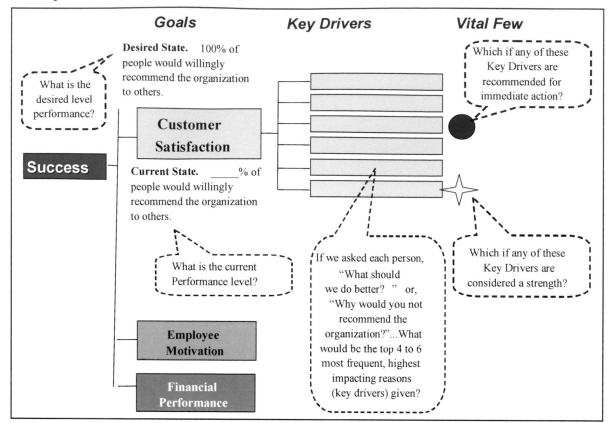

Figure 1-7, The Customer Satisfaction Branch

Employee Motivation

The words of those who do the organization's work also must be allowed to give strong input to the prioritization efforts. To capture this vital employee information in actionable form, employees must be regularly surveyed and/or interviewed. Experience has shown that most of the employee satisfaction survey results achieved today are either useless or sub-optimal.

What the leaders really should want to know about employee motivation is simply the answers to these questions:

- **What per cent of the employees are positively motivated, as characterized by such measures as: "Would you willingly recommend working for the organization to qualified others?"**
- **Of those who respond in the negative, we need to know what the prioritized reasons for their reticence to recommend are. "If the organization could improve one or two things, what would you recommend they be?"**
- **Finally, we need to know what the exceptional people-related things that the organization is doing are. "What are the things our people say that we should be touting?"**

With this information in hand, the leadership team can select what the "vital few" employee defined issues are, and allocate talent and resources to address them with confidence that these are some of the "right" things. By focusing on these "vital few," the gap between the current motivation levels and the desired levels can be most efficiently and effectively impacted.

Again, it has been our experience that very few, if any, employee satisfaction studies provide information in needed actionable form. See Figure 1-8, <u>The Employee Motivation Branch</u>, for a snapshot and Chapter 6, The Employee Motivation Branch for more "how-to" details.

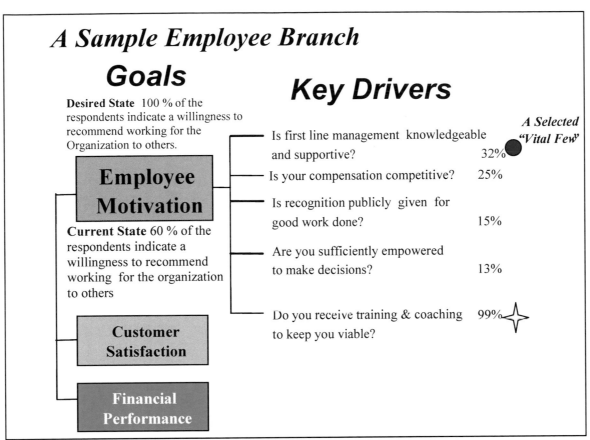

Figure 1-8, The Employee Motivation Branch

Financial Performance

It has been our experience that few, if any, leaders have truly isolated and ear-marked for action, the "<u>vital few</u>" measures of the organization's financial success. Few leaders seem able to zero in on the handful of key drivers or gap-closers that are absolutely critical to financial success. Rather, they tend to act as if dozens and even hundreds of measures are absolutely critical. Thus they would have to focus on the "trivial many." Not going to happen! They act on the next crisis or the "squeakiest wheel." Motion is mistaken for progress.

It is essential to separate the true financial "vital few" and the true key drivers from the clutter. An effective way to accomplish this is to engage a small team of key players who are intimately involved with, or have a great deal of interest in the financial aspects of the organization's operation. They are asked to develop and gain agreement on only the <u>most important</u> issues or opportunities that have the greatest effect on the selected key financial performance measures.

Answers to the following simple questions are all that are needed to cull out key drivers from the trivial many and get down to critical financial gap-closing actions:

Step 1.	What are the <u>one or two</u> key, overall, all encompassing measures of the financial contribution of a group, or the performance of an organization? (E.g. Is it earnings per share, profit, market share, cost, revenue, donations, <u>etc?</u>)
Step 2.	For each of the one or two such selected measures, what are the current levels and processes? Where are we now and how is it we get here?) and what are the desired levels and processes? What is it that defines financial success and what processes are needed to get us there?
Step 3.	What are the four to six key drivers which if improved, will have the greatest impact on the gaps between the desired financial performance and the current levels of performance for the selected measures?
Step 4.	If the organization were to attack one or two of these drivers first, which ones should they be? Where should we best apply out resources to positively impact our financial performance?
Step 5.	Finally, we can also answer these questions: What are the key areas of positive financial performance that the organization should be most proud of?" What is it that we should be touting and using for rewards and recognition of employees?

See Figure 1-9, <u>The Financial Performance Branch</u>, for a graphic portrayal, and Chapter 7, Financial Performance for more details.

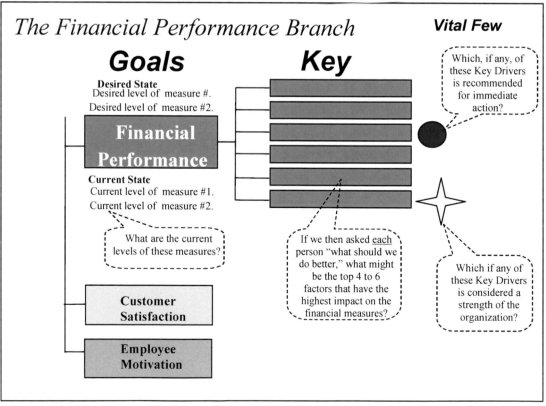

Figure 1-9, The Financial Performance Branch

Once the highest-priority issues or opportunities have been isolated, and before resources are allocated, a simple, but conscientious examination should be made to confirm that selected candidates for action pass Mission, Vision, and Constituent screens.

Is the candidate selected for action:

- Aligned to, or supportive of the organization's published directive mission and vision?
- Consistent with the shared values?
- Representative of progress toward an agreed Prescription Vision?
- Responsive to the major, prioritized improvement messages that have been obtained from the directions as given by customers, employees, and stakeholders?

Doing Things… Right

The selected priorities/initiatives/projects should be approached by a focused, organized individual, and/or team efforts. This constitutes the start of the execution, second half of "Doing The Right Things…**Right**" part of the Success Tree® System. There are two major execution elements in this part of the system:

- The Eight Step Breakthrough Process™
- The Organizational Report Card™

First is the Eight Step Breakthrough Process™, a simple, logical, step-by-step process which, when followed produces remarkable improvements that are required to close the "vital few" gaps. This is overviewed in the next section and includes an extremely valuable tracking tool, the Stoplight Report™. This subject is covered in "how-to" detail in Chapter 8, The Breakthrough Process™.

Second is the Organizational Report Card™. This is a simple survey, customized for each organization. It allows leaders and/or groups (and the readers of this guide for that matter) to be polled to determine whether the organization is actually seeking the "Right Things" and then "Doing Them Right." Chapter 9, The Organizational Report Card, covers full details of this important system element.

See Figure 1-10, <u>Doing Things Right</u>, below for a snapshot of the positioning of the "**doing**" part of the system.

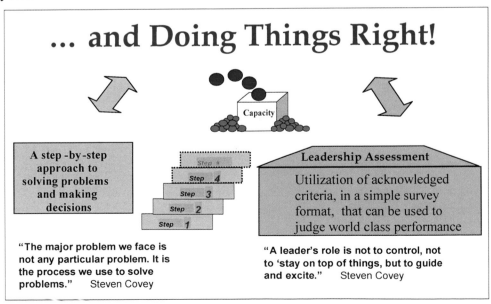

Figure 1-10, Doing Things Right

The Breakthrough Process^{TM}

The Breakthrough Process consists of a simple, logical and structured problem solving and/or opportunity-capturing set of steps that will enable leaders to efficiently close identified Customer, Employee and Financial gaps. These steps are:

Step 1. Select a specific high priority challenge needing breakthrough improvement.

Step 2. Communicate the leadership's specific expectations and requirements. *This step introduces the **Job Ticket**, a single system element that is so powerful and so useful that it warrants additional comment at the end of these steps.*

Step 3. Assemble and organize the talent and resources needed to work the initiative.

Step 4. Determine factually the current undesirable level of performance and the processes or procedures that deliver this level.

Step 5. Come to consensus on the desired level of performance and the processes that must be put in place to deliver same.

Step 6. Develop a transition plan which, when executed with excellence, will move performance from the current process with its inadequate results, to the needed process and desired results.

Step 7. Resource and execute the recommended changes according to the transition plan.

Step 8. Monitor to determine the level of success/recycle if necessary. If the results are as desired or needed, celebrate and go on to the next priority challenge.

The Job Ticket is basically a communications vehicle and an enabler that defines clearly, and in sufficient detail, the specific requirements and expectations that leadership places on a vital task assigned to an accountable team leader and team. With a job ticket in place, can the team be fully empowered with confidence to carry out the task, but they can do so with a sense of comfort that their efforts and outputs will gain rightful respect from those who are to judge the quality of the team's work.

Sometimes, a logical, dispassionate step-by-step process seems to stress the patience of action-oriented individuals. We sometimes are asked, "Do we have to follow all of the eight steps?" "Can we skip steps to save time?" To best address these questions, consider:

- "Do we <u>have</u> to understand the problem or challenge?"
- "Do we <u>have</u> to ensure that the accountable problem solvers understand what is being expected of them?"
- "Do we <u>really</u> need to determine the facts relative to the current state?"

Of course the answer to each question is a resounding "yes." <u>Each</u> of the eight steps is <u>essential</u>. Surely any step can be covered in a rapid manner depending on the situation. To skip any step entirely is just risking the "gap-closing" failure that has plagued so many problem solvers today.

See Figure 1-11, <u>The Breakthrough Process</u>™, for a snapshot, and Chapter 8, The Breakthrough Process for more detail. The Job Ticket is featured in detail later in this chapter. It warrants the reader's special consideration as a powerful means for ensuring the precise assignment of key projects.

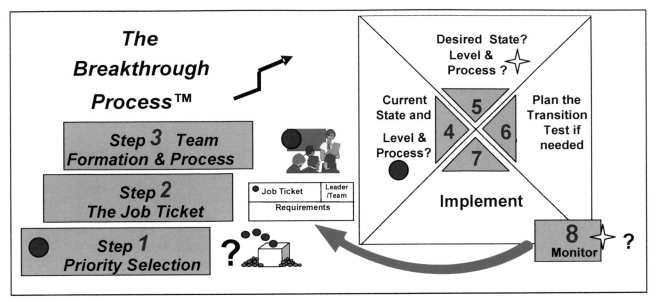

Figure 1-11, The Breakthrough Process

Bumps in the Road

Experience shows, and research confirms that a preponderance of organizational plans, initiatives and projects fail to meet leadership's expectations or requirements. The root causes of such failures are now well understood. All failure modes are fully addressed by the simple and logical steps of the Strategic Triangle's Breakthrough Process™ as outlined below:

Step 1. Failure to Focus – The rigorous application of the "Doing the <u>Right</u> Things" approach, as in the Success Tree® System, isolates the "vital few" areas that are consistent with priorities as expressed by customers, employees, and stakeholders, and are aligned to the mission, vision and values of the organization.

Step 2. Loss of Focus – The use of the Job Ticket provides clear leadership direction to accountable individuals and teams, thus enabling the leader to keep efforts focused.

Step 3. Failure to Resource – Focus on the prioritized "<u>vital few</u>," attacked sequentially, avoids the trap set by innumerable initiatives that outrun available talent and resources.

Step 4. Team Breakdown –The Breakthrough Process, step 2, includes proven counsel relative to team organization, start up and management approaches that counter the common causes of team failure.

Step 5. Failure to Execute – The application of the fishbone Change Management Model addresses expected and predictable change resistance elements. Countermeasures for use during execution are provided. Further, the discipline to focus on only a <u>few</u> key initiatives that are sequentially implemented ensures that limited execution resources are respected.

Step 6. Failure to Evaluate/Recycle – The use of the "gap-closing" approach, the commitment to fact-based measures, and the use of Job Tickets combine to avoid the common failure to assess whether the original goals have actually been approached.

See Figure 1-12, <u>Bumps In The Road</u>, for an overview and Chapter 8, The Breakthrough Process™ for more "how-to" details.

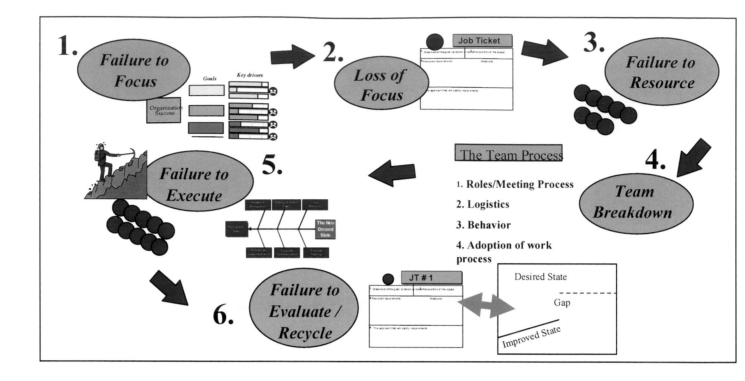

<u>Figure 1-12, Bumps In The Road</u>

The Team StopLight Report™

This is an opportune point to share a summary of the very effective monitoring approaches incorporated in the Breakthrough Process™.

Figure 1-13, <u>The Team StopLight Report™</u>, overviews a simple, painless way for teams to track, and report step-by-step progress and to highlight issues and/or the need for leadership help. Simple, timely, one-page reports to management are made easy. The Breakthrough Process forms the basis for this tool and utilizes symbols to indicate the condition at each phase or step of each effort. See Chapter 8, The Breakthrough Process for more detail about the StopLight Report as a means for tracking key projects. These are the referenced symbols:

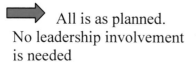 All is as planned. No leadership involvement is needed

Some issues that will affect schedule quality or cost are present, but are under control

 There are issues that jeopardize the success of the team. Leadership intervention is needed.

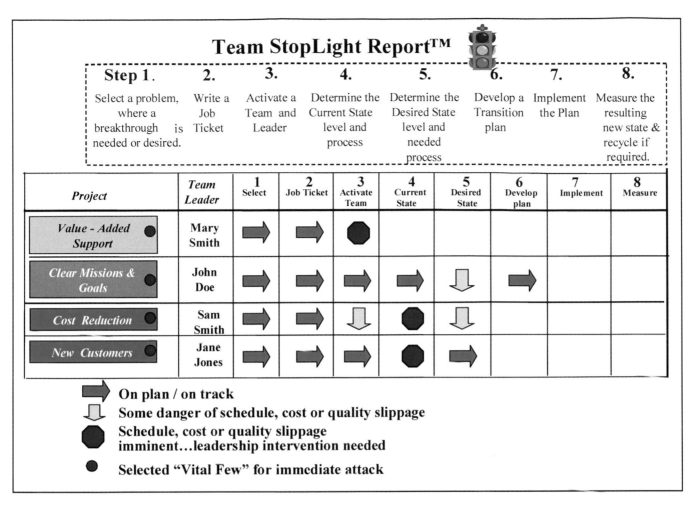

Figure 1-13, The Team StopLight Report™

The Organizational Report Card™

The second of the two key elements of the "Doing Things Right" half of the Success Tree® System is the Organizational Report Card. This is a simple, quick, assessment tool, built on acknowledged standards for world-class organizational performance. It allows leaders, employees, or others to quickly determine the perceived effectiveness of an organization's current processes and procedures, and the current levels of performance through the use of a comparison to processes and performance in leadership organizations that meet recognized standards of excellence. The specific statements in the report card are situation sensitive and can be readily customized to fit any organization. The card is normally comprised of eight categories, each containing five statements. Figure 1-14, The Organizational Report Card, depicts a summary of the derivation, content, and the structure of the tool. More "how-to" detail, including useful model report cards are shown in Chapter 9, The Organizational Report Card.

The eight standards of organizational excellence categories are:

1. Leadership
2. Strategic Plans
3. Customer Focus
4. Human Resources

5. Process Management
6. Information & Analyses
7. Business Results
8. Organizational Customized Items

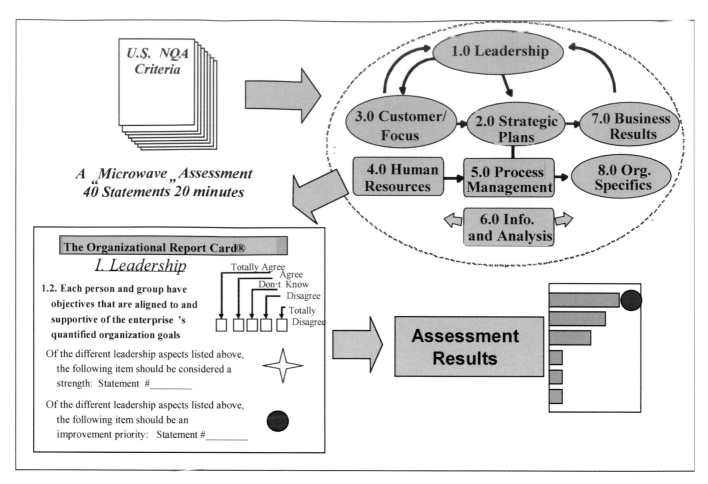

Figure 1-14, The Organizational Report Card™

Change Resistance and Change Management

> *"If you think you are going to be successful running your business in the next 10 years the same way you did in the last 10 years, you're out of your mind. To succeed, you have to disturb the present."*
> Roberto Goizueta, Former CEO, Coca Cola, Inc.

While all leaders seem to agree that change is not only important, but inevitable, most change initiatives result in abject failure! Failures also often produce unintended negative consequences that actually magnify the normal negative effects of the failure. Intense competition and the dynamic pace of the world will inexorably muscle unpleasant changes through even a change-resistant organization. The alternative is organizational demise. Every substantive change initiative faces daunting organizational resistance. Experience in the trenches has taught that recognizing change resistance up front and planning to overcome these natural barriers to change can produce successful change adoption.

Applying a change model using a classic "fishbone" or cause-and-effect diagram has consistently produced very positive results. To ensure that desired changes will become operational, there are eight elements in the model that must be assessed and addressed. See Figure 1-15, <u>The Change Management Model</u>, for an overview. The fishbone change tool is covered in the text that follows.

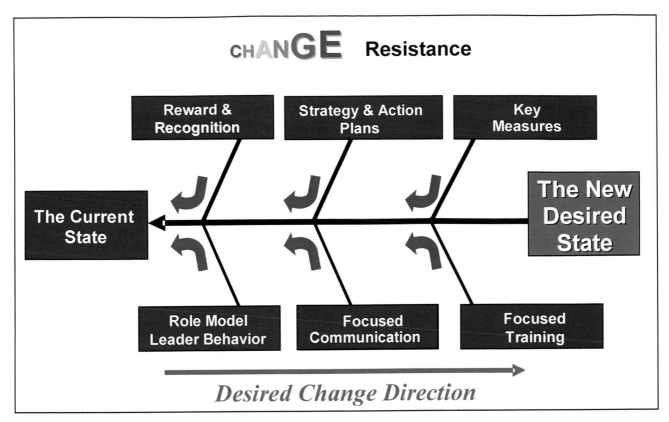

Figure 1-15, The Change Management Model™

The head and tail of the fish begin the explanation of this powerful Change Management tool:

- **The Current State** is at the tail of the fish. When contemplating change, it is important to understand and communicate a clear picture of the current state, emphasizing the negatives to all impacted by the change. The message is, "We cannot stay here!"
- **The Desired State** is the head of the fish. This is a clear picture of what it will be like when the change is adopted, emphasizing the positives. The message is, "See how beautiful it will be when we get there?" This must be communicated to all involved or impacted.

The six bones of the fish address specific resistances that will likely be encountered when breakthrough change is desired. Note that in Figure 1-15, The Change Management Model, the bones are depicted in a reverse angle indicating that they are resistant to the change. Thus, they favor the maintenance of the status quo. These bones are:

- **Reward and Recognition.** The current way we reward and recognize the contributions and behavior of our people must be examined. Any such elements that foster the current way to the detriment of the desired change must be replaced by implementing change-inducing reward and recognition means.
- **Key Measures.** The organization's key measures in the change arena must be examined. Measures that support the desired change must be added to the list. Measures that appear to sustain the old way must be modified, downplayed or eliminated. The intent is to feature measures that display progress of the change initiative.

- **Strategies and Action Plans.** Specific <u>change</u> <u>attack</u> strategies and plans that will efficiently move the organization and its leaders from the current state and processes to the desired state and new processes must be developed and deployed.
- **Focused Training.** Focused training that provides key individuals and groups with needed change-related understanding and desired state skills must be developed and deployed.
- **Role Model Senior Leader Behavior.** "Do what we say and not what we do" will not cut it! Leaders must be the first to role model behaviors that are expected in the Desired State.
- **Focused Communications.** Intense and continuous communications making graphic the change information (the "why," "how," "when," and "who") must be shared and repeated over and over again. It is said that the first thing to go under change-induced stress is hearing. Thus the need to be clear and repetitive.

See Chapter 10, The Change Management Model™, for more "how-to" details about this most important subject and tool.

Lessons Learned

We all have had successful and not–so–successful experiences. Successful individuals try to repeat what worked and avoid what didn't work. A comic once said that "History is unfortunately repeated because no one is paying attention."

It is just human nature to celebrate successes without really examining the processes that produced them. Equally normal is trying to forget failures as fast as possible. It's a shame, since <u>all</u> lessons are fully paid for. Every benefit extracted from good and bad experiences should be treasured and multiplied by freely sharing them with others in the organization.

It is always wise to pause and reflect on both successes <u>and</u> failures to extract the maximum in increased knowledge from each experience. Informal sharing of experiences combined with periodic, structured, formal sharing sessions can be a major asset for the organization. Basically we seek to understand what the results were, and what the processes were that produced these results. Experience has shown that a true personal and organizational commitment to learning and a formal lessons learned sharing process can yield remarkable benefits. Even so, the evidence of actual well-structured, organized sharing in practice is sparse indeed.

A formal organizational Sharing Forum™ has these objectives:

1. Clearly/simply communicate key success and failure results and process experiences.
2. Provide insights relative to counter measures that were employed as well as their effect
3. Offer recommendations for future avoidance.
4. Display dispassionate facts and reasoned opinions.
5. Ensure that there is no "finger-pointing" and no "witch-hunting".
6. Facilitate the adoption of new, more effective business processes.
7. Enable the growth of people through learning .

See Figure 1-16, <u>Sample Sharing Forum™ Agenda</u>, and Chapter 11, Lessons Learned for more "how-to" information

---

<u>Sample Sharing Forum™ Agenda</u>

8:00 - 8:10 AM	★ *Introductions/ expectations/meeting process*
8:10 - 9:00	*Project description, history, & chronology including processes followed & practices used*
9:00 - 10:00	★ *Key <u>successes</u> shared including what, how, impacts.*
10:00 -10:15	*Break*
10:15 - 11:15	★ *Key <u>improvement</u> opportunities shared*
	-- Causal Analysis techniques & finding what happened, when, where, how, who?
	-- Team recommendations / Q & A
11:15 - 12:00	★ *Sr. management observations / meeting evaluation & wrap-up*

Figure 1-16, Sample Sharing Forum Agenda

Many valuable lessons have been gleaned during hundreds of coaching experiences with teams around the world. A few of the most informative coaching lessons learned about teams are listed below. More detail about each experience is covered in Chapter 11, Lessons Learned.

- **Every project, team, leader, customer is different.**
- **Focus, focus, focus is essential to the success of the team.**
- **Common team process steps expedite progress and results.**
- **Leaders can be doers on teams.**
- **Teach by coaching, not supervising**
- **Set very aggressive goals.**

- **Pay now or pay a lot more later.**
- **Asking, "Why? Why? Why?" gets you to the root causes .**
- **Consensus not "majority rules".**
- **More, shorter team meetings vs. fewer longer meetings.**
- **There is no such thing as a short break.**
- **Measures, measures, measures.**

The Full Success Tree® System Vs Element-By-Element

To recap, **the first half** of the Success Tree® System, *Doing The <u>Right</u> Things*, includes six elements that together provide any organization with a capability to enable needed understandings of its prioritized, aligned, key performance drivers and the selected "vital few" that warrant special leadership attention. These elements are:

- The Directive Mission.
- The Prescriptive Vision.
- Organizational Shared Values.

- The Voice of those who are served .
- The Voice of those who do the serving.
- The Voice of the financial stakeholders.

The second half of the system, *Doing Things Right*, includes the Breakthrough Process™ that enables teams to efficiently and effectively address identified critical issues and opportunities, and the Leadership Report Card™ that provides an assessment of performance levels versus a world class standard.

See Figure 1-17, The Success Tree® System Elements, for a graphic summary of the eight key pieces.

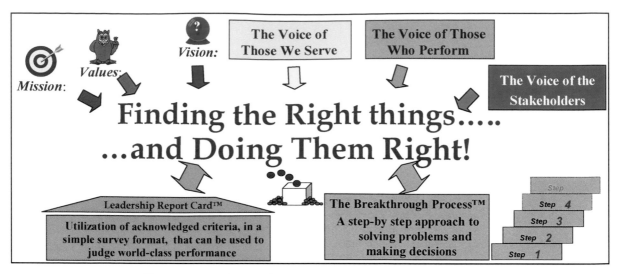

Figure 1-17, The Success Tree® Elements

Not all situations are the same and no two management teams are the same. Sometimes the change challenges associated with the adoption of all eight of the system elements are desired and are successful. Sometimes a slower, more conservative approach is desired. These two situations are important to examine. The first **(Case A)** is where the full concept and all elements of the Success Tree® System are embraced by a leader and/or a leadership team. The second **(Case B)** is where uncertainty and doubt cause the leaders to pursue only one or two elements of the system at a time, building confidence as they go.

Case A. When a leader and the leadership team:
• Embrace the full suite of Success Tree® System elements
• Rigorously deploy and apply the Breakthrough Process™
• Regularly conduct performance assessments using the Report Card™ and adopt a spirit of continuous improvement

In Case A, the leadership team has sufficient confidence to accept the full system. In this case, the organization will reap full world-class performance benefits sooner. Delighted customers, motivated employees, and outstanding financial returns are inevitable outcomes. What could be better?

Case B. When a leader and the leadership team:
• Feel that this is not the time for a complete revolution
• Have not yet developed confidence in the complete system
• Decide that only a specific element or a few elements of the system warrant immediate attention and pursuit

In Case B, the organization will see benefits in the form of improvement in the selected element. Over time, the leadership team will thus develop confidence in the concept and will select additional elements of the system and proceed to the next adoption step. Here, upward progress is sure but slow.

The Success Tree® System Element Assessment

A convenient assessment form has been developed for the purpose of determining which of the eight Success Tree® is in need of immediate attention.

See Figure 1-18, <u>System Element Selection</u>, for a guide to this approach. Using this type of form, an organization can quickly isolate elements of importance that are not fully in place, and commit to immediate action for each. Confidence will develop with success in each of these selected elements. An invaluable by-product can ultimately be acceptance of the complete fact-based, gap-closing approach. This then can foster movement toward adoption of the full system with concomitant major organizational benefits

System Element Selection			
<u>**_Element_**</u>	<u>_Importance_</u>	<u>_Status_</u>	<u>_Chapter_</u>
A Directive Mission	_10_	_1_	_2_
A Clear, Prescription Vision			_3_
Organizational Shared Values			_4_
Capturing the Words of the Customer			_5_
Capturing the Words of the Employees			_6_
The Words of Financial Stakeholders			_7_
Structured, Common Problem Solving			_8_
Organizational Performance Assessment			_9_

**Importance Scale**: 1 = Not Important; 10 = Vital;
**Status Scale**: 1 = Non-existent; 10 = Fully Operational

**Ratings of Importance 7 or more having a Status of 5 or less highlight Candidates for action**

Figure 1-18, System Element Selection

The reader will find it useful to record their own personal assessment of the importance of each element and the status of these elements in their own organizations. The chart in Figure 1-19, <u>System Element Selection</u>, below shows which chapters of this text address each element in detail. Thus, for one that is judged to be very important to the success of the organization and where the status is unsatisfactory, ready reference to a helpful chapter is readily available.

As an example, if your assessment gives the Directive Mission an Importance of 10, (Vital), and a current Status of 1 (Non-existent), this is an obvious candidate for immediate action.

A world class leader knows that **all** **eight** system elements are important. A world class organization has **all** **eight** systems in place and operational. Think about it. Rate yourself and your organization. If you disagree that all eight are vital to the success of an organization, try to rationalize why anyone of them (the Directive Mission, a Prescriptive Vision, a set of Organizational Shared Values, or the fact-based advice of customers, employees and/or financial advisors) are not important to have in place. It cannot be done rationally. Leaders must commit to having each Success Tree® System element at an operational state and at a high level of performance.

Chapter Conclusions

At this point, the stated objectives of this chapter have been addressed:

The origins and make-up of the Success Tree® System have been shared.

The stage has been set for more in-depth learning by reading each of the chapters in this guidebook.

Graphics and real world examples have been used in an effort to provide clarity as well as to create a sense of enthusiasm and confidence in each element of the system.

 Finally, I am absolutely convinced that adoption of all eight elements of the Success Tree® System, followed by diligent, continuously improved operational execution, will produce exceptional advances in all facets of an organization's performance. This will prove to be rewarding for all your constituencies, and intriguing to analysts, assessors, academics, and pundits.

As the system is embraced, a calm serenity falls over the leadership. Control of one's organizational destiny is a bonus that no doubt will prove to be personally rewarding to the leaders involved.

"Bottom line, each of you current and aspiring "jugglers," will be able to efficiently and effectively find the right things, and then do them right, thereby achieving the ultimate in efficiency and effectiveness in carrying out the mission and achieving the vision of an organization."
R.C. Palermo

Do The **Right** Things ... Right!

It Is That Simple!

Chapter 2
The Directive Mission

Chapter Objectives:

To illustrate and make the case that a solid Directive Mission is a very important facet of an organization's success.

To provide an approach to examine, revise, or create an Organization's Directive Mission statement that gives guidance or explicit direction for resource decisions and issue resolution.

To help the leader and the organization focus and "stick to the knitting".

© 2003 The Strategic Triangle Inc.

Do The **Right** Things ... Right!

It Is That Simple!

Chapter 2

The Directive Mission

"The Secret of Success is constancy of purpose."   Benjamin Disraeli

Positioning. An organization's mission or charter should be a statement of the reasons for its existence. As such, the mission is one of the six key guides for determining the "right" things for an organization to focus on. The mission is often misunderstood or confused with visions or even worse with slogans. This section is intended to clear up that confusion.

.It may help to think of the difference between a mission and a vision using these definitions:

- The <u>Directive Mission Statement</u> describes <u>what</u> is done or provided...<u>who</u> is served, taught, treated, or supplied...<u>how</u> it all gets done...and <u>why</u> it is done. Its intent is to communicate a clear understanding of the "business" of the organization in order to give some guidance as daily and long term decisions are made. It enables great questions be asked, such as: "Is this decision consistent with our directive mission?"
- The <u>Prescriptive Vision Statement</u> is the description of the organization's <u>destination</u>. It depicts how we want the organization to be perceived, positioned, performing, and described three or more years from now. It gives guidance as questions are asked, such as: "Does this decision move us positively toward our Prescriptive Vision?"

Much more on the vision topic is in Chapter 3, The Prescriptive Vision.

Experiences with Missions. Some managers openly state that the mission of their organization is obvious or just understood, and need not be written in detail. Therefore these leaders feel that a mission need not be drafted, word-smithed, embraced and communicated. This position is unsubstantiated by facts gleaned from discussions, interviews, and surveys involving employees, investors or suppliers. All of these constituencies are vocal in their belief that an understanding of the organization's "business" is not only of interest, but is also essential. Increasingly, customers also indicate a need to understand the mission of the organizations that they do business with..

Some leaders state that they really don't want to be hamstrung by a detailed mission. They want the freedom to turn on a dime and strike out in new directions, or reach for new opportunities without having to be handcuffed by a mission. This position risks the same fate as the legions of past leaders embarrassed by failures, and the multitude of organizations that have crashed, because of the ugly results of an inability to stick to a game plan.

Does this mean that once the game starts that you can't change the game plan? No, of course not! If needed, one just has to take the time to modify the mission and share it with important constituencies. Your customers, employees, and financial backers might just be interested in the changes in the mission that will impact them in major ways.

 Some managers state that there isn't time for a mission session or that the world is too fast moving and dynamic to stop and try to formulate a detailed mission. Real world experiences dispute this. Even in the most contentious situations, leadership consensus can be reached on a Directive Mission in four hours or less. Surely the benefits of having the leadership team come to a common understanding of why an organization exists and the benefits of having the entire workforce share the same understanding is worth four hours or less!

Finally, other leaders indicate that what is needed is a simple, one-sentence mission that inspires, captures the imagination, and can be used in public relations and advertising initiatives. We call these, "slogans," not missions. Granted there is a use for slogans. "We bring good things to life" may be cute and catchy and sound great in advertising, but it doesn't give sufficient direction to General Electric's leaders for resource allocations, prioritized judgements, or organizational and operational decisions.

We must therefore, make a distinction between a "sound bite" that might better be called a "Motivational Mission," intended to shape public sentiment, and that of a Directive Mission that gives specific guidance to the organization's leaders as they journey onward and hopefully upward. The Directive Mission needs to be clear and explicit. It must provide some "bounds" that define the operational domain of the organization. Motivational Missions and Directive Missions can and do coexist, but should never be considered interchangeable. At this point, a rather profound thought, or maybe an accusation, relative to leaders and missions is offered:

 The value of offering <u>fewer</u> products or services that meet or exceed customer-defined requirements, far exceeds the value of offering a broad or full line of products or services having mediocre or poor quality and/or questionable reliability in order to claim a "full product line." Bottom line:
Do only what you will do well!

To exemplify this case, consider a common leadership goal of aspiring to be a "full line" supplier. If an organization mission does not include a commitment to benefit owners or financial backers, the leader is basically given a license to move into low or negative margin products or services that he or she feels are needed to achieve the status as a "full line" supplier. A ridiculous example helps make the point: If an organization makes and markets laser eye surgery equipment that produces solid margins and substantial revenues, does it make financial sense to also market surgical masks? One could argue that it is consistent with a goal of being a "full line" supplier. By having a mission without a commitment to earnings, a commitment to customer satisfaction or employee motivation, this leader making such an unfortunate decision could still be operating within the mission.

If, on the other hand, a mission were to contain a specific statement of commitment that captured and related the boundaries that conform to the interests of the owners or financial backers and other constituencies, the leader would have been obliged to make decisions consistent with those explicit commitments. The organization would rightfully be expected to operate within those bounds. Thus, while marketing surgical masks and other such items might increase revenues and contribute to a full line supplier image; if it degrades margins to a point where it negatively impacts the stock price, the decision could be to reject this product addition, as guided by the directive mission.

Sad to say, the behaviors and decisions of many organizations and leaders seem to indicate that they assume that financial returns are optional or worse, not of consequence. Again, successful leaders and thriving organizations consistently demonstrate by word and deed with year-after-year great results, that the needs of all three constituencies – those who are served, the servers, and the "owners" – must and can be constantly addressed.

To ensure solid organizational guidance from missions, we have found that it is best to develop and come to consensus on a Directive Mission Statement. It must explicitly cover:
- **What** the organization produces or provides.
- **Who** the users or recipients of the goods and/or services of the organization are.
- **How** the goods or services are acquired or developed and delivered
- And **Why** the work of the organization is conducted.

Whether some leaders like it or not, every person in an organization will be called upon to make organization-related decisions almost every day. It is not enough to hope that they make the "right" decisions that are best for the organization. It is true that leaders sometimes go to extraordinary means to restrict a worker's power to act independently, and that "empowerment" is then just a catch phrase. It is also true that such dictatorial organizations develop and seem to succeed...at least for a while. An underlying reason for this control behavior is a belief that people cannot be trusted to make the "right" decisions. Experience shows us that there is much unused and unchallenged brainpower in all organizations. What a shame! If and when this talent is unleashed by enlightened leadership, the results are truly astounding.

Further, it is axiomatic that the people closest to the action (the doers) know much more about how things really run, than do the leaders in the executive suite. Who better then, to find the root causes of problems and to apply fixes? Who better to know where to help cut costs or to help improve productivity in a continuous improvement mode? Who better to know how processes, procedures can realistically be changed to produce excellent results?

A valid reason for leadership's reticence to exhibit faith in employees to do the right things is that the workers do not know what "right" is. A Directive Mission starts to address this barrier by allowing clear communication of what the organization does, whom it serves, how it does its work, and why it operates. Everyone in such an organization can be coached and encouraged to make or acquire better offerings, delight more customers, motivate more workers, or generate more revenue or profit. The Directive Mission can be a rallying point.

Steps to Produce a Directive Mission

A Directive Mission is developed by following each of the steps noted below in a disciplined manner. The initial step is to determine whether a mission statement for the organization already exists.

Case A. A mission already exists

If there already is a mission in place, the existing mission is examined against the directive mission's format requirements. The examination involves four basic questions:

- **What** exactly does the organization provide?
- **Who** are the recipients or users of the goods or services?
- **How** are the offerings acquired, developed or delivered?
- **Why** does the organization perform its duties?

Thus, the adequacy of the existing mission statement can be assessed and if required, be supplemented. If the current mission is judged to adequately cover the "what, who, how, and why" criteria, move on to the next challenge.

As any of the four questions receive incomplete or inadequate answers, a suitable statement for the item is developed, consensus is sought and achieved. The enhanced statement(s) are added to the current mission. The revision is labeled "The Organizational Directive Mission" to distinguish it from an existing mission.

Case B. An organizational mission statement does not exist

The leader of such an organization should draft, achieve consensus, and record answers to the following four questions:

- **What** exactly does the organization provide?
- **Who** are the recipients or users of the goods or services?
- **How** are the offerings acquired, developed, or delivered?
- **Why** does the organization perform its duties?

In both Case A, modifying an existing operational mission, and Case B, creating a new mission, the team proceeds to construct and gain consensus on paragraphs that capture the essence of four ideal answers. It then can be appropriately labeled, "The Organizational Directive Mission." Thus, Directive Mission statements are the explicit explanation of what we are doing and where we need to focus actions. It is totally appropriate and desirable to periodically assess whether the organization is operating in conformance to a Directive Mission.

If the following mission assessment questions are asked of any management team, don't be surprised at the inadequate answers:

- **Is conformance to the Directive Mission Statement elements measured?**
- **How, and how often?**
- **What is the current performance level for each element?**
- **What is the desired level or needed level for each?**
- **How large are the Current/Desired gaps?**
- **Which are the key causes that lead to these gaps?**
- **Which improvement need will be addressed first?**
- **How will it be addressed?**
- **Who is accountable for corrective actions?**

If it is judged that statements in the constructed Directive Mission are such that they cannot be measured, one has to question why they should be included in a mission. How would we know if we were operating in a manner consistent with them? How would we know if we were making acceptable progress with them? Again we reiterate the absolute importance of measures and measuring.

From the many areas for improvement, the one or two "vital few" actions that need to be taken to ensure conformance to the stated mission should be isolated. If they are not already in progress, they are candidates for major breakthrough efforts and should be put in the queue for priority action.

See Figure 2-1, <u>The Directive Mission</u>, for a snapshot of the mission format and some key questions that are fairly asked of it.

The Directive Mission 🎯

For each of the first three bulleted questions

- ***What do we do?***

    How is this measured?
    What is the current level?
    What is the desired level?

- ***For whom do we do it?***

    How large are the gaps?

- ***How do we do it?***

    Which are the key causes or barriers that lead to these gaps?

...and Why do we do it?

Figure 2-1, The Directive Mission

A consensus Directive Mission must be cascaded throughout the levels in the organization. At each opportunity, the mission and its intent must be shared. These questions should constantly be posed:

- **Given this Directive Mission, what does or will your group do to support it?**
- **What is your <u>supportive</u> mission, using the What, For Whom, How, and Why format? In order to assure alignment, the "Why" response should feature the support of the organization's mission.**

Some Real-World Examples

It is instructive to examine the published mission statements of some well-known organizations using this Directive Mission concept as a critique. It is important to note that while the mission examinations that follow may be critical of the Mission Statement of an organization, it is not necessarily critical of the organization itself. However, the difficulties that some of the organizations in question have been facing recently may indeed be partially related to a faulty or inadequate mission statement and an inadequate or non-existent mission deployment process.

Actual randomly selected organizational mission statements are examined in:

- Figure 2-2, <u>The Kodak Mission</u>
- Figure 2-3, <u>The Xerox Mission</u>
- Figure 2-4, <u>The Johnson & Johnson Mission</u>
- Figure 2-5, <u>The Harvard College Mission</u>
- Figure 2-6, <u>The American Cancer Society Mission</u>

They were captured from web sites during 2002. Some relevant comments and observations are included in each figure. The reader is urged to similarly critique their own organization in a similar manner.

<u>First, the published Kodak mission:</u>

<u>Kodak Mission</u>

"Build a world -class, results -oriented culture...by providing customers and consumers with solutions to capture, store, process, output, and communicate images to people and machines anywhere, anytime... bringing differentiated, cost - effective solutions to the marketplace quickly and with flawless quality through a diverse team of energetic employees with the world -class talent and skills necessary to sustain Kodak as the World Leader in Imaging ."

Source: www.Kodak.com

<u>Directive Mission Check</u>

What: Providing solutions to capture, store, process, output and communicate images to people and machines anywhere, anytime

For Whom: Customers and consumers

How: By bringing differentiated, cost -effective solutions. to the marketplace quickly and with flawless quality and through a diverse team of energetic employees with the world - class talent and skills necessary

Why: To build a world -class, results -oriented culture and to sustain Kodak as the World Leader in Imaging

---

Figure 2-2, The Kodak Mission

Further observations and suggestions about the Kodak mission are provided next:

What: The mission statement shown in Figure 2-2, allows Kodak to develop, license, buy, or otherwise acquire <u>any</u> image solutions. The inclusion of the term "image solutions" does confine Kodak's interests to images. Very broad latitude is granted by the phrases "from capture to communication" and "anywhere, anytime." It is <u>too</u> broad. In this world today, it is not enough to have a presence in all areas of a market; you have to really <u>excel</u> in each one of them. No firm can be #1 or #2 in all the businesses that this mission allows. There is a danger that Kodak has and/or will spread itself too thin and lack focus.

For Whom: The term *"customers and consumers"* basically designates an organization's distribution intermediaries, and end users as customers. Measuring the satisfaction level of each of these constituencies is relatively straightforward and if done, would allow Kodak to pursue customer satisfaction improvement based on facts. Identifying satisfaction levels and the causes for dissatisfaction are essential to ensure focus.

How: The use of the term *"differentiated"* relative to Kodak's solutions would seem to push the firm away from its bread-and-butter commodities like color film for consumers and toward the more complex *"solutions selling."* There is an obvious danger in short-changing the "golden goose." The inclusion of the description of its employees as energetic with world-class talent and skills is a good indication that the firm recognizes the importance of people. It would be interesting to see whether employee surveys indicate that this belief is put into practice. The failure to mention partners or alliances may imply that Kodak can continue to go it alone or will treat partners in an inadequate manner. This is dangerous in our connected business world.

Why: It would be interesting to see what metrics the firm uses to measure a *"world-class, results-oriented culture"* and *"World Leader in Imaging."* Don't be surprised if they don't or cannot measure them.

 Mission statements or parts of mission statements that cannot be, or don't intend to be measured, are slogans or sound bites. They have little value in giving direction or guidance.

It is surprising and disappointing that the stockholder is not even mentioned in the mission statement, much less featured. This can imply that the firm is not particularly sensitive to the expectations of its owners. Is this a reason for Kodak's financial troubles or is it a manifestation of the thinking that exists in Kodak's leadership team?

A Better Direction-Giving Kodak Mission would be:

What: The mission of Kodak people is to develop/acquire, deliver/distribute, and maintain, image-related products and service solutions that anticipate, meet, or exceed user needs and expectations.

For Whom: The key image needs of enterprises and individuals around the world.

How: Its motivated, talented, empowered employees work individually and in teams with a commitment to continuous work improvement and personal growth. Its alliance partners are treated as a part of an extended Kodak family.

Why: In doing so, Kodak generates consistent and predictable earnings and produces an above-average return for its stockholders. It earns a deserved reputation as the world leader in imaging by producing great image products that delight customers, through the work of motivated employees, while exhibiting above average financial performance.

Next, the 2002 Xerox Mission Statement:

Xerox Mission Statement	Directive Mission Check
Our strategic intent is to help people find better ways to do great work by constantly leading document technologies, products and services that improve our Customers' work processes and business results *Source: www.Xerox.com*	**What:** Help people find better ways to do great work **For Whom:** Customers **How:** By constantly leading in document technologies, products, and services. **Why:** To improve our customers' work processes and business results

Figure 2-3, The Xerox Mission

In a manner similar to that employed with Kodak earlier, the following are observations and suggestions about the Xerox mission

What: The phrase *"Help people find better ways to do great work"* can encompass almost any endeavor. It is not at all definitive or descriptive. It does not mention marks on paper, images, or documents or any tangible product or service. How would one measure "help?" As such, it gives no valuable guidance. It could be a major consulting company's statement as much as that of the "Document Company."

For Whom: The use of the term *"Customers"* basically means that anyone or any entity that pays for a Xerox product, anywhere in the world, is a customer. No one is excluded from Xerox' market. Again, this gives license for Xerox to sell to anyone, anywhere regardless of the profit implications.

How*: "By constantly leading in document technologies, products and services"* Note that there is no mention of the value or use of Xerox' employees, alliance partners, or suppliers. How do they measure "leading?"

Why: *"To improve our customers' work processes and business results."* Note that this permits the provision of consulting services that require different skills from those of the usual Xerox sales representatives. This implies substantial risks. Is Xerox really ready for consulting?

Note also that there is no mention of the interests of the stockholders in this mission. Here too, this may is an indication that the firm is not particularly sensitive to the expectations of its owners. Is this a reason for Xerox's 1990 to 2000 financial troubles, and is it a manifestation of the inherent thinking that exists in Xerox's leadership team? I doubt it, but this is the mission that is offered to the public by Xerox leadership.

A better Xerox Direction-giving Mission would be:

What: The strategic intent of the Xerox Corporation is to develop/acquire, deliver, and maintain product and service solutions that address the identified key document management challenges

For Whom: Major enterprises around the world.

How: Its motivated, talented, empowered employees work individually and in teams with a commitment to continuous work improvement and personal growth.

Why: In doing so, Xerox generates consistent and predictable earnings, thereby facilitating an above-average return for its stockholders.

The Johnson and Johnson Credo (mission) presents an interesting and informative example:

J & J Credo

We believe our first responsibility is to the doctors, nurses, and patients, to mothers and fathers, and all others who use our products and services. In meeting their needs everything we do must be of high quality. We must constantly strive to reduce our costs in order to maintain reasonable prices. Customers' orders must be serviced promptly and accurately. Our suppliers and distributors must have an opportunity to make a fair profit.

We are responsible to our employees, the men and women who work with us throughout the world. Everyone must be considered as an individual. We must respect their dignity and recognize their merit. They must have a sense of security in their jobs. Compensation must be fair and adequate, and working conditions clean, orderly, and safe. We must be mindful of ways to help our employees fulfill their family responsibilities. Employees must feel free to make suggestions and complaints. There must be equal opportunity for employment, development, and advancement for those qualified. We must provide competent management and their actions must be just and ethical.

We are responsible to the communities in which we live and work, and to the world community as well. We must be good citizens – support good works and charities and bear our fair share of taxes. We must encourage civic improvements and better health and education. We must maintain in good order the property we are privileged to use, protecting the environment and natural resources.

Our final responsibility is to our stockholders. Business must make a sound profit. We must experiment with new ideas. Research must be carried on, innovative programs developed and mistakes paid for. New equipment must be purchased, new facilities provided and new products launched. Reserves must be created to provide for adverse times. When we operate according to these principles the stockholders should realize a fair return.

Source: www.jnj.com

Directive Mission Check

What:

High quality products and services needed by doctors, nurses, patients, mothers and fathers

For Whom:

• First for the doctors, nurses, and patients, to mothers and fathers and all others who use our products and services.

• Second for our employees

•Third to our communities

• Last to our stockholders

• Our suppliers and distributors

How:

• By offering prompt and accurate services

• By having everything be of high quality

• By reducing cost

• By considering employees as individuals whose dignity is respected and recognizing their merit

• Through fair and adequate compensation

• By supporting good works and charities

• By protecting the environment

• By experimenting with new ideas,carrying on research, developing innovative programs, making and paying for mistakes, buying new equipment, providing new facilities, launching new products and creating reserves for adverse times.

Why:

• To meet customer needs

• To meet community responsibilities

• To have the stockholder realize a fair profit

Figure 2-4, The Johnson and Johnson Mission

Over the years, Johnson & Johnson's 50-year old Credo has received much attention and acclaim. It is unique in that it puts customers first, and stockholders last...yes, it <u>does</u> mention the stockholder! J & J apparently understood that both putting the customer first <u>and</u> still paying attention to the stockholder were essential elements of the firm's enviable long-term success.

The Johnson & Johnson Credo is a good example of a Directive Mission Statement in that it sets boundaries and gives direction and guidance. This one-page document outlines responsibilities in great detail in order to have them applied as part of the everyday J & J business philosophy. This was true in 1943 and is still true today. It is indeed a Directive Mission model that is worth emulation.

The J & J Directive Mission could have been slightly improved through the addition of a descriptor of the services that J & J <u>will</u> supply. To make this criticism clear, recognize that the people served by J & J obviously need health insurance, tax advice, office equipment, lawn mowers, etc. Hopefully J & J does not intend to develop or acquire and market these products and services with a Johnson & Johnson label as being consistent with offerings that are "needed by doctors, nurses, patients, mothers and fathers."

Figure 2-5, The Harvard College Mission Statement is also informative:

Harvard College Mission Statement	Directive Mission Check
Harvard College adheres to the purposes for which the Charter of 1650 was granted: "The advancement of all good literature, arts, and sciences; the advancement and education of youth in all manner of good literature, arts, and sciences; and all other necessary provisions that may conduce to the education of the ... youth of this country..." In brief, Harvard strives to create knowledge, and to enable students to take best advantage of their educational opportunities.	**What:** In brief, Harvard strives to Create knowledge Open the minds of students **For Whom:** The youth of this country **How:** The College encourages students by:
To these ends, the College encourages students to respect ideas and their free expression, and to rejoice in discovery and in critical thought; to pursue excellence in a spirit of productive cooperation; and to assume responsibility for the consequences of personal actions. Harvard seeks to identify and to remove restraints on students' full participation, so that individuals may explore their capabilities and interests and may develop their full intellectual and human potential. Education at Harvard should liberate students to explore, to create, to challenge, and to lead. The support the College provides to students is a foundation upon which self-reliance and habits of lifelong learning are built. Harvard expects that the scholarship and collegiality it fosters in its students will lead them in their later lives to advance knowledge, to promote understanding, and to serve society.	• Respecting ideas and their free expression • Rejoicing in discovery and in critical thought; • Pursuing excellence in a spirit of productive cooperation • Assuming responsibility for the consequences of personal actions • Fully participating without restraints • Having individuals explore their capabilities and interests develop their full intellectual and human potential • Providing support to students upon which self-reliance and habits of lifelong learning are built. **Why:** To enable students to take best advantage of their educational opportunities. Harvard expects that the scholarship and collegiality it fosters in its students will lead them in their later lives to advance knowledge, to promote understanding, and to serve society. Education at Harvard should liberate students to explore, to create, to challenge and to lead.
Harry R. Lewis *Dean of Harvard College* *February 23, 1997* *Source: Harvard web site* *www.harvard.edu*	

Figure 2-5, The Harvard College Mission Statement

Some observations and comments about the Harvard mission from the perspective of a Directive Mission follow:

What: In brief the mission states, "Harvard strives to create knowledge and to open the minds of students to that knowledge." Pretty flowery language. How would one measure the creation of knowledge? Better yet, how would one measure the extent to which the minds of students have been opened? Note that opening the mind to learning does not necessarily mean that the mind absorbs the learning.

For Whom: "The youth of this country" is an interesting phrase. The number of foreign students would seem to violate this part of the mission. It would seem that Harvard administration does not heed the mission constraint. The mission would appear to need updating.

How: "The College encourages..." Interesting verb choice, using the word "encourages." Doesn't Harvard teach? Coach? Mentor? Note that there is no mention of the faculty, facilities, equipment, financial aid, endowment, etc in the mission.

Why: "Harvard expects that the scholarship and collegiality it fosters in its students will lead them in their later lives to advance knowledge, to promote understanding, and to serve society. Education at Harvard should liberate students to explore, to create, to challenge, and to lead." Given the verb "expects," this really isn't a reason why Harvard does what it does. The use of this verb precludes results measurement. If measures were employed, what might well be examined is if Harvard did indeed expect this. A better phrase might be "the scholarship and collegiality "enables"," "fosters," or "promotes."

On balance this mission statement is a pretty weak statement of intent and thus, it appears that Harvard pays no attention to its published mission.

A more Directive Mission for Harvard College would be:

What: Harvard College provides a unique educational opportunity and environment.

For Whom: For a diverse group of talented, national and international students.

How: Through the efforts of, and the interaction with, a world-class faculty and selected other individuals in world-class facilities.

Why: To provide scholastic experiences that challenge thinking, foster creativity, offer exposure to those in leadership positions, and to develop leadership skills. In doing so, Harvard is a major source of national and world leaders who serve society well.

Another informative mission example is that of the American Cancer Society:

American Cancer Society Mission

The American Cancer Society is the nationwide community -based voluntary health organization, dedicated to eliminating cancer as a major health problem by preventing cancer, saving lives, and diminishing suffering from cancer through, research, education, advocacy and service.

Source ACS web site 2002

Directive Mission Check

What:

Exactly what the ACS does or provides is is not clear from this statement. One can deduce that it provides funding for cancer research, cancer related educational literature, and advocacy for cancer -related issues but these are not stated in the mission.

For Whom:

The specific people who are served by the offerings of the ACS are not clear from the statement. One can deduce that it is the American public in general and cancer victims in particular, but there is no such mention.

How:

How is also not clear from this mission. Personal knowledge of the ACS leads one to understand that it conducts its work by seeking donations from a variety of sources and distributes the funds to worthy cancer related medical institutions. Further, it funds an active web site and produces publications that meet the needs of cancer victims. Finally, it produces and distributes cancer preventative communications and information that can ease the burden of current patients. None of this is included in the mission.

Why:

This could use elaboration to better give direction to its leaders, employees, and volunteers

Figure 2-6, The American Cancer Society Mission Statement

A better ACS Direction-Giving Mission would be:

What: The American Cancer Society secures funding for cancer research, cancer-related educational literature, and provides advocacy for cancer-related issues on behalf of the American public in general and cancer victims in particular.

For Whom: It conducts its work by soliciting donations and grants from a variety of sources and distributes the funds to cancer-related medical institutions and organizations that are judged to be worthy. Further, it funds an active web site and produces publications that meet the needs of cancer victims and their families.

How: It produces and distributes cancer-preventative communications and information that can ease the burden of current patients. It relies on a dedicated, impassioned, staff and talented volunteers.

Why: Its goal is to make positive contributions to the prevention of cancer, its early detection, and the quality of life of cancer victims and their families. Ultimately its goal is to assist in the ultimate elimination of cancer as a major health problem.

A Directive Mission Statement provides clear direction for goal setting, strategy development, and decision making purposes. Upon completing and after consensus by leadership, the statement can and should be cascaded to all levels in the organization as well as to important other constituencies. This includes all employees, customers, suppliers, partners and customers where appropriate. It can and should be constantly referred to for these purposes. In this way, every action, and every decision has the benefit of being considered in light of the mission.

Because of the importance of effective mission-direction, it is advisable to periodically check on an organizatioin's actual performance against its Directive Mission. To do this, we have found it exceptionally useful to develop and execute a simple assessment vehicle that isolates key phrases of the mission for leadership and if desired, employee, customer, Board member and others to provide their judgment of conformance. A sample, using the proposed Draft American Cancer Society Directive Mission is shown below in Figure 2-7, <u>Assessing Conformance to the Organization's Mission</u>.

A Sample Mission Conformance Check

Your opinion will help us select the vital few areas that need improvement action and those that should be noted as having "bragging rights". You have four choices:

❏ Work	❏ Pride	❏ OK	❏ Don't Know
(Needs priority improvement focus)	(Performance we should now be proud of)	(No action needed for now)	(Not in a position to judge)

The American Cancer Society :

	Work	Pride	OK	Don't Know
M-1. Secures funding for cancer research.	❏	❏	❏	❏
M-2. Secures funding for cancer-related educational literature.	❏	❏	❏	❏
M-3. Provides advocacy for cancer-related issues on behalf of the American public in general.	❏	❏	❏	❏
M-4. Provides advocacy for cancer victims in particular.	❏	❏	❏	❏
M-5. Conducts its work by soliciting donations.	❏	❏	❏	❏
M-6. Solicits grants from a variety of sources.	❏	❏	❏	❏
M-7. Distributes funds to cancer-related medical institutions.	❏	❏	❏	❏
M-8. Distributes funds to organizations that are judged to be worthy.	❏	❏	❏	❏
M-9. Funds an active web site.	❏	❏	❏	❏
M-10. Produces publications that meet the needs of cancer victims	❏	❏	❏	❏
M-11. Produces publications that meet the needs of cancer victim's families.	❏	❏	❏	❏
M-12. Produces and distributes cancer preventative information that can ease patients' burdens.	❏	❏	❏	❏
M-13. Relies on a dedicated, impassioned staff.	❏	❏	❏	❏
M-14. Relies on dedicated, impassioned, talented volunteers.	❏	❏	❏	❏
M-15 Makes positive contributions to the prevention of cancer .	❏	❏	❏	❏
M-16. Makes positive contributions to cancer's early detection.	❏	❏	❏	❏
M-17. Goal is to assist in the ultimate elimination of cancer as a major health problem.	❏	❏	❏	❏

Comments

_____
_____
_____
_____
_____
_____
_____

Use reverse side if needed

Name (Optional) _____

Figure 2-6, Assessing Conformance to the Organization's Mission.

Chapter Conclusions

At this point, the objectives of this chapter have been addressed:

The case that a solid, descriptive mission is a very important facet of an organization's success is illustrated.

An approach to examine, revises, or create an organization directive mission statement that gives guidance and/or explicit direction for resource decisions and issue resolution is provided.

The leader and the organization's focus in order to "stick to the knitting" are stressed.

Once again, the Directive Mission Statement describes <u>what</u> is done or provided...<u>who</u> is served, taught, treated, or supplied...<u>how</u> it all gets done...and <u>why</u> it is done. Its power is to enable the communication of a clear understanding of the "business" of the organization in order to give guidance to all involved as daily decisions are made. It enables great questions such as "Is this decision consistent with our directive mission?" this to be asked.

We examined examples of mission statements of existing organizations and considered their implications. The mission statements selected showed both well-written and poorly written statements. Well-written statements were hard to find. With the exception of Xerox, no first-hand knowledge of the organizations was used to critique or comment on the values. This put the author in much the same position as the general public or an individual stockholder.

The reader can use a similar questioning approach shown in this text to critically examine the missions of organizations that they invest in, or work for. They can evaluate the non-profit organizations that they give to, or volunteer for, by examining the published missions and then asking questions. Many of the organizations that were researched for this book did not publish their mission statements. If the reader finds this to be true of organizations that you are interested in, what this lack of mission visibility portrays is for you to decide.

 To have a common mission, you must first have a mission. To get guidance from a mission, you must have one that actually <u>gives</u> guidance. Until the organization mission is focused, logical and easy to understand... successful deployment and empowerment are not only impossible, the empowerment attempt can result in dysfunctional outcomes!! Thus, a Directive Mission fully provides this needed guidance.

"When you have a critical job to do, it is probably helpful to know precisely what the mission is."
R.C. Palermo

Chapter 2. The Directive Mission

Do The **R<u>igh</u>t** Things ... Right!

It <u>Is</u> That Simple!

Chapter 3
The Prescriptive Vision

Chapter Objectives:

To make the case that a clear, descriptive picture of the desired state three years hence is a very important facet of an organization's success.

To provide a simple, effective method for creating an organization vision statement that will enable all the key constituencies of an organization to understand the three-year goals, thus allowing them to direct appropriate supportive efforts toward the achievement of this desired state.

To help the leader and the organization to stay focused on the three-year horizon.

© 2003 The Strategic Triangle Inc.

Chapter 3. The Prescriptive Vision

Do The **Right** Things ... Right!

It Is That Simple!

Chapter 3
The Prescriptive Vision

"Where there is no vision, the people perish." Old Testament

Positioning. The Prescriptive Vision Statement is one of six key guides that help an organization determine what the "right" things are, thus enabling laser-like focus. The other remaining five guides are the Directive Mission, Shared Values, and the words of customers, employees, and the financial community. As an aggregate, they are the organizational "directors."

A vision is basically a picture of the desired future state of an organization. It can be characterized as a detailed answer to the question, "How do we want to look, be perceived, perform, and/or be positioned three years from now?"

This is a good point to address some common questions about the vision time frame. "Why three years?" "Why not five years?" "Why not one year?" Simply put, one year is too short to investigate, plan, and execute initiatives that are intended to produce breakthrough results. Five years is often too long for people to retain focus and momentum. Further, the rapid pace of the competitive world may not tolerate a five year period between plans. Finally, people can lose interest and intensity after just a few months on a project. Leadership support can wane. Thus, longer term plans often fail to come to fruition. Experience has shown, and logic supports a three-year vision horizon.

Vision statements are often misunderstood. They are sometimes confused with mission statements. A vision statement is profoundly different from a mission statement. Think of it in this way: the mission describes an organization's <u>mode</u> of transportation, while the vision describes its <u>destination</u>. Both are equally important to "finding the <u>right</u> things."

The Prescriptive Vision Statement is the description of a destination. It depicts how we want the organization to be perceived, positioned, and described three years from now.

The Directive Mission Statement describes <u>what</u> is done or provided, <u>who</u> is served, taught, treated, or supplied, <u>how</u> it all gets done, and <u>why</u> the work is done. Its intent is to communicate a clear understanding of the "business" of an organization. It provides guidance to all involved in the organization as daily decisions are made, and work actions are taken. More on this can be found in Chapter 2, The Directive Mission.

Vision Work Experiences

Some leaders state that the vision for their organization doesn't have to be made explicit. They feel that this would restrict their creative options and opportunities. They want the freedom to turn on a dime, and strike out in new directions, or reach for new opportunities without having to be handcuffed by a stated vision.

Others feel that a vision even three years hence is too difficult to develop, articulate, and even more difficult to come to agreement on. One client indicated that he would rather have a root canal than sit through one more agonizing visioning session.

A few feel that a clear declaration of stated goals for three years out can "come back to bite you" when it doesn't pan out. These leaders will view a written vision as something to be avoided.

 For whichever reasoning led to it, the "a specific vision is not needed" position is unsupported by insights gleaned from customer, employee and financial surveys. These insights are supported by discussions with selected constituencies of a variety of organizations. All these constituencies consistently express a <u>strong</u> desire to understand the intended destination of an organization in which they have a vested interest. The numbers of organizations that have crashed because they failed to have developed and/or articulated and disseminated a longer-term destination are legion. Failure to develop and drive a game plan that is consistently supportive of a stated vision is often fatal.

Some leaders state that there just isn't time for a vision session, or that the world is too fast moving and dynamic to stop and try to formulate and gain agreement on a vision. In even the most contentious situation, I have facilitated consensus on an organizational vision in less than a four-hour group session. Updates to such a vision can be accomplished in one or two hours. Surely the benefits of having the leadership team come to a common understanding of where its organization needs to, or wants to head, and the benefits of having all the workers share the same understanding, is worth four hours or less.

 Does this mean that once the journey starts that you can't change the destination? No, of course not. A vision is never carved in stone! In fact, it should be revisited at least annually to see if an update or course correction is needed. All that has to be done is to take the time to re-examine the vision, gain consensus on any needed changes, share the new vision with constituencies, and then redirect resources as may be appropriate to the updated vision. Your customers, alliance partners, suppliers, and financial backers have a vital interest in any substantive vision change.

Finally, other leaders indicate that what is needed is a simple one sentence vision that inspires and captures the imagination. This can be used in public relations and advertising initiatives. These are "slogans," not vision statements. Granted there is a use for slogans. "We aspire to be the very best" may be cute, catchy, and may be useful in advertising, but it doesn't give sufficient direction to people for resource allocations, prioritization judgments, or organizational decisions. The phrase "will aspire" is synonymous with "we try"…not very convincing.

 A distinction must be made between a motivational sound bite that is intended to be used for inspiration and to shape public sentiment, and that of a Prescriptive Vision that gives specific guidance to the organization's citizens as they journey forward as a unit. The vision needs to be clear and explicit and should unambiguously describe the intended destiny of the organization.

The metaphor of a crew of rowers and their coxswain is a good one to graphically portray the positioning and value of a prescriptive vision. See Figure 3-1, The Prescriptive Vision. Here, if the organization's employee, customer, supplier, and financial rowers clearly understand the good and the bad about the current state, and have a common picture of the boat's destination. The leader can encourage the crew rather than police them and efficient progress to the end point can be achieved.

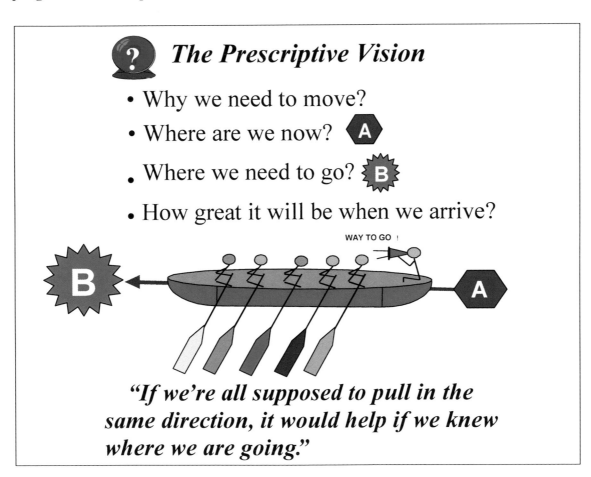

Figure 3-1, The Prescriptive Vision

Producing A Prescriptive Vision Statement

After years of development, testing, and application in practice, a simple, painless, and yet effective approach for producing a Prescriptive Vision has been perfected. This approach provides a leader and/or the senior team with an efficient way to come to consensus on a solid, direction-giving, Prescriptive Vision statement. A graphic portrayal of this approach is shown in Figure 3-2, The Prescriptive Vision Process. Specific step-by-step guidance for developing a Prescriptive Vision is presented below:

Step 1. The leader and/or the senior team brainstorm and come to agreement on a list of terms that in the aggregate describe all key facets of the organization. What are the measures or descriptors that can fully characterize the enterprise or group today, in the past, and/or in the future? These can include, but are not limited to descriptions of the organization's: products, services, revenues, profits, market share, margins, budgets, number and types of customers, employees, and organizational style.

Step 2. Current data for each of the selected descriptors are gathered. The resulting numbers are checked for accuracy and completeness.

Step 3. Facts, if possible, and opinions only if necessary are used to describe the organization as it existed 3 to 5 years ago. The results are checked for perceived accuracy and completeness.

Step 4. Comparing the information from Steps 2 and 3, the up, down, or level historical trends that are suggested by the two points (current and three years past) are recorded in the form of up, down, lateral trend arrows.

Step 5. Is the direction of each of these trends desirable? Is this the direction we want the enterprise or group to follow in the future? If current trends continue, will the resulting future state of the organization be big enough, good enough, or strong enough? The desired state level for each of the descriptors is determined using future directional arrows.

Step 6. Using the arrow directions, numbers are agreed that reflect these desired state levels.

Step 7. Using the desired results in Step 6, brainstorm key words or phrases that should be present in the Prescriptive Vision Statement in a manner that will fairly represent these data. Group similar items, and eliminate less important words or phrases. Gain consensus on the priority phrases and words that must be in the final statement. Craft a concisely worded Prescriptive Vision Statement from the surviving words and phrases.

Step 8. The resulting Prescriptive Vision Statement is communicated throughout the organization. Subsequently, each group in the organization is asked to study the Prescriptive Vision Statement and feed back their planned actions that will help the organization's journey toward that destination. In this way, the "rowers" can start pulling in the same direction.

See Figure 3-2, <u>The Prescriptive Vision Development Process,</u> for a sample graphic useful in a visioning exercise.

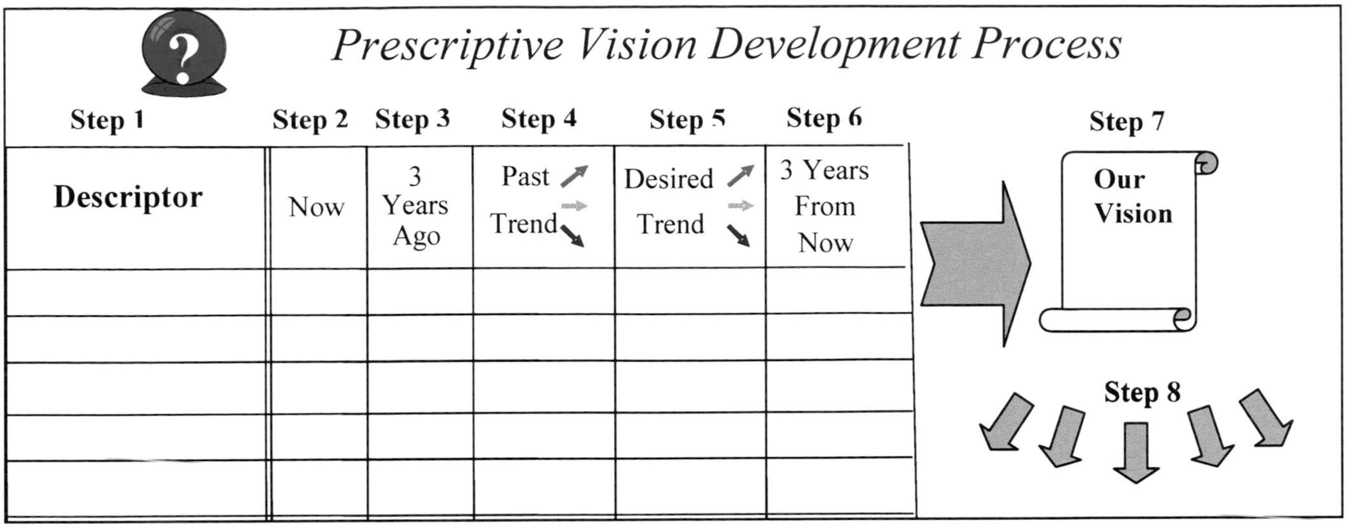

Figure 3-2, The Prescriptive Vision Development Process

A Sample Vision Exercise

Organizations will rarely display a detailed vision statement in the public domain; they rightfully feel that their vision work is to be held in confidence. Thus the following section presents a sample vision exercise that is derived from real-world examples, suitably altered to protect client information.

Step 1. The selected key organization performance measures for this example are:

- # of Customers
- Geography Served
- Revenue In U.S. Dollars
- # of Employees
- # of Products

- # of Services
- Operating Geography
- # of Alliances
- Earnings Per Share
- Stock Price

Step 2. The current state levels for each measure are found to be:

- # of Customers   10,000
- Geography   U.S.
- Revenue $ 100M
- # of Employees   2000
- # of Products   11

- # of Services   10
- # of Alliances   0
- Earnings Per Share $ 1.00
- Stock Price $ 10.00

Steps 3 and 4. The levels for three years prior and the deduced trends [past-to-today] were:

	Past	Now	Past Trend	
• # of Customers	8000	10,000	Up 25%	↗
• Geography	U.S.	U.S.	Flat	→
• Revenue	$ 160M	$ 100M	Down 37.5%	↘
• # of Employees	2000	1000	Down 50%	↘
• # of Products	10	11	Up 10%	→
• # of Services	5	10	Up 100%	↑
• # of Alliances	2	0	Down	↓
• Earning Per Share	$ 1.50	$ 1.00	Down 30%	↘
• Stock Price	$ 25.00	$ 10.00	Down 60%	↘

Steps 5 and 6. The past levels, current levels, past trends, desired future trends, and the resulting desired levels for each measure are shown in Figure 3-3, The Vision Analysis.

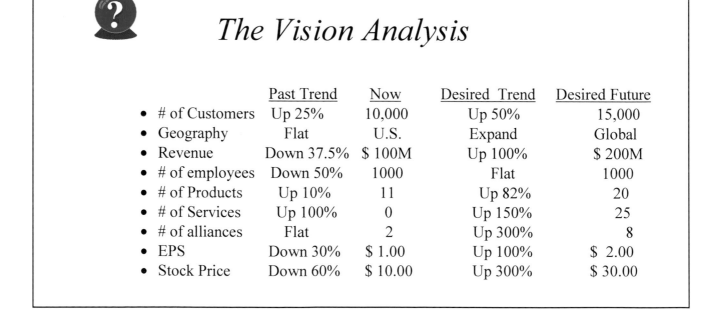

The Vision Analysis

	Past Trend	Now	Desired Trend	Desired Future
• # of Customers	Up 25%	10,000	Up 50%	15,000
• Geography	Flat	U.S.	Expand	Global
• Revenue	Down 37.5%	$ 100M	Up 100%	$ 200M
• # of employees	Down 50%	1000	Flat	1000
• # of Products	Up 10%	11	Up 82%	20
• # of Services	Up 100%	0	Up 150%	25
• # of alliances	Flat	2	Up 300%	8
• EPS	Down 30%	$ 1.00	Up 100%	$ 2.00
• Stock Price	Down 60%	$ 10.00	Up 300%	$ 30.00

Figure 3-3, The Vision Analysis

Step 7. Given the information shown in Figure 3-3, <u>The Vision Analysis</u>, the following XYZ Inc. Prescriptive Vision Statement is reflective of the desired trends, and is drafted for leadership review, and modification. The resulting statement is shown in Figure 3-4, <u>The XYZ Company Prescriptive Vision.</u>

The XYZ Company Prescriptive Vision

During the next three years, XYZ Inc. will expand to become a global company, relying on world-class alliance partners to leverage the skills of our core domestic workforce. Rapid growth in revenues will be achieved by combining an increased penetration of existing markets using current products, the doubling of product offerings, the addition of new services, with the penetration of new global markets. Current employees will receive continuous skills improvement training with talent retention being key. In combination with cost reduction and cost maintenance efforts, we will consistently increase earnings per share, thereby receiving a favorable stock evaluation to fully benefit our stockholders.

Figure 3-4, The XYZ Company Prescriptive Vision.

Step 8. The resulting XYZ Prescriptive Vision Statement and the back up specific data are communicated throughout the organization. Each group in the organization is asked to study the Prescriptive Vision Statement and desired future data and then feed back their planned actions that they believe will help the organization's journey toward that destination. Management comment and approval follow.

In conclusion, after following, step-by-step the Prescriptive Vision process, the XYZ organization has a clear destination that can be deployed and communicated to employees, suppliers and investors. Further, the desired state data are available for use in the development of operating plans, business plans, and target setting.

Two Real-World Vision Examples

It is instructive to examine the published vision statements of some well-known organizations. Again, I recognize that the sensitive nature of vision statements may preclude them from being fully disclosed. However, some successful organizations share enough in such vehicles as Annual Reports or 10-K disclosures, or even on web sites to be useful for examination.

In Figure 3-5, The American Express Vision Statement was captured from the firm's web site, *www.americanexpress.com* in 2002. In Figure 3-6, The Microsoft Corporation Vision Statement is examined. It was captured from their web site, *www.microsoft.com*, in 2002.

As stated earlier, a useful vision statement is supposed to offer leaders, managers, employees, investors, donors, and other interested constituencies, a clear view of the intended future destination of an organization. As such, it is appropriate to examine an organization's vision statement using the following questions:

1. Does the statement describe an intended future state of the organization in sufficient detail to adequately inform and/or give direction as decisions are made by appropriate groups such as:

- Leaders, managers and employees?	- Market analysts?
- Prospective employees?	- Investors?
- Selected Customers?	- Donors?

2. Does the statement provide encouragement, instill confidence in the organization, and/or energize the reader?

3. Can progress toward the vision and its elements be measured?

Using these three questions, some relevant comments and observations follow each of the two sample vision statements.

American Express

The published American Express vision is shown in Figure 3-5, The American Express Vision Statement. A brief commentary follows and a suggested improved version is presented for the reader's consideration.

"The American Express Vision is to become the' world's most respected service brand'. We plan to realize our vision through becoming a top 25 employer, improving service quality, and deepening customer relationships".

Source: www.AmericanExpress.com

Figure 3-5, The American Express Vision Statement

Comments/Observations

If the American Express name weren't at the top of the vision, no one could guess whose vision this is. Basically it could be any one of thousands of organizations' vision statements. Perhaps American Express has a private, internally distributed vision that gives specific direction and insights to its employees and partners. If this one is the only corporate vision, it is useless in giving guidance to resource allocation and decision making.

First, it gives little direction or bounds that will guide operational and strategic decisions. Note that American Express leaders can choose to add any service offering, get into any service business, serve any markets or customers and still make the case that the initiative is consistent with this vision. Note also, that there is no mention of profit, return-on-investment, financial health or return to the stockholders.

Finally, lacking any statement of financial performance goals, it is hardly supportive of or encouraging for its investors.

A more effective Draft American Express Prescriptive Vision Statement start point for the leaders to consider is shown in Figure 3-6:

American Express' vision is that we be perceived by worldwide Financial and travel services' customers, global merchants, employees and our stakeholders as the world's most respected financial and travel service brand.

This vision is accomplished by:

- *Maintaining a position of a top employer — as judged by the results of a survey of our employees — compared to those of similar firms.*
- *Never being satisfied with existing service quality or performance committing to a measured, continuous improvement philosophy.*
- *Establishing and maintaining strong, positive, close, on-going relationships with our customers, emphasizing two -way communication and ensuring that the value of our services are judged by our customers to exceed their costs.*

In doing so, American Express provides consistent earnings that support above - average returns for our investors.

Figure 3-6, A Draft American Express Prescriptive Vision Statement

Microsoft

Some observations and comments about the Microsoft vision statement follow Figure 3-7, The Microsoft Vision Statement. A draft of a new more directive vision is offered for the reader's consideration.

" Microsoft's vision is to empower people through great software - any time, any place, and on any device. As the worldwide leader in software for personal and business computing, Microsoft strives to produce innovative products and services that meet our customers' evolving needs. At the same time, we understand that long -term success is about more than just making great products. " Source: www.microsoft.com

Figure 3-7, The Microsoft Vision Statement

Comments/Observations

If the word "mission" were substituted for "vision" in the Microsoft statement above, it could also be a mission statement. It fails to meet the definition of a vision as being a description of the organization's desired <u>destination</u>. Perhaps they have a private, internally distributed vision that gives specific direction and insights to its employees and partners. If this one is the only corporate vision, it has little value for giving guidance to resource allocation and decision making.

First, the phrase *"Microsoft strives to produce"* is not appropriate as part of a statement of where an organization <u>desires</u> to be positioned or perceived in the future. Does it want to be perceived as *"striving"* or perceived as *"succeeding?"* Also, won't it acquire or license other products that it doesn't "produce?" "Acquire" is a better word choice than "produce."

Note the sentence *"At the same time, we understand that long-term success is about more than just making great products."* This is quite cryptic. If Microsoft is about more than just making great products, to what does this refer? Could it be providing acceptable returns for its stockholders? It is disappointing that the stockholder's interests or any specific references to the value of employee are omitted. Microsoft leaders can add any service offering, get into <u>any</u> service business, serve <u>any</u> markets or customers and still make a valid case that the initiative is consistent with this vision.

One wonders about Microsoft's verification measures. That is, how does Microsoft measure whether its customers feel that they are "empowered-any time, any place and on any device?" Does Microsoft measure this? I doubt it is done.

A more effective Microsoft prescriptive vision start point for the firm's leaders to consider is shown in Figure 3-8, <u>A Microsoft Prescriptive Vision Satatement</u>.

Microsoft's vision is a future where:
Customers see their productivity and satisfaction optimized through the use of our software for personal and business computing. Our delighted customers willingly and regularly recom mend Microsoft to others.

Employees consistently indicate that it is a great place to work, learn and grow. Associates and partners willingly recommend working with Microsoft to qualified others.

We produce and/or acquire innovative software products and services that meet or exceed our customers' current and evolving needs. We are never satisfied with current quality or productivity.

We maintain a position as the worldwide leader in software for personal and business computing as measured by dollar sales.

We reward loyal financial backers by seeing that they get returns on investments that exceed industry averages.

Figure 3-8, A Microsoft Prescriptive Vision Statement

Because of the importance of having an effective vision, it is advisable to periodically check on an organizatioin's actual performance against its Prescriptive Vision. To do this, I have found it exceptionally useful to develop and execute a simple assessment vehicle that isolates key phrases of the vision for conformance assessment by leadership, employees, customers, Board members and others. A sample, using the proposed Draft Microsoft Prescriptive Vision is shown below in Figure 3-9, A Sample Vision Confromance Check.

A Sample Vision Conformance Check

Your vote will help us select the "Vital Few" that need focused improvement action and those that should be featured as "bragging rights". You have four choices:

❑ Work
(Needs priority improvement focus)

❑ Pride
(Performance we should now be proud of)

❑ OK
(No action needed for now)

❑ Don't Know
(Not in a position to judge)

		Work	Pride	OK	??
Vi-1	Customers see their productivity and satisfaction optimized through the use of our software for personal and business computing.	❑	❑	❑	❑
Vi-2	Our delighted customers willingly and regularly recommend Microsoft offerings to others.	❑	❑	❑	❑
Vi-3	Employees consistently indicate that Microsoft is a great place to work, learn and grow.	❑	❑	❑	❑
Vi-4	Associates and partners willingly recommend working with Microsoft to qualified others.	❑	❑	❑	❑
Vi-5	We produce and/or acquire innovative software products & services that meet or exceed customers 'current and evolving needs.	❑	❑	❑	❑
Vi-6	We are never satisfied with current quality or productivity.	❑	❑	❑	❑
Vi-7	We maintain a position as the worldwide leader in software for personal and business computing as measured by dollar sales.	❑	❑	❑	❑
Vi-8	We reward loyal financial backers by seeing that they get positive returns on investments that exceed industry averages.	❑	❑	❑	❑

Comments:

Name (Optional) _____

Figure 3-9, A Sample Vision Conformance Check

Chapter Conclusions

At this point, the objectives of this chapter have been addressed:

Make the case that a clear, descriptive picture of the desired state three years hence is a very important facet of an organization's success.

Provide a simple, effective method for creating an organization vision statement that will enable all the key constituencies of an organization to understand the three-year goals, thus allowing them to direct appropriate supportive efforts toward the achievement of this desired state.

Help the leader and the organization to stay focused on the three-year horizon.

It just makes common sense that if each involved individual and team in an organization is made to understand where the enterprise needs to head and given the proper leadership encouragement, people will work toward a common end. Further, it is logical to conclude that the vision will thereby be approached more rapidly than might otherwise be the case.

Surely there are many ways to have a leader and/or leadership team develop and come to consensus on a vision. The proposed Prescriptive Vision method is simple, data-based, and has proven to be very effective.

I am absolutely convinced by experience that a clear, well-defined Prescriptive Vision is a key element that measurably contributes to the success of an organization and, thereby, the success of the leader.

The reader should consider using these questions to study the visions of companies that they invest in, or work for. They could also evaluate the non-profit organizations that they give to or volunteer for, in a similar manner.

- **Does the vision statement describe an intended future state of the organization in sufficient detail to adequately inform and/or give direction as management decisions are made?**
- **Does the mission statement provide encouragement, instill confidence in the organization, and/or energize the reader?**
- **Can progress toward the vision be measured?**

" I push in one direction, not in every direction."

Rita Montalcini, Nobel Laureate Medicine, 1988

Do The **Right** Things ... Right!

It Is That Simple!

Chapter 4

Organizational Shared Values

Chapter Objectives:

To share an effective approach for examining, revising or creating an organizational set of values.

To examine examples of value statements of existing organizations and consider their implications.

To help the leaders and all constituencies gain assurance that, as the organization's work is performed, all of the leaders and employees behave in a manner consistent with the agreed values.

© 2003 The Strategic Triangle Inc.

Do The <u>Right</u> Things ... Right!

It <u>Is</u> That Simple!

Chapter 4

Organizational Shared Values

"Following the abuses of the '90s, executives are learning that trust, integrity, and fairness do matter --and are crucial to the bottom line."

Business Week Aug.'02

Positioning. An organization's values are sometimes called a philosophy, a set of beliefs, or ethics. They are basically a guide for the behaviors that are expected to be exhibited by the employees of an organization. The statement of values can be characterized as an answer to the question, "How are we expected to behave as we do the work of the organization?" With a set of values in hand, the leaders can communicate the behaviors that are expected to all members of the organization, as well as to its suppliers, customers, stakeholders, and the public.

 Thoughtfully developed and carefully communicated values can provide a true guiding light that enables the employees of an organization to actually behave in much the same way as the founders or leaders expect. This is not to say that having and communicating values is sufficient. Unless the leaders "role model" the values through their every day behavior and decision-making, published values are worthless. Unless the leaders also monitor to ensure that all leaders and employees are actually putting these values into practice, the values can too easily be ignored or forgotten.

Experiences with Values. Today, it is more important than ever that an organization come to consensus on what it truly values and then ensure that the values are embraced. Where there is hypocrisy ("Do what I say, not what I do"), and where the leaders are not role models for value-centered behaviors, the dangers are obvious. The ultimate results can be disastrous. During years of interactions with organizations around the world, I have encountered many situations where words and deeds do not match. Figure 4-1, <u>Values Hypocrisy</u> depicts a summary of this incongruity.

Values Hypocrisy

What do we believe? How should we act?

Words	*Reality*
• An open -door policy	• It's not safe to speak your mind
• Empowered employees	• Most employees can't be trusted with information
• Honesty above all	• The end justifies the means
• Motivated employees make the machine run	• Fear is the best motivator
• We are responsible to our stakeholders, customers, employees, and stockholders	• Profits are the alpha and the omega
• "Quality suppliers first"	• Lowest cost is all that counts

Figure 4-1, Values Hypocrisy

After the painful Enron and Andersen experiences of 2002, it can be confidently noted that stated values are important and that <u>every</u> employee and leader in a firm <u>must</u> understand them and exhibit behaviors that are consistent with them. We have all seen an alarming reality associated with ignored organizational values. Experiences, especially recent ones, have shown that although a statement of values may have been developed, and may have been communicated throughout an organization, the values are just not fully put into practice. Simply put, they are often treated as short-lived sound bites instead of guiding elements.

Some leaders feel that the values of their organization need not be made explicit. Some feel values such as honesty and integrity are just understood and need not be stressed. Others feel that a published set of values is conventionally required and, therefore, value development sessions are a small sacrifice.

 An organization must continually reinforce its values. It is wise to regularly survey employees to see if they perceive that the organization's values are being put into practice by their co-workers, managers and leaders. Customers can also be queried to see if the organization is perceived to be modeling published values. Without these assessment actions, the leaders are either behaving as if the values are merely words on paper or are operating on faith that the values will be embraced. Both are dangerous paths. It is interesting to note that the challenge: "Don't act like that!" has little meaning if expectations of behavior are not well understood in an organization.

Informal discussions, interviews and surveys of many organizations' employees, customers and suppliers have been revealing. All these constituencies consistently express a strong need to believe that the senior management of their suppliers, of their bosses, and their colleagues act in a manner consistent with published organizational values.

Granted, that there is natural skepticism or even cynicism about the subject of values. When an organization proves by its performance that it does indeed embrace its values, (e.g., they "walk the talk"), their constituencies often reward it with outstanding performance and loyalty. Consider the role model behavior of Johnson and Johnson leadership during the Tylenol contamination crisis of a few years ago and the benefits that subsequently accrued to the organization. When an organization demonstrates hypocrisy relative to stated values, it is inevitably punished. The number of leaders who have been embarrassed and the number of organizations that have crashed because of a leadership failure to ensure that values are practiced seem to be growing daily.

Does this mean that once the values are stated that they cannot change? No, of course not. New values can be added as conditions warrant, but deletion of a prior published value requires care. For example, if "honesty" is stated in a prior version of an organization's values, and it is deleted in a later version, does that mean that the organization no longer values honesty?

A word about deployment of values in a large organization is appropriate. Experience has shown that once the leadership of an organization comes to consensus on a set of values, then all of the sub-groups within the organization must embrace the same values. Group values that differ from those of the parent organization should be discouraged. For example, if a group's value set indicates that "integrity" (which appears in the organization values) is not included in a sub-group's value set; this may seem to imply that "integrity" is not held to be of value to this particular group.

Finally, I believe that an organization's values should be limited to eight or less in number. Committees who work to produce a set of values tend to reach consensus by including everyone's desired value in the organizational set. This can lead to sets containing 10 to 20 or more values. The more values there are, the more devalued is the currency of each one.

Steps to Produce an Effective Statement of Values

It is important to recognize that an organization may already have a set of values in place. If so, the following screening questions are appropriate:

- Are the listed values adequately described and easily understood?
- Can all employees fully explain each value's meaning and intent if asked?
- Are the values embraced and demonstrated visibly in practice?
- Does the leadership want (need) to rework or update the values or develop a new set of values?

If the decision is to rework or develop a new value set, the organizational leaders can proceed using an effective Values development process as described in the following outline:

Step 1. Gather the leadership team together and brainstorm a list of word candidates for possible inclusion in the organization's value set.

Step 2. Eliminate redundancies and logically group words to narrow the candidate list. If any new candidate words arise, add them.

Step 3. Consider which of the candidate words best describe the desired or needed behaviors that must be exhibited in the course of the organization's work.

Step 4. Give each participant 10 total votes, allowing no more than five on any one candidate word. Five votes for a candidate would indicate that it is an essential value and/or it represents a perceived weakness or threat in current performance.

Step 5. Sum the votes. Come to a consensus on the priority set of values (5 to 8 of them) giving due consideration to those that received the most votes and that raise the most passion.

Step 6. Draft an explanatory paragraph for each of the selected values.

Step 7. Develop and execute an effective values communication strategy.

Step 8. Develop and execute an annual employee survey that determines:
- If the employees feel that the values are being reflected in the behavior of the leaders, managers, and co-workers.
- The values that most often appear to be ignored or overlooked in practice.
- The reasons for believing that some values are being ignored.
- Priority candidates for improvement.

Figure 4-2, Values Worksheet, is a form that is easily used to guide the first six of the above eight-Step value statement development approach.

Values Brainstorming

Potential key words or phrases that should be included in a Set of Values	# of votes
A	
B	
C	
D	
...	

1. Brainstorm potential key words or phrases that should be included in a Set of Values for the organization. Write them on the chart.

2. Eliminate redundant items. Group similar items.

3. Cast votes for the most important words or phrases. "If I could ensure that only one word or phrase was included, it would be letter __ ."

4. Add up the votes and record them in the column provided. Mark with an * those words or phrases that are key candidates (the ones that got the most votes). Discuss and come to a consensus on five to eight words or phrases that will constitute the organization's values.

Figure 4-2, Values Brainstorming

Some Real-World Value Statement Examples

It is instructive to examine the published value statements of some well-known organizations, especially those that have had recent ethical issues. Note that while the value examinations that follow may be very critical of the Value Statement of a particular organization, it is not necessarily critical of the organization's people. Rather, such poor performance is an indictment of the leadership. The difficulties that two of the organizations in question have been facing are clearly related to a faulty or inadequate values process.

In Figure 4-3, Enron Values are shared and discussed. They were captured from *www.enron.com* in 2002. In Figure 4-4, Andersen Values are shared and discussed. They were captured from *www.andersen.com* in 2002. Finally, in Figure 4-5, is Wegmans Philosophy (Values) from *www.wegmans.com* in 2002 are shared and discussed.

As stated earlier, a statement of values is supposed to offer leaders, managers, employees, customers, investors, donors, and others, a clear view of the behavior that is expected from the an organization. As such, it is appropriate to challenge any set of organization values with the following group of questions:

1. Is the set of values in sufficient detail to adequately inform and/or give direction to leaders, managers, and employees as they go about the work of the organization? Does it give adequate information to investors, customers, donors, the community, or prospective employees so they can expect certain behavior as they interact with the organization?
2. Do the values provide encouragement, instill confidence, create a sense of pride in the organization, and or energize the readers?
3. Can adherence to each value be measured? Are they measured? Is there evidence that the values have been embraced? Ignored? If required, what corrective action was taken? What was the outcome? What lessons were learned?

 Enron Values

Enron Corporate Values

Communication. We have an obligation to communicate. Here, we take the time to talk with one another and to listen. We believe that information is meant to move and that information moves people.

Respect. We treat others as we would like to be treated ourselves. We do not tolerate abusive or disrespectful treatment.

Integrity. We work with customers and prospects openly, honestly, and sincerely. When we say we will do something, we will do it; when we say we cannot or will not do something, then we won't do it.

Excellence. We are satisfied with nothing less than the very best in everything we do. We will continue to raise the bar for everyone. The great fun here will be for all of us to discover just how good we can really be.

Source: 2001 Enron Annual Report

Comments:

The fact that only four values are included is very positive. It makes them easy to remember and easy to cascade throughout an organization. The explanation that follows each value is brief but informative. The intent of each and the direction that they offer relative to expected behavior is clear.

The values are such that the employees and those who deal with the company would feel confident that they are working for and with the "right" kind of company.

Adherence to the values can readily be assessed via surveys and observation that are conducted by internal or preferably external examiners.

While we have no first -hand information about the adherence of Enron leaders and employees to their values, the news media have made it quite clear that communication and integrity were compromised by the leadership. We note that the Integrity value specifically mentions customers and prospects and omits mention of stockholders. We doubt that investors would have been so supportive if they knew that reported financials were improved by what may be legal but questionable practices to benefit the leaders.

Figure 4-3, Enron Values

Values

 Andersen Values
Comments

- Quality Service

- Quality People

- Meritocracy

- One Firm Approach

- Integrity

- Innovation

- Openness and Trust

- Stewardship

- Empowerment / Accountability

- Entrepreneurial

- Continuous Learning

- Sharing

Source: www.Andersen.com

One thing is clear from a first glance at the values. There are too many of them. It appears as if the values may have been developed by a committee, with consensus reached by including everyone's favorite value. It is impossible to cascade 12 values and expect universal absorption and acceptance.

It is important to note that no representation of "profit" appears in the values. Yet, we know from experience, and from many of Andersen's own publications that partners and employees were driven to maximize their personal financial return above all else. Since there are no stock grants or no stock options, partners maximized their income by annually increasing distributed profits. Indeed, to even become a partner, candidates must generally have had to develop and/or bring with them current clients that generated substantial and continuing large annual fees. Thus, from day one, the financial performance measure dwarfed all other values in importance. Granted, a satisfied client is vital to a partner, but extracting maximum fees is equally important. To others aspiring to become partners, it appeared to be all that counted.

It appears clear from the alleged document shredding and the ensuing legal difficulties, that the "Integrity" value was not embraced. "Walking the talk" was an unmet challenge.

Finally, it is ironic that "Stewardship" was a value. Rather than preserving the Firm for the next generation as it had been preserved for them by their predecessors.

Figure 4-4, Andersen Values

Wegmans Values

<u>*Wegmans' Co. Philosophy*</u> *[Values]*

(written more than 25 years ago):

At Wegmans, we believe that good people, working toward a common goal, can accomplish anything they set out to do.

In this spirit, we set our goal to be the very best at serving the needs of our customers. Every action we take should be made with this in mind.

We also believe that we can achieve our goal only if we fulfill the needs of our own people.

To our customers and our people we pledge continuous improvement, and we make the commitment:

"EVERY DAY YOU GET OUR BEST " Source: www.wegmans.com

<u>Implied Values</u>

Common Goals

Motivated People

Customer Focus

Continuous Improvement

<u>**Comments**</u>

Wegmans is a major regional supermarket chain, and one of the largest private companies in the U.S. It is enormously popular in its store areas and is perceived to be world class in every thing it does.

The values stated in the philosophy are few in number and easy to comprehend. Given that it is privately owned with no stockholders, it is understandable that financial results are not included as publicly communicated values.

Personal observations and shopping experiences of the author support a contention that all the leaders from the board chair, the CEO, and all employees, put into practice all of these "Customer Focus, Motivated Employees, and Continuous Improvement " values stated in the philosophy ...every day.

Figure 4-5, Wegmans Values

Because of the importance of effective Organizational Values, it is advisable to periodically check on an organizatioin's actual performance against its values. To do this, I have found it exceptionally useful to develop and execute a simple assessment vehicle that isolates key phrases of the values for conformance judgment by leadership, employees, customers, Board members and others. A sample, using the Wegmans set of values is shown below in Figure 4-6, A Sample Values Conformance Check.

A Sample Vision Conformance Check

Your vote will help us select the "Vital Few" that need focused improvement action and those that should be featured as "bragging rights". Your have four choices:

❏ Work   ❏ Pride   ❏ OK   ❏ Don't Know

(Needs priority improvement focus)   (Performance we should now be proud of)   (No action needed for now)   (Not in a position to judge)

		Work	Pride	OK	Don't Know
Vi-1	Customers see their productivity and satisfaction optimized through the use of our software for personal and business computing.	❏	❏	❏	❏
Vi-2	Our delighted customers willingly and regularly recommend Microsoft offerings to others.	❏	❏	❏	❏
Vi-3	Employees consistently indicate that Microsoft is a great place to work, learn and grow.	❏	❏	❏	❏
Vi-4	Associates and partners willingly recommend working with Microsoft to qualified others.	❏	❏	❏	❏
Vi-5	We produce and/or acquire innovative software products and services that meet or exceed customers' current and evolving needs.	❏	❏	❏	❏
Vi-6	We are never satisfied with current quality or productivity.	❏	❏	❏	❏
Vi-7	We maintain a position as the worldwide leader in software for personal and business computing as measured by dollar sales.	❏	❏	❏	❏
Vi-8	We reward loyal financial backers by seeing that they get positive returns on investments that exceed industry averages.	❏	❏	❏	❏

Comments:

Name (Optional) _____

Figure 4-6, A Sample Values Conformance Check

Chapter Conclusions

At this point, the objectives of this chapter have been addressed:

Share an effective approach for examining, revising or creating an organizational set of values.

Examine examples of value statements of existing organizations and consider their implications.

Help the leaders and all constituencies gain assurance that, as the organization's work is performed, all of the leaders and employees behave in a manner consistent with the agreed values.

While there are many ways to come to consensus on an updated set of values or to create a new values statement, the approach outlined in this chapter has proven to be effective and relatively painless.

The value statements were selected to show both well written and poorly written value statements and to demonstrate good deployment/leadership role model behavior, and evident poor deployment/poor leadership role model behavior. Other than the one for Wegmans, no personal knowledge of the organizations was used in the critique or comments on the values of an organization. This puts the author in much the same position as the general public or an individual stockholder. The reader can use the questioning shown to examine the values of companies that they invest in or work for. They can evaluate the non-profit organizations that they give to, or volunteer for by examining the published values. Many of the organizations that were searched for this book did not publish (or may not have) value statements.

Enron and Andersen are just recent examples of firms that failed to put the values of their organization fully into practice.

 "It is not enough to say that the organization has shared values. It is not enough to write them down and communicate them. The leaders need to role model behaviors that are consistent with the organization's values every single day."

R.C. Palermo

Do The <u>Right</u> Things ... Right!

It <u>Is</u> That Simple!

Chapter 5
Customer Satisfaction

Chapter Objectives:

    To provide an approach that is effective in capturing the words of the customer to produce actionable improvement information.

    To help leaders gain assurance that, as the organization's work is planned and conducted, the priority needs of the customers will be sufficiently, efficiently, and effectively addressed.

© 2003 The Strategic Triangle Inc.

Do The **Right** Things ... Right!

It Is That Simple!

Chapter 5

Customer Satisfaction

"It will not suffice to have customers that are merely satisfied. A satisfied customer may switch. It is necessary to innovate, to predict the needs of the customer and give him more."
Dr. W. Edwards Deming

 The basic premise, supported by numerous examples and experiences and consistent with the words of the late Dr. Deming, is that customer obsession is the most appropriate principle for a world class leader. Customer obsession is defined here as accepting no less than <u>delighted</u> customers as the ultimate desired state, and then continuously driving toward that goal with a single-minded passion.

Positioning. This chapter shares a proven and effective way to approach the desired state of customer delight. The key messages of this chapter can be summarized as follows:

- The bottom line financial and operational performance of any organization will absolutely improve when the management team puts effort and heart into being customer focused–or better yet, customer obsessed. This in itself will move dedicated employees to feel good and thereby be even more motivated. The overall result is a wonderful, reinforcing, "virtuous cycle" that advances customer, employee, and financial performance.

- Customer obsession continues to be a true organizational differentiator today. Any organization that works to capture, understand, and react positively and definitively to the words of the customer on a regular basis –will be an awesome force.

- Customer obsession <u>has</u> to begin at the top. It can be the top of an enterprise, group, or team, but it has to be supported by a committed leader.

- In order to be assured that an organization is "doing the <u>right</u> things," the words of those who are served <u>must</u> regularly be captured. This will allow customers to give strong direction to an organization's improvement efforts in an actionable form. This customer information has a short half-life, so regular surveys and continual contact are a mandatory requirement. Experience has shown that most of the customer satisfaction surveys that are done today are expensive, and provide either useless or sub-optimal information.

What customer obsessed leaders really should want to know are the simple answers to these three customer questions:

1. **What percent of those people who are served are delighted? E.g., "Would willingly recommend the organization to others?"**
2. **If the serving organization could improve one or two things, which would the customers recommend? E.g. "If you're going to fix something, fix these."**
3. **Finally, "What are the things that the organization is perceived to be doing exceptionally well?"**

With this information in hand, the leadership team can select which of the "vital few" customer-selected issues to attack first, and then allocate talent and resources to them with confidence. By sequentially focusing on these "vital few," the gap between the current satisfaction levels and the desired perfect levels can most efficiently and effectively be closed.

Those areas indicated by customers as being exceptionally well done can be used in advertising the value and benefits of the organization to prospective customers. They can also be utilized for recognizing worthy teams and individuals within the organization. Again, it has been our experience that very few, if any, customer research studies provide information in an actionable form that will lead to corrective or improvement actions.

Three Personal Experiences with Customer Obsession

I openly admit to a strong bias in favor of the customer. It stems from countless interactions with loyal customers and clients over the years and from decades of being mistreated as a customer. Over the years, this bias reached the level of an obsession with satisfying customers. The term "Customer Obsession" connotes a passion for settling for nothing less than <u>delighted</u> customers. The term "delighted customers" is assigned to those customers who would willingly recommend an organization's services or products to others. The obsession is a passion stemming from a fundamental belief that it is the most profitable thing to do. It's also just the "right thing to do"

Three real life personal examples of the behavior of a customer-obsessed leader follow:

Example 1. The Business Card Survey. Consider the impact of a business card containing a personal customer satisfaction "survey" on its reverse side. I used it at every opportunity to engage customer and potential customers in dialogue. As business cards are exchanged over lunch or on airplanes, any response to the questions resulted in an immediate action on my part. If dissatisfaction was indicated, details were collected and communicated immediately to the appropriate local organizational personnel for resolution. If positive comments were related, a "Thank You" note was sent to the parties involved. If no knowledge of the Firm's offerings was indicated, product brochures were happily produced on the spot.

A replica of the business card survey is shown in Figure 5-1,   A Business Card Customer Survey.

		Satisfied	Neutral	Dissatisfied
1.	Overall, how satisfied are you with Xerox?	❏	❏	❏
2.	How satisfied are you with the quality of Xerox products?	❏	❏	❏
3.	How satisfied are you with the quality of support you receive from Xerox?	❏	❏	❏

Figure 5-1, A Business Card Customer Survey

Example 2. The Inverted Pyramid Chart. My group's organization chart was an inverted pyramid. That is, the customers served were at the top of the chart and I, as the leader was at the bottom with the group managers placed in the middle. It was amusing to hear fellow executives and customers ask if this wasn't demeaning to the leader? My facetious response was, "Not at all. Without me supporting the organization, it all collapses." See Figure 5-2, The Customer Pyramid.

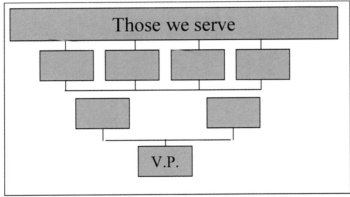

Figure 5-2, The Customer Pyramid

Example 3. The "Red Phone." A staff member noted that while Xerox customers were annually surveyed, it is often during new machine installations that an organization's reputation is made or broken with a new customer. As such, as a test, I made the decision to include my business card in the installation kits of all equipment being installed during a six-month period. New customers who had an installation or start-up complaint were asked to call me at my office number or at home if it was after hours. A separate red phone was installed in my home to ensure that there would be few busy signals confronting customers who called. A typed instruction sheet was placed next to the phone if another family member were called upon to answer the phone in my absence.

Only two calls were logged in the ensuing 6-month period. This was a marvelous testimonial to the quality of Xerox technicians and products. A major positive by-product was that it clearly demonstrated to all employees that total commitment to customer delight and that the leader was a role model for expected behavior.

Model Organization-Wide Customer Initiatives

In the 1980's, there were many Xerox organization-wide customer initiatives designed to make the organization and its executives more customer sensitive. Some worthy of consideration were:

- **The Focus Executive Program.** Each Xerox senior executive was assigned two or more major accounts. The program required that the Xerox senior executive meet with the senior executives of their assigned customer accounts to establish contact, and then meet with their assigned executives on a quarterly basis. In this way, solid rapport and mutual understanding were established. The positions and opinions of assigned account executives could be aired at major Xerox decision meetings. It was an enlightening opportunity to get out of the "toner tower" and meet the street.

- **Customer Satisfaction Measurement.** As a corporate officer, I was accountable for the management of an intensive customer satisfaction measurement process. This included an annual survey of <u>every</u> Xerox customer compiled on a rotating basis every month. As such, customer complaints were exposed to the highest levels of management and follow up corrective action plans were assured. Equally important was the fact that the results of these annual surveys directly impacted bonus levels from senior executives to district managers.

- **The "Day In the Furnace."** On a rotating basis, customer complaint calls to the corporate office in Stamford Connecticut or the U.S. headquarters in Rochester, New York, were routed to the office phone of a selected senior executive. That executive was required to <u>personally</u> take the calls, identify themselves, and, as senior executives, ensure that corrective action was taken. This assignment was affectionately labeled "the day in the furnace". Again, in this way, leadership commitment to customer obsession was role modeled.

- **Customer Guests.** As a part of the Corporate Customer Satisfaction Process, a senior executive chaired a monthly meeting of V.P.s from engineering, manufacturing, marketing, sales, and customer service to review the status of major customer issues as highlighted in customer surveys. Selected customers were occasionally invited to attend those meetings to assess whether we were working on the right issues and whether we were making suitable progress.

It is a sad footnote that this Xerox customer obsession passion apparently waned over time. In the 90's the unique customer obsession initiatives were largely discontinued.

Leader Reaction To Customer Obsession

Everyone seems to agree that satisfying customers is important to the success of any organization. That is where general agreement seems to end. Some leaders disagree that exceeding the expectations of or fully satisfying 100% of an organization's customers is what the desired state should be. This is so, they argue, because "perfection cannot be achieved." Note that the advocacy of customer obsession as a <u>desired</u> state, does <u>not</u> mean that "delighting all customers" should be an annual performance appraisal target or a bonus level. It does <u>not</u> assume that perfection <u>will</u> be achieved. Simply put, a commitment to customer obsession means having 100% delighted customers should <u>always</u> be the <u>desired</u> state. Surely it would seem silly to argue the inverse that a firm's <u>desire</u> is to have some percent of customers <u>not</u> be delighted.

Some executives disagree with the importance of, and/or the expense of operating a customer satisfaction measurement system that:

- Regularly surveys customers.
- Isolates their perception of prioritized areas needing improvement.
- Drives focused improvement actions.
- Monitors results and compares them to stated objectives.

Yet this is exactly what is needed to ensure that customers will willingly recommend an organization to others and who will continue to do business with the same organization year after year. This is exactly what world-class organizations accomplish.

Everyone needs to rebel against the customer mistreatment that we all see and experience daily. We need to move from a quiet, rueful acceptance attitude to that typical of a zealot. Consider the following translation that makes the point:

What We Hear	**What They Really Mean**
A. "Your call is very important to us. Please stay on the line and we will get to you as soon as we can."	"Money is more important than you are so we're not gonna hire enough people to help you when you need it."
B. "Please continue to hold. Your call is very important to us."	"Hold on, we're doing something more important than your call."
C. "Pick from the following seven options"	"You're going to have to put up with this obstacle course before we will let you talk to a human being." "We hope you will get tired and stop trying."

The Words Of The Customer

 When leaders listen to customers, they often don't really <u>hear</u> the words of the customer. Rather, they consciously or unconsciously "translate" customer words (which are often quite clear and even brutal) to "organization speak." "It's awful" becomes "There are still some challenges." The lesson: Do not translate customer words! Listen and react to the actual <u>words</u> of the customer.

If you catch your self saying, "Here's what they mean…" Stop! Remember that it is the <u>words</u> of the customer, not your interpretation that counts. Consider this real live experience when a question was posed to a customer who had bought the newest, fastest technical device from a company and had used it for nine months: "How do you like the new unit?" the senior executive asked. Expecting to hear "great machine" or "great quality," what was heard was "Sometimes when I need it, it is down."

How could this be? This was the most reliable unit in the world! It was twice as reliable as its predecessor, and had even more impressive reliability performance when compared to that of current competition. What a ridiculous customer! How could this assessment ever be conveyed back to the home office? Then came a pause....the customer didn't say that the device was unreliable! The <u>words</u> of the customer were: "Sometimes when I need it, it is down." When asked, "When do you need it and find that it is down?" The response was "April."

This was a large accounting firm that needed uninterrupted service during tax time...during April! When a second, back-up unit on short-term rental for the month of April was offered as a solution to the April challenge, the customer was delighted. This second unit was quickly converted to a sale when volumes rose. Everyone won!

The obvious message? Listen and react to the words of the customer. See Figure 5-3, <u>The Words of the Customer</u>, for a humorous, but meaningful depiction of situations where translations cause trouble. (This figure is not attributed because the original source could not be located).

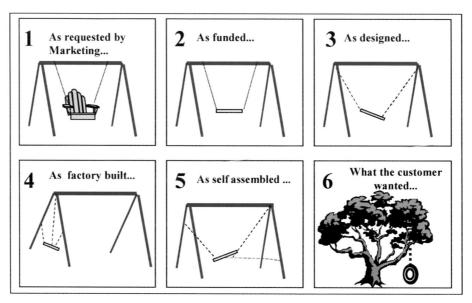

Figure 5-3, The Words Of The Customer

Customer Obsession Results

Of course, customer obsession must extend to all organizational groups. This means that all of the company's organizations:
- Capture the words of their customers.
- Apply the current-state/desired-state/gap-closing strategy.
- Utilize excellent team processes.

The results of applying the gap-closing process produced marvelous results. Note the following:

Xerox produced remarkable product quality improvements as shown in Figure 5-4, Product Quality Improvement. Each generation of copiers exhibited substantially better quality and greater performance with shorter and shorter development and production time cycles. Note also that for three years in a row, Xerox products received Product Line of the Year awards for copiers from Buyers Lab, a respected independent office-equipment-rating agency.

The wide-spread use of the "listen and close the gaps through the efforts of excellent team processes" pays big dividends.

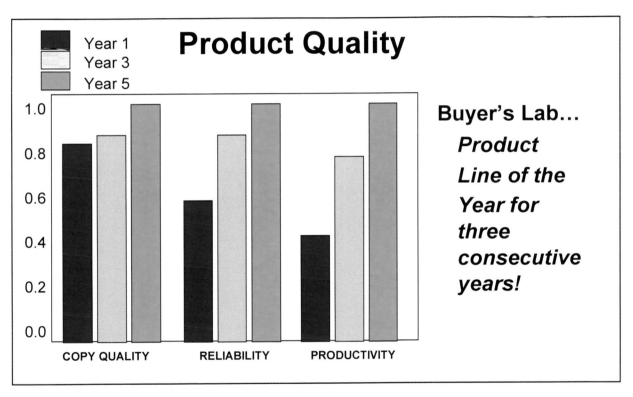

Figure 5-4, Product Quality Improvement

The Customer Satisfaction Branch

The most efficient and effective means of executing Customer Obsession is to transform this important but ethereal concept into a simple game plan. To do this, the tree diagram is employed. The tree diagram is a marvelous approach that takes a complex idea or challenge and breaks it into bite-sized, digestible pieces that can be prioritized for serial action. The old saw, "Q. How do you eat an elephant? A. One spoonful at a time," applies here. In this way, even the most daunting organizational challenges can be comfortably and successfully addressed.

See Figure 5-5, <u>The Customer Branch</u>, for a depiction of Customer Satisfaction Branch of the Success Tree®

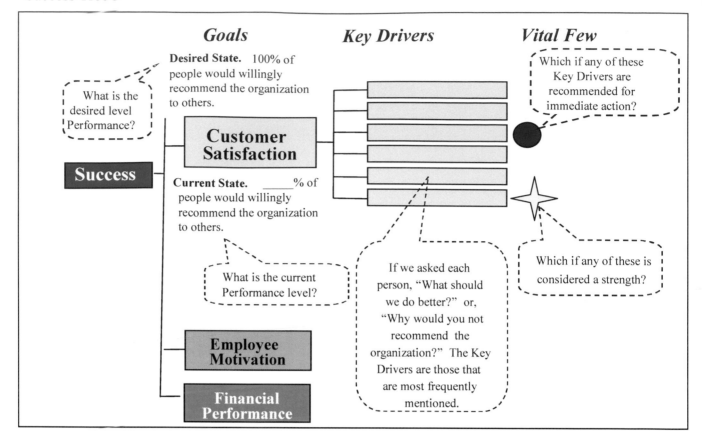

Figure 5-5, The Customer Branch

Customer Satisfaction Research

A concise summary of the wisdom gained from years of reviewing customer research reports is as follows:

- High cost
- Lots of data
- Little useable information

- Long delivery time
- Little ultimate impact
- A waste of paper

As indicated above, much of the customer satisfaction research that we have seen is seriously deficient. Reports are inches thick and contain meaningless comparisons to other organizations and/or other groups. Any action-oriented leader who really wants to improve the performance of the organization will likely be disappointed. If the leader wants to know what the biggest, and/or most frequent issues that its customers have, will again likely be disappointed.

In many firms, the audience for customer satisfaction presentations and the readers of customer satisfaction research are often heard to utter such banalities as:

"Aha, we knew that was a problem."

"We are surprised at that outcome."

"What did they mean by that?"

"How could they feel that way?"

"I thought we fixed that!"

Having completed this required, staged performance, the operational leaders generally go back to work, putting the information out of their minds until the next survey. The only people who seem to really care are those who have "customer" in their job title. Even they are left without actionable information.

An Effective Closed-Loop Customer Satisfaction Process

In order to capture vital customer input in actionable form, customers must be regularly surveyed and/or interviewed in the most cost-effective, unobtrusive manner.

A simple, clear, customer survey that provides as its key output, a single page of needed, action-ready information has been developed and has been executed over the past 10 years with excellent results. The summary survey guide below is worth careful scrutiny.

- Customer surveys must be carefully constructed to yield results that are "actionable." The fundamental objective is to determine the level of motivation or satisfaction, <u>and</u> the key prioritized reasons for dissatisfaction.
- Some common sins:
  - Too many questions, unnecessary complexity.
  - Failure to include a key, overarching question such as, "How willing are you to recommend our organization to qualified others?"
  - Failure to allow the respondent to judge and relate the priority of the dissatisfiers.
  - Tendency to focus on comparisons to internal groups or to "industry norms" as opposed to the focus on the gap that needs to be closed to approach perfection, i.e. surveys are designed to yield data, not action information.
  - Failure to quickly follow through with visible countermeasures for key dissatisfiers.
  - Failure to feed back survey results and committed improvement actions to those surveyed.

What leaders really should want to know from customers is simply conveyed by the answers to four questions:
- **What per cent of those served are delighted (e.g., would willingly recommend the organization to qualified others)?**
- **Of those who respond in the negative, what are the prioritized reasons for dissatisfaction?**
- **If the organization could improve one or two things, what would the customers recommend as a change priority?**
- **Finally, what are the things that the customers perceive that the others do very well today?**

A Simple Approach To Securing Actionable Customer Information

Fortunately, needed actionable customer information can be obtained in a very short time frame. The approach is based on a very rapid, cost-effective survey. Such an effective, simple customer survey approach is described in the following paragraphs.

There are usually eight sections in a survey with five statements in each section. A respondent reads each statement and indicates whether he or she would:

Totally Agree   Agree   Don't Know   Disagree   Totally Disagree.
❏   ❏   ❏   ❏   ❏

Then, as appropriate, the respondent can indicate an area of strength by noting the statement number in a blank space provided as:

"Of the different aspects listed above, I consider the following item to be strength today_____."
Next, an area of weakness can be noted by having the respondent write the selected statement number in the blank space provided as:

"Of the different aspects listed above, I consider the following item to be an improvement priority_____."

Once the completed surveys have been returned, a scoring system may used to produce a numerical set of results:

- +3 points for each "Totally Agree"
- +1 for each "Agree"
- 0 for each "Don't Know"
- -1 for each "Disagree"
- −3 for each "Totally Disagree"

The score for each respondent is added up. The average score is placed on the Customer Branch as the current state.

The statement numbers that were written in the blanks by the respondents are totaled, and the top four to six "areas for **priority improvement** vote-getters" are placed on the branch. The same is done for any strength.

A sample of the portion of the customer survey form is displayed in Figure 5-6, <u>An Actionable Survey Example</u>.

An Actionable Survey Example

3. The Customer Process	Totally Agree	Agree	Don't Know	Disagree	Totally Disagree
3.1 Is the company responsive to your needs?	☐	☐	☐	☐	☐
3.2 Are you receiving value in proportion to the price?	☐	☐	☐	☐	☐
3.3 Have you experienced late deliveries?	☐	☐	☐	☐	☐
3.4 Does the product perform as advertised?	☐	☐	☐	☐	☐
3.5 Is the company easy to do business with?	☐	☐	☐	☐	☐

Of the different aspects listed above, I consider the following item to be a strength today:

Statement #_____

Of the different aspects listed above, I consider the following item to be an improvement priority

Statement # _____

Figure 5-6, An Actionable Survey Example

Actionable Customer Information

The voluminous customer satisfaction surveys and reports available today bring to mind the old Clark Gable quote from "Gone With the Wind": "Frankly my dear, I don't give a damn." All that is needed for action is one-page that provides just two bits of information:

- The % of customers who are say that they are delighted.
- The major reasons given by those who are not delighted, in prioritized order.

With such customer feedback in hand, a leader can confidently allocate resources to attack each prioritized item, one at a time, each time measuring the resulting impacts on customer satisfaction.

A simple, clear, customer survey that provides this vitally needed, action-ready, single page of information is shown next.

A sample is shown in Figure 5-7, Actionable Customer Information. This exhibit is worth very careful study.

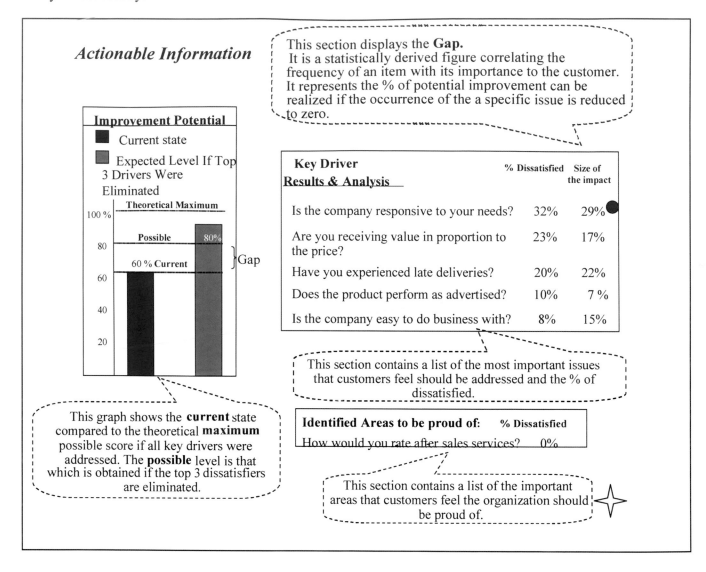

Figure 5-7, Actionable Customer Information

One can readily see how actionable information directly feeds the Customer Satisfaction Branch by comparing Figure 5-7, Actionable Customer Information to Figure 5-8, The Sample Customer Satisfaction Branch below. Again, these two figures warrant careful study.

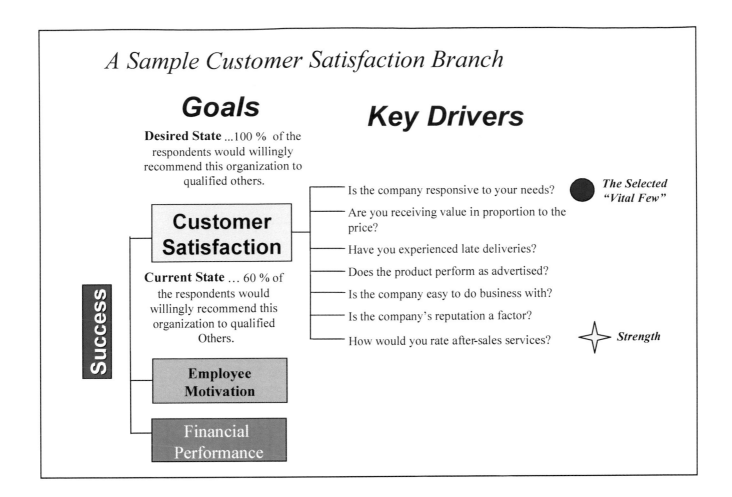

Figure 5-8, A Sample Customer Satisfaction Branch

Given this action-ready information in tree form, the only thing left for the leadership team to do is to come to consensus on which of the identified key drivers will be attacked first. We say it in this way because all organizations have limited talent and resources, and therefore, prioritizing and sequencing action assignments is mandatory. From this point, an effective problem-solving process, like the Breakthrough Process™, discussed in Chapter 8, is brought to bear.

The Closed-Loop Customer System

The survey, the resulting actionable information, and the creation of the branch together form the elements of a closed-loop system. That is:

(1) Constructing a simple customer survey vehicle that is designed to determine, in the words of a customer, their level of satisfaction, the prioritized issues that they feel most need to be addressed, and the areas that an organization should consider a strength.
(2) Examining the Action Sheet results.
(3) Constructing the tree branch.
(4) Employing a team process to produce results that measurably close the current/desired gap.

See Figure 5-9, <u>A Closed-Loop Customer Satisfaction System.</u>

Figure 5-9, A Closed – Loop Customer Satisfaction System

Three Realistic Action Options

Customer satisfaction questions must provide answers in an actionable form if efficient improvement progress is to be made. Since very few, if any existing customer research studies provide such information, an organization's leaders must consider three options:

1. **Opinion-Driven.** An empowered group can be convened and asked to brainstorm and gather <u>opinion-driven</u> estimations of what customers would likely say, and then proceed to work selected issues based on their <u>opinions</u> on the four questions below.

   a. What do we think that the current levels of customer satisfaction are?

   b. If we had asked each customer "what should we do better?" or if we asked them "why would you not recommend XXXX?" ...what might be **the top 4 to 6 most frequent, highest impacting reasons** given? Label these as "Key Drivers."

   c. Which of these Key Drivers should be considered a priority area for improvement by the organization?

   d. Which of these Key Drivers should be considered strengths of the organization?

Of course, this is not the most desirable situation, but it can produce results in time-urgent, research-poor situations and it is better than ignoring the subject altogether.

2. **Existing Research Interpretation.** If some research is available that can assist in estimating the current levels of satisfaction and approximating key prioritized drivers, the empowered group can extract information and produce answers to a, b, c, d, above. This can allow the organization to proceed to work key drivers with a modicum of confidence. Again, not the best, but better than guesses or no action at all.

3. **Action-oriented Research.** Agree to develop simple, specific surveys, acquire facts, and move forward with great confidence that the "right", prioritized customer issues will have surfaced. Obviously this is the most desired option.

Whichever option or combination of options is selected, it is essential that the customer satisfaction gap be defined and gap-mitigating actions be identifed before proceeding to spend time and resources.

Chapter Conclusions

At this point, the objectives of this chapter have been addressed:

Provide an approach that is effective in capturing the words of the customer to produce actionable improvement information.

Help leaders gain assurance that, as the organization's work is planned and conducted, the priority needs of the customers will be sufficiently, efficiently, and effectively addressed.

The simplest approach to capturing the words of the customer should be the goal. The only answers that truly matter are:
a. Would you willingly recommend us to others?
b. If not, what are the few things we most need to change in order to get you to say 'yes'?
The inclusion of the actionable customer survey and the adoption of the closed-loop improvement process will assure delighted customers and the benefits that come from that state.

A final thought or maybe a warning:

"If your organization doesn't have the commitment to make customers delighted, you had better hope that you don't compete with an organization that does."

R.C. Palermo

Chapter 5. Customer Satisfaction

Do The **Ri<u>gh</u>t** Things ... Right!

It **I<u>s</u>** That Simple!

Chapter 6
Employee Motivation

Chapter Objectives:

To provide an approach to examine, revise, or create an employee -motivation process that can ensure that employee perceptions, requirements, and satisfaction levels are fully and regularly understood and are acted upon in a timely manner.

To help leaders gain assurance that, as the organization's work is organized and conducted, the priority needs of the employees will be addressed in an efficient and effective manner.

© 2003 The Strategic Triangle Inc.

Chapter 6. Employee Motivation

Do The **Right** Things ... Right!

It Is That Simple!

Chapter 6

Employee Motivation

"Motivate employees, train them, care about them, and make winners of them. At Marriott, we know that if we treat our employees correctly, they'll treat our customers right. And if the customers are treated right, they'll come back again."

J. W. Marriott

Employee Motivation Positioning

The key messages of this chapter can be summarized as follows:

The fundamental performance of any organization will dramatically improve if the management team puts honest effort and heart into ensuring that employee-related issues are identified, prioritized, and sequentially attacked. Improved employee motivation has to begin at the top. Any lower level initiative can either suffer from neglect or quickly be snuffed out by unsupportive management.

There is absolutely no doubt that a balanced focus on delighting customers, producing healthy financial results, <u>and</u> at the same time ensuring that an organization's employees are positively motivated, is essential <u>and</u> profitable. Taking full advantage of the available brainpower of employees continues to be a true competitive advantage today. Any organization that works to capture, understand, and react positively and definitively to the words and counsel of the employees on an annual basis, can expect to have the employees produce impressive results. It's also just the right thing to do!

The term "employee motivation" is preferred rather than the usual "employee satisfaction." In our experience when asked, "Are you satisfied working here?" many employees respond "no," and when asked, "Why?" they say "Inadequate pay." Yet, when these same people are asked, "Would you willingly recommend working here to qualified others?" many people now respond in the affirmative. Of course, this doesn't mean that employees should not receive fair pay for the work done. It merely deals with the reality of human nature. Experience has shown that, a positive response to the "willingness" question is a better measure of positive motivation.

Experiences with Employee Motivation

Everyone agrees that having energized, motivated employees is important to the success of an organization. This is where general agreement seems to end. The following observations make this point. Some leaders:

- **Disagree that having 100% of employees indicate that they are energized and motivated by their work can be the desired state.** Two of the many unfortunate quotes from this cadre are:

  "Getting paid should be sufficient motivation" or

  "They get their recognition every pay day"

  Others assert that 100% employee motivation is just not achievable and should therefore be discarded as a concept. It is important to note that supporting the position that a desired state that 100% of employees should indicate a willingness to recommend working in the organization to qualified others is not advocated as a bonus target or performance appraisal measure. There is no inference that 100% could always be achieved. Simply put, having 100% motivated employees should be the desired state with an emphasis on the word "Desired. Surely no one desires the inverse…e.g. having an acceptable percentage of employees who are not motivated! It is clear that employees who don't feel good about their work will eventually produce poor quality and lesser quantity, whether consciously or unconsciously. This negatively influences other workers, cascading and multiplying the negative impacts of untreated dissatisfaction.

- **Feel that an employee motivation measurement and improvement system is, in essence, a waste of time and money.** Yet this is exactly what is needed to ensure that employees will willingly recommend working for the organization to qualified others, and who will continue to stay and grow with the organization.

- **Say that they value their employees, but they restrict their employee motivation improvement efforts to occasional speeches interspersed between performance critiques.** Here, workers use the pejorative phrase "They don't walk the talk" to describe such leaders. Employees react to this by saying, "We are managed by the 'mushroom' theory: Keep us in the dark and occasionally sprinkle some manure on us." This quote from a professional describes the perception of such management. "We punch in, hang up our brains at the door, do what we are told, don't make trouble, and pick up our brains on the way out".

Experiences absolutely leave no doubt that people have much more to offer than they are permitted to deliver. For the most part, employees aren't managed, they are mismanaged. They are a grossly under-utilized asset of the organization. As a famed industrialist once said,

"You can take my factories, burn up my buildings, but give me my people and I'll build the businesses right back again."
Henry Ford

An Example of Employee Focus

While at Xerox, a rather unique employee motivation improvement process proved to be effective when executed well. It was called an Executive Interview. Its elements were:

1. All managers were expected to schedule and conduct annual, one-hour interviews with the people who reported to the people who reported to the manager. To clarify, consider an organization where a person leads a group having 10 direct reports, each of these having 10 direct reports of their own. There would therefore be total of 100 people two levels below the senior person in the organization. Thus, this leader was expected to interview those 100 second level people annually. Far from a burden, the 100 hours per year invested in this way produced tremendous returns.
2. The interviews were to be conducted in the employee's workplace.
3. The interviews were to take one hour or less as dictated by the employee's interests.
4. There was to be no management agenda. The topics to be discussed were to be determined by the employee.
5. The major role of the leader was to listen, respond and take appropriate follow-up action if required..

This proved to be an invaluable additional source of employee information while generating increased respect for management. It enabled a leader to keep in contact with the organization, to share business information, to see that irritants were raised and resolved quickly, to evaluate future leaders to mentor, and in the process, to role model expected leader behavior. The 100 hours per year were an excellent investment, not a burden.

Employee Motivation Survey Experiences

As in the case of customer research, most employee surveys that are done today are expensive, and are either useless, or at best, produce sub-optimal action information. Reports are inches thick and are a burden to carry, much less read and digest. Comparisons to other organizations and/or other groups are presented in the report in order to have the client feel good or bad about the comparison. Topics or statements where the employee assessment was much better than a selected comparison entity – no matter how poor the absolute measure was – are posed as a reason for management feeling good. How foolish!

One particularly annoying finding is that the surveys often include statements or questions that organization has no intention of, or no capability of addressing. This only winds up casting doubt on the motivation of management and ultimately asks for trouble. It will not take long for employees to state that they expect little or no action from the survey effort. Often, a question is inserted in the survey that produces telling and even alarming negative results. The question is:

"Do you believe that the results of this survey will be used to produce positive changes?"

In one case that I am familiar with, the client removed the question from future surveys to avoid negative feedback.

Typical research study outputs sorely disappoint action-oriented leaders who really want to know if the organization is doing a good job in the eyes of its employees. It will frustrate leaders who want to understand the largest, most frequently encountered issues that its employees want addressed. The usual outcomes of common employee research are:

- High cost
- Lots of pages
- Lots of tables and graphs
- Little actionable information
- Cynicism from the employees
- Low ultimate return on investment.
- Frustrated Leaders

Employee Survey Observations

What follows is a real world example of such an employee survey. Usually, the results of employee surveys are not made public. However, a University of Louisville Employee Satisfaction Survey was displayed on the University's web site. This offered an opportunity to examine a real-world, publicly available example, and use it to make some important points.

The survey report is 113 pages long. While this size may justify the fees charged by the research firm, and while it may meet the expectations of the client, it is a burden, not a boon. Its quantity doesn't insure that the needs of action-oriented university leaders will be met.

- The results show the top ten, positively-scored questions that are so rated by respondents. There is no indication of which, of all these, are the key ones that should be touted as positives by the university. It would have been easy enough to have asked the respondents, "Which of these statements represent a strength that the university should be proud of?"
- Further, when the university finds out that both staff and faculty felt they were underpaid, will pay increases result? Will the administration seek to prove that the perception of low pay is unfounded? What action is expected on the part of the respondents? Why ask the question?
- Also shown are the top ten negatively-rated questions. Again, there is no indication of which, if any, of these questions should, in the judgment of the respondents be given high priority for the university to address. It would have been easy enough to have asked, "Which, if any, of these items should be the highest improvement priority for the university?"
- Like most surveys and their published results, this report can leave an action-oriented individual frustrated. What would best be done to improve the employees' perception most efficiently and effectively? Where should precious improvement resources be best allocated? How much improvement in motivation can be expected if a specific item is fixed? No clear answers are evident in this report. Lots of interpretation will be needed to deduce this information and this is rarely undertaken.

Let's try a graphic extract from this survey report. If you were responsible for the satisfaction improvement of the full-time faculty at the University of Louisville, which action would the survey data lead you to pursue first? What incremental action is suggested for you by the data presented? How sure are you that the impact would be significant?

Full-Time Faculty Data

This is the information that the university leaders have to determine the key improvement actions to raise the motivation of the full-time faculty:

- The Law department returned 82% of the surveys while the Business and Public Administration department returned only 33%.
- The majority respondents were white males with over 15 years of service who expect to stay until retirement .
- Three-quarters are tenured, Ph.D. professors and associate professors.

- The most negative overall and high impact satisfaction questions for all faculty (full-time data are not presented separately) were:
    - Would recommend U. of L. for employment = 42 % positive.
    - Employees attitude at U. of L. is positive = 39% positive.
    - There is not too much stress in job = 33% positive.
    - Working conditions have improved in the past 5 years = 31% positive.
- 73 % of the faculty like their jobs.
- The males are generally more negative than the females.
- The eighteen respondents from the Allied Health Sciences Faculty were the most negative.
- The ten lowest average scores (from lowest to highest) were for these questions:

    1. You are paid fairly relative to your responsibilities.
    2. Department is staffed to cover regular workload.
    3. Administration gives high priority to employee satisfaction.
    4. We are paid fairly relative to experience.
    5. There is not too much stress in the job.
    6. Benefited from mentoring opportunity.
    7. Salary increases are determined fairly.
    8. There is a high priority on faculty success.
    9. There is support of faculty at the U. of Louisville.
    10. Value of benefits is better than available elsewhere.

Once again, the intent of this critique is to provide the reader with some process insights and to pose thought-provoking questions. It is not intended to demean the university's attempt to gather employee satisfaction information. Rather, the university should be complimented because they care enough to even do a survey. Unfortunately, surveying faculties and staff members is not common among many universities...make that among many organizations. Also, there is no intent to condemn the consultant for the report or the survey work. Clearly the conventional survey detail and process represent an agreement between the client and the consultant. Indeed, it is clear that the university was pleased with the work done, or the results would not have been shared on the web site. After all, satisfying the client is what a consultant tries to do.

Finally, all of the insights gathered from the University of Louisville survey were gleaned from public web site information. No attempt was made to contact university personnel or the consultant for more detailed information.

What Next?

So, what do you, as the faculty leader? Note that three of the top ten issues are about pay…no surprise here! What specific direction do you give to problem-solving teams? It's not a simple decision given the form of the data that the standard survey provides.

Imagine the benefit that an action-oriented faculty leader would accrue from having a single sheet of paper that provides the following actionable information:
- **The % of the faculty that would willingly recommend the university to qualified faculty candidates.**
- **The top five statements that the respondents feel, if improved, would have the greatest influence on a positive move in opinions relative to "willingness to recommend".**
- **The percent of improvement that can be expected from each improvement action.**

Like the customer survey presentation discussed in Chapter 5, the "victims" of employee satisfaction presentations, and the readers of massive survey reports are often heard to utter observations such as:

"Are they still upset about that?"
"Now there's a new one."
"That's not possible!"
"How could they feel that way?"
"They're never satisfied!"
"What the heck did they mean by that?"
"Are you sure that there isn't something wrong with your data?"

Save this list for use at your next employee survey report meeting or merely hand out the list and go back to productive work.

Recommended Closed-Loop Employee Motivation Process

In order to capture vital employee input in actionable form, employees must be regularly surveyed and/or interviewed in the most cost-effective manner.

A simple, clear, employee survey that provides a single page of action-ready information is available for the leader's use. A guide for developing such a survey is shown in Figure 6-1, An Employee Survey Construction Guide. It is worth careful study.

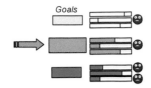

Employee Survey Construction Guide

Goals

100 % would willingly recommend the organization to qualified others.

Those Who Serve

_____ % who willingly recommend the organization to qualified others.

• Employee surveys must be carefully constructed to yield results that are "actionable". The fundamental objective is to determine the level of motivation or satisfaction, and the key reasons for dissatisfaction.

• Some common sins:

- Too many questions, unnecessary complexity.

- Failure to include a key, overriding question that seeks an answer to a question like, "how willing are you to recommend working here to qualified others?"

- Failure to request the respondent to relate the priority of the dissatisfiers.

- Tendency to focus on comparisons to internal groups and to "industry norms" as opposed to the focusing on the gap that needs to be closed.

- Failure to quickly follow through with visible countermeasures for key dissatisfiers and to communicate the same to all employees.

Figure 6-1, An Employee Survey Construction Guide

What leaders really should want to know from employees is simply portrayed by the answers to four questions:

1. **What percent of those who serve are delighted (e.g., would willingly recommend the organization to qualified others?).**
2. **Of those who respond in the negative, what are the prioritized reasons for dissatisfaction?**
3. **If the organization could improve one or two things, which would the employees recommend?**
4. **Finally, what are the things that the employees perceive are done very well?**

An Actionable Employee Survey

An effective, simple employee survey approach is described in the following paragraphs. There are usually eight sections in this survey with five statements in each section. A respondent reads each statement and indicates whether he or she:

Totally Agree   Agree   Don't Know   Disagree   Totally Disagree.
❏   ❏   ❏   ❏   ❏

Then, if appropriate, the respondent can indicate an area of strength by noting the statement number in a blank space provided next to the statement,

"Of the different aspects listed above, I consider the following item to be strength today_____."

Next, an area of weakness can be noted by writing the statement number in the blank space provided next to the statement: *"Of the different aspects listed above, I consider the following item to be an improvement priority____."*

Once completed surveys have been received, a scoring system is used to produce a numerical set of results:

+3   points for each "Totally Agree"
+1   for each "Agree"
 0   points for each "Don't Know"
-1   for each "Disagree"
−3   for each "Totally Disagree"

A partial such survey form is shown in Figure 6-2, <u>An Actionable Employee Survey Sample</u>.

An Actionable Employee Survey Sample

<u>The Process</u>

	Totally Agree	Agree	Don't Know	Disagree	Totally Disagree
3.1 An efficient process for resolving employee issues is effectively utilized.	☐	☐	☐	☐	☐
3.2 An efficient process for preventing reoccurrence of a problem is effectively utilized.	☐	☐	☐	☐	☐
3.3 Employees wishing to communicate with the organization's leadership find it easy to contact the right people.	☐	☐	☐	☐	☐
3.4 Employee retention is tracked, valued losses are identified and understood—with process changes put in place to minimize repetition.	☐	☐	☐	☐	☐
3.5 Employee -focused leadership organizations are regularly benchmarked in order to identify quantum employee process improvements.	☐	☐	☐	☐	☐

Of the different aspects listed above, I consider the following item to be a strength today: Statement #_____

Of the different aspects listed above, I consider the following item to be an improvement priority: Statement #_____

Figure 6-2, <u>An Actionable Employee Survey Sample</u>

This information is captured and uses a simple vote-count system to determine the size of the impacts... The single-page sheet is shown in Figure 6-3, Actionable Employee Information. It is also worth careful study.

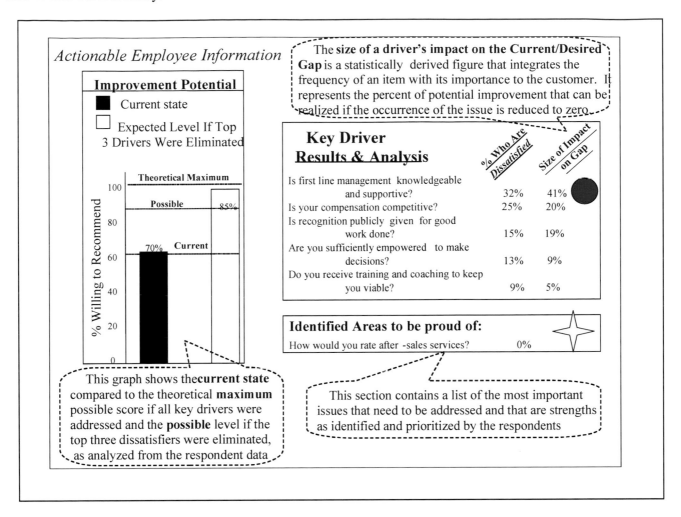

Figure 6-3, Actionable Employee Information

The employee action information that is gathered in the actionable survey is best depicted using the form of a tree diagram. This in invaluable for use in subsequent improvement efforts. The suggested improvement statement numbers that were written in the blanks by the respondents are added up, and the top four-to-six areas that got the most votes are placed on the branch as Key Drivers. The same is done for the strengths. The average score is placed as the current state on the tree.

Figure 6-4, The Employee Motivation Branch Model, displays how the results of the survey will be positioned to answer key leader questions.

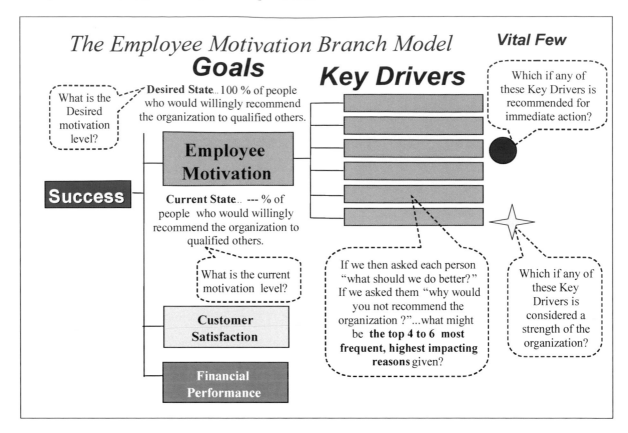

Figure 6-4, The Employee Motivation Branch Model

Those areas indicated by employees as being exceptionally well done can be used in advertising the value and benefits of the organization and also for recognizing appropriate teams and individuals.

A sample employee branch is shown in Figure 6-5, A Sample Employee Branch.

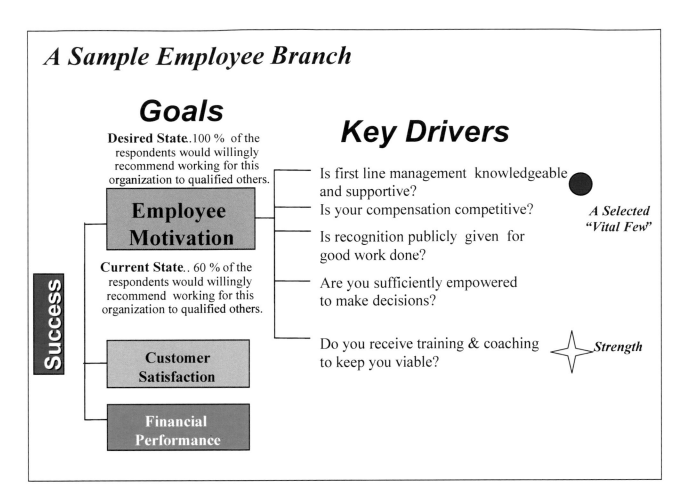

A Sample Employee Branch

Goals

Desired State..100 % of the respondents would willingly recommend working for this organization to qualified others.

Employee Motivation

Current State.. 60 % of the respondents would willingly recommend working for this organization to qualified others.

Customer Satisfaction

Financial Performance

Success

Key Drivers

Is first line management knowledgeable and supportive?

Is your compensation competitive?

A Selected "Vital Few"

Is recognition publicly given for good work done?

Are you sufficiently empowered to make decisions?

Do you receive training & coaching to keep you viable? *Strength*

Figure 6-5, A Sample Employee Branch

Given this action-ready data, the only thing left for the leadership team to do is to come to consensus on which of the identified key drivers will be attacked first. I say this because all organizations have limited talent and resources. Prioritizing and sequencing action assignments is mandatory. By focusing on these "vital few," the gap between the current satisfaction levels and the desired perfect levels can be closed most efficiently and effectively. From this point in the process, a problem-solving approach like the Breakthrough Process™ discussed in Chapter 8, can be utilized to produce and execute solutions.

By putting the survey's actionable information, the creation of the branch, and the execution of a problem- solving process together, we have the elements of a closed-loop system. That is, we start by constructing an employee survey vehicle that is designed to determine, in the words of employees:

- Their level of motivation.
- The prioritized issues that they feel most need to be addressed.
- Isolate the areas that an organization should consider strengths.
- Then, the results of the survey are formatted for easy communication and consensus using a tree diagram.
- The Vital Few candidates for initial attack are identified and the problem-solving efforts can then applied to the selected Vital Few.

The System is depicted in Figure 6-6, <u>A Closed-Loop Employee Motivation System</u>. The effective, efficient corrective action step depicted in the system is detailed in Chapter 8, The Breakthrough Process™.

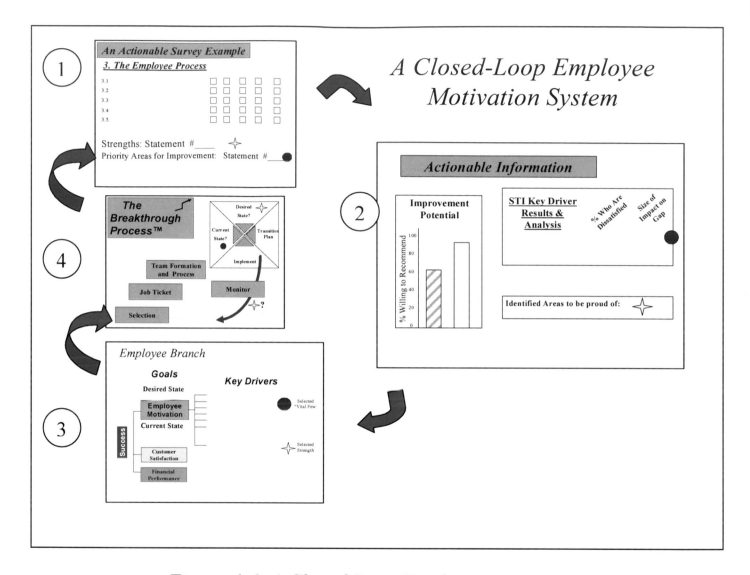

Figure 6-6, A Closed Loop Employee Motivation System

Chapter Conclusions

At this point, the objectives of this chapter have been addressed:

Provide an approach to examine, revise, or create an employee-motivation process that can ensure that employee perceptions, requirements, and satisfaction levels are fully and regularly understood and are acted upon in a timely manner.

Help leaders gain assurance that, as the organization's work is organized and conducted, the priority needs of employees will be addressed in an efficient and effective manner.

The best approach for securing the words of employees is through a simple, easy-to-use survey. It must determine the level of employee motivation using such statements as "Willingness to recommend that qualified others work for the organization. For those who say "no" the survey must extract the key, prioritized reasons for saying "no". Massive, expensive survey reports of 100 pages or more are unnecessary.

It is hoped that the theory, the examples, and the counsel provided in this chapter will encourage current and future leaders to give strong consideration to adopting the Employee Branch approach and focus on the Vital Few drivers as a means of realizing breakthrough employee performance.

A closing thought:

"Treating employees as one treats a valuable asset does not demean people. Far from it. A wise leader sees that valued assets get good care, are well maintained and are continuously upgraded. Many employees would like to be treated as well as inanimate organizational assets are treated."

R.C. Palermo

Chapter 6. Employee Motivation

Do The <u>Right</u> Things ... Right!

It *Is* That Simple!

Chapter 7
Financial Performance

Chapter Objectives:

To share details of a financial management process for revising or creating financially prioritized goals that can be deployed, fully understood, and acted upon by all in the organization.

To help leaders gain assurance that, as the organization's work is organized and conducted, the priority financial issues and opportunities will be given appropriate attention and resources.

© 2003 The Strategic Triangle Inc.

Do The <u>Right</u> Things ... Right!

It <u>Is</u> That Simple!

Chapter 7

Financial Performance

"If it is not growing, it's going to die."   Michael Eisner, CEO Disney

Positioning. The key messages of this chapter are summarized as follows:

 The financial bottom line of every organization will improve if the management team puts both effort and heart into ensuring that <u>prioritized</u> financially related issues and opportunities are identified, shared throughout the organization and sequentially attacked with a passion. This is as opposed to the shotgun approach of trying to influence or act on all elements of a financial picture.

There is absolutely no doubt that a balanced focus on delighting customers, ensuring that employees are energized and motivated, and <u>at the same time</u> generating healthy financial results are essential to the long-term success of an organization. Simply put, to get delighted customers, you need great products and/or great services. To get these, you need motivated employees and allies. To pay for employees and products or services, money is needed. To recruit, hire, train, and retain great talent and get financial backing, you need consistently positive financial results. This is a powerful, reinforcing success cycle.

Experiences with Financial Performance

Leaders readily agree that fact-based financial information is essential to the success of an organization. This is, however, where general agreement seems to end. The following experiences support this point:

Some leaders disagree with focusing improvement attention on only a handful of the most important financial drivers. They cannot see giving up the multitude of measures that they have pursued in the past. They tend to feel that <u>every</u> aspect of financial performance must be listed, tracked, reviewed, and regularly addressed. They maintain that all financial measures are vital. Chasing the "important multitude" has produced mediocre results at best and painful failures at worst.

 This "Important Multitude" approach is just plain foolish. No one has the resources to adequately address all the financial issues, challenges, or opportunities that an organization faces. Communicating them and exhorting staffs to manage all of them or worse criticizing and berating staff because of a failure to improve the "important multitude" won't cut it over the long run. Using a focused, sequential attack on a selected "vital few" is a powerful, effective approach to increased financial performance results.

It is alarming to note that some organizations have more resources in their financial function than they have in marketing or sales! The "police" mentality ("Catch them doing something wrong") existing in these organizations clearly and unnecessarily adds to overhead costs. The honesty or capability of employees is clearly impugned by such behavior. The fault lies in management, not in the financial staff.

People in the finance group consistently welcome the opportunity to analyze financials and produce the one or two overarching financial measures with current and desired state levels determined. With this in hand, senior leaders can come to consensus on the "Vital Few" actions that will be resourced to efficiently and effectively close the identified gaps. Once addressed, the next candidate on the priority list will be resourced for attack. The financial staff support for this disciplined approach is always unqualified.

 Some leaders question the desirability of having 100% of their employees informed about the financial <u>key</u> drivers of their organization. They lack confidence that making each person aware of the numbers, will lead to dramatic financial improvement of their organization or group. One leader encountered was proud to state that he uses the "Orange Theory of Financial Management." That is, "You just keep squeezing your employees, suppliers, and customers. It's the way to get the most juice," in his words. It is sad to note that the "Orange Theory" did not keep his firm from Chapter 11.
Simply put, organizations adopting this squeezing approach can not hope to compete with organizations that have fully engaged all of their employee assets in an attack on the financial "vital few."

The details of the financial health of an organization should not be seen as top-secret information, reserved for senior management. Clearly some data are proprietary, but not all. Every employee can contribute to lower costs, higher quality or increased production. People know where opportunities from incremental change lie. It is these people, organized into focused, breakthrough teams that produce remarkable results.

A Pro Forma for Financial Performance Analyses

As is the case with Customer Satisfaction and Employee Motivation, great financial progress can be achieved through the use of a tree diagram. See Figure 7-1, A Financial Performance Branch Model for a graphic portrayal.

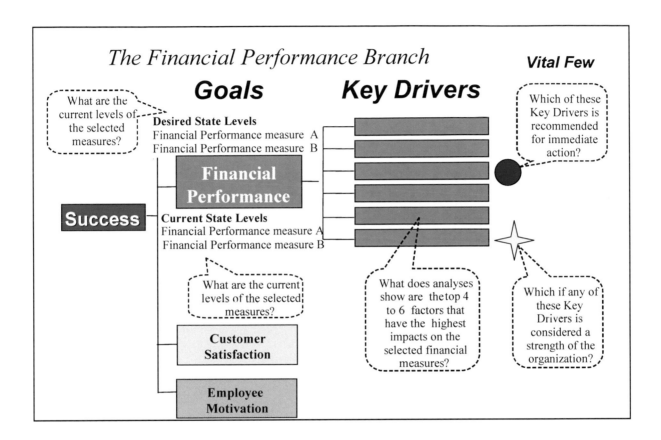

Figure 7-1, A Financial Performance Branch Model

Some Financial Branch Examples

It is difficult to acquire real world financial data in the Success Tree® System format for use in providing financial branch examples for the reader. Much of such information is sensitive and is understandably confined within an organization. An extensive search of the web for such details came up empty. Therefore, with the permission of a few clients, real Financial Branch details are presented in this chapter. Changes have been made to ensure that the identities of the contributing organizations and their data are kept in confidence. The essence of their work is retained and is most informative. Please also note that the comments on each case are intended to encourage readers to develop and examine their own financial branches using this technique.

A Successful Non-Profit Organization Financial Branch

The first example is that of a very successful non-profit organization. This group has been using the Success Tree® System approach to managing their enterprise for over a seven year period. Their financial branch is depicted in Figure 7-2, <u>A Non-Profit's Financial Branch</u>.

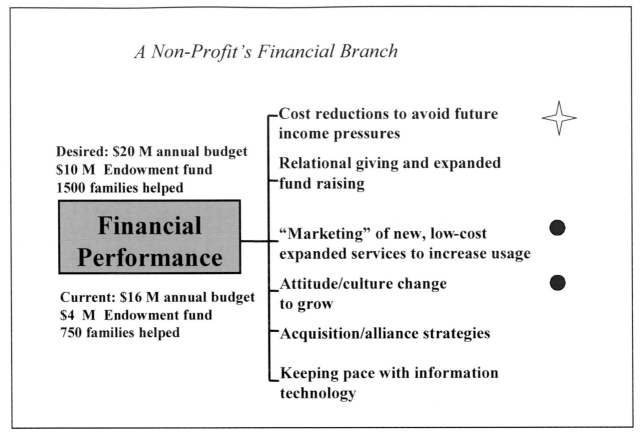

Figure 7-2, A Non-Profit's Financial Branch

Note that:

- By having reduced costs, running lean, and still producing high quality services, there is a sense that the organization now has a well-positioned cost base for the challenges of the future. The star on the figure highlights this as a strength.
- The "number of families helped" is included among the financial branch goals. This is considered an indication of "market share" for this type of organization.
- Two drivers have been selected as "Vital Few" for focused improvement efforts. First the "number of families helped" is targeted to be substantially increased via the marketing of expanded low cost services. Second, there is recognition given to the need to overcome resistance to the change inherent in the growth culture initiative. Both the targeted drivers are connoted by dots. The leaders believe that the two projects are sufficiently different from each other that both should be provided resources required for simultaneous attack. They will use a star to designate successful conclusion of each project. As each project is completed, they will return to the branch to get another driver to attack.

A Start-Up Organization

This organization's ambitious leaders have adopted the Success Tree® System approach for driving their enterprise to the next success plateau. The financial branch is shown in Figure 7-3, A Start-Up Public Firm's Financial Branch.

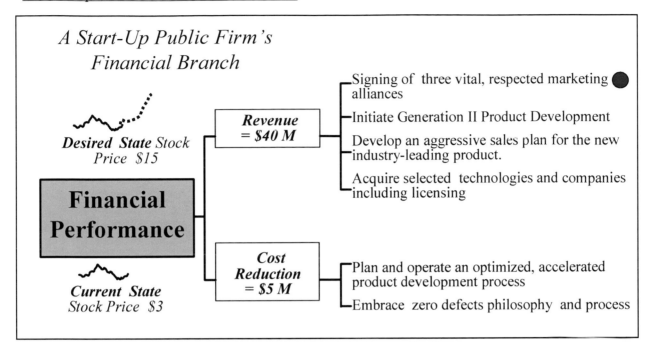

Figure 7-3, A Start-Up Public Firm's Financial Branch

Note that:

- The stock price is the selected overall financial measure. Most senior teams reject this measure because "it is not directly under our control" and is subject to the vagaries of the market. They tend to prefer Earnings Per Share or Profit. The leaders of this firm are realists. They say that they have "bitten the bullet" and chosen the price of the stock as their single measure of financial success since that is what their investors deem most appropriate.
- The selection of alliances as a key driver was made because the limited cash of the organization combined with the aggressive revenue targets made total internal development impossible.
- Two projects have been selected as the "Vital Few" for team attack. They are indicated on the figure by two dots.
- The leaders believe that these projects are sufficiently different that they each should have the resources required to provide two teams with quality personnel. As each project is completed, the leaders return to the branch to focus on another driver for improvement attack.

The Support Function Financial Branch

Figure 7-4, <u>A Support Function's Financial Branch</u>, represents a different case. Here, the organization is a financial administrative support function, the Information Technology department, in a large firm. As an aside, it is interesting to note that its "customers" are internal to the organization.

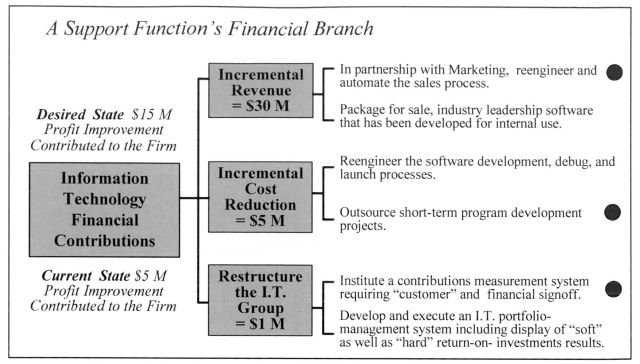

Figure 7-4, A Support Function's Financial Branch

Note carefully these interesting facets of the chart:

- The financial branch is correctly labeled "Financial Contributions" since the group, unlike the full organization, does not directly interact with paying clients. Rather, it supports those who do. The people they serve, their customers, are employees of the Firm.
- The Current and Desired States use the "amount of measured dollars contributed to the bottom line by Information Technology personnel" as the group's measure of contribution. A very interesting and insightful choice.
- The key drivers selected to increase the group's contributions are:
  - Helping their internal customers to become more sales-productive
  - Reengineering their customer's production processes
  - Becoming more productive as a function, and acting in a more fiscally responsible manner
- The dots indicate that three projects have been selected as the "Vital Few" for team attack. The Information Technology's leaders believe that the projects are sufficiently different that they will provide the resources and talent required for these two actions. As each project is completed they will return to the branch to get another driver.

A Large Enterprise Financial Branch

Figure 7-5, <u>A Large Enterprise Financial Branch</u>, represents another interesting case. Here, the organization has decided to assign one "Vital Few" breakthrough assignment to each of their six functional organizations. Their logic was that each function was large enough in talent and resources to staff and carry out at least one major priority improvement project/group to support their "25% Improvement Program."

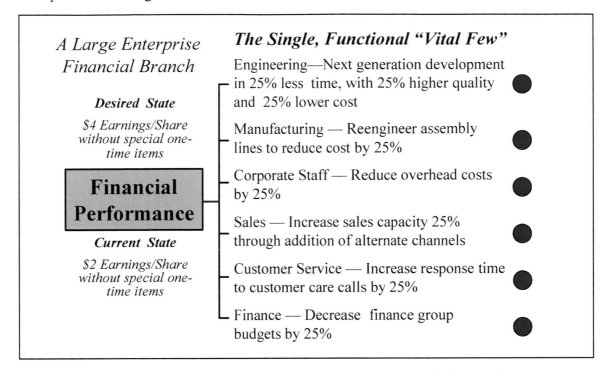

Figure 7-5, <u>A Large Enterprise Financial Branch</u>

Note the following interesting facets associated with the chart:

- The single, overall financial goal of the organization is Earnings Per Share (EPS). The expectation is that doubling its EPS would result in a minimum doubling of the firm's stock price.
- The gap-closing drivers are a mix of cost reductions and revenue-increasing projects. There are two to three more drivers for each function that await full completion of the initial selections before they are addressed.
- The six dots indicate that six projects have been selected as the "Vital Few" for focused attack. The organization and functional leaders believe that the projects when successfully executed will be sufficient to deliver the desired Earnings Per Share levels.

As each project is completed, the leaders will return to the branch to get another driver. The Earnings Per Share Desired State level will be constantly adjusted upward. In this way, the tree process is evergreen and can easily be updated as time passes and projects are completed.

The Step-By-Step Branch Construction

A very effective approach to the construction of an organization's Financial Branch is described in the paragraphs below. Employing an experienced facilitator to conduct the meetings as provided in the steps, and utilizing meeting tools such as brainstorming, weighted voting, the priority matrix, and the Pareto chart, will prove to be most beneficial in producing high-quality, consensus outputs. See Chapter 8, The Breakthrough Process™ for more information on these tools and approaches. These are suggested financial branch construction steps:

1. **Come to agreement on the one or two success measures relative to the organization's financial performance.**
   Use brainstorming by a team that is made up of the finance group and other selected departmental individuals. The teams' objectives are to select the one or two measures that appropriately reflect the overall financial health of the organization. The measures selected should constitute an aggregate of most, if not all, of the key financial measures for the organization. For example, Earnings Per Share would contain all revenues and costs. Some commonly selected measures are: Stock Price, Earnings Per Share, Annual Donations, Profits, Cash Flow, Annual Income, Annual Budget, and/or Market Share.
2. **Determine the current levels of the selected measures.**
3. **Come to agreement on the desired levels of the selected measures for three years hence.**
   Some clues: What levels will make the leaders proud? What levels will meet or exceed the "owners" expectations? What levels will put the organization in an elite category? Do not select levels that are readily achievable.
4. **Determine the four to six key drivers or elements that make up each of the selected success measures. These selected measures, if attacked successfully, will most efficiently close the gap between the current and desired states.**
5. **Have the team agree on the one or two "vital few" drivers that are to be assigned to teams for initial solution development and execution.**

The Closed-Loop Financial System

When the key drivers that can close the gap between the current and desired states of the financial goals have been determined; and the leadership team has come to a consensus on which of the identified key drivers will be attacked first, a problem-solving approach like the Breakthrough Process™ can be profitably (pardon the unintended pun) brought to bear. It consistently produces effective and efficient solutions.

Putting the creation of the financial branch together with a problem-solving process forms the elements of a closed-loop system. The steps are:

- Construct a financial branch.
- Select the "Vital Few" candidates for initial attack.
- Apply a problem-solving effort to the selected Vital Few.
- Monitor results and recycle if needed.

Thus, the loop is formed. The system is depicted in Figure 7-6, A Closed-Loop Financial System. The effective, efficient, corrective problem-solving approach part of the loop is detailed in Chapter 8, The Breakthrough Process™.

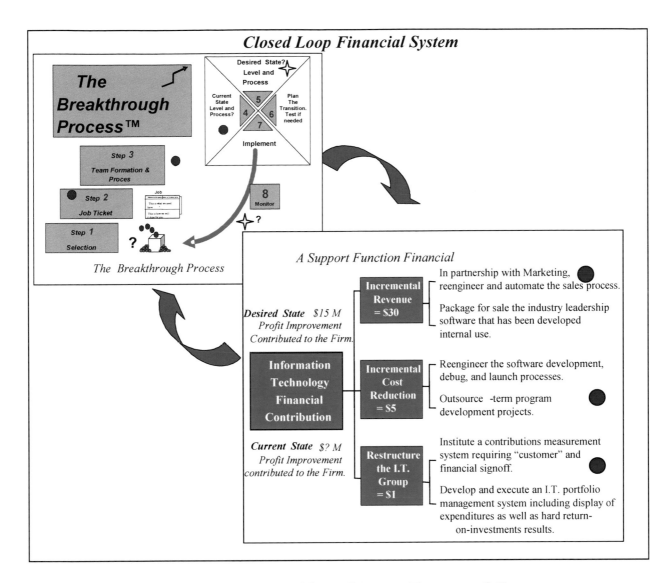

Figure 7-6, A Closed-Loop Financial System

Chapter Conclusions

At this point, the objectives of this chapter have been addressed:

Share details of a financial management process for revising or creating financially-prioritized goals that can be deployed, fully understood, and acted upon by all in the organization.

Help leaders gain assurance that, as the organization's work is organized and conducted, the priority financial issues and opportunities will be given appropriate attention and resources.

The distillation of the key drivers and the "Vital Few" for sequential attack is a proven, extremely effective means of producing remarkable breakthrough improvements in the financial health of an organization.

It is hoped that the theory, the examples, and the counsel produced in this chapter, will encourage current and future leaders to adopt the Financial Branch approach and focus on the vital few financial drivers as a means of realizing exceptional breakthrough financial performance.

A closing thought:

"Understanding the factual current state of finance is a critical first step to financial success. Sorting through these current financials and zeroing in on a few overarching measures enables focus. Subsequent deployment of this information to teams throughout an organization can produce remarkable financial improvements."

R.C. Palermo

Do The **Right** Things ... Right!

It Is That Simple!

Chapter 8

The Breakthrough Process™

Chapter Objectives:

To share details of a proven, efficient and effective, logical step -by-step approach for problem solving, working issues, and capitalizing on opportunities.

To help leaders gain assurance that issues and challenges can be uniformly addressed by each leader in the organization.

© 2003 The Strategic Triangle Inc.

Do The <u>Right</u> Things ... Right!

It Is That Simple!

Chapter 8

The Breakthrough Process™

"The major problem we face is not any particular problem; it is the process we use to solve problems."

Steven Covey

Positioning The Breakthrough Process is the first of the two halves of the "doing things right" part of the Success Tree® System. It was developed and has been constantly improved on the firing line over a period of 10 plus years.

 The Breakthrough Process is a simple, logical, proven, versatile, and effective approach to working challenges and resolving issues that have been highlighted in any organization. The process is readily applied to the selected "right things" that have been derived from the organization's mission, vision, values, customer words, employee words, and/or the selected financial drivers. It lets accountable individuals and teams attack assigned issues and challenges with confidence that the challenges are vital to the success of the organization. It also allows leaders to effortlessly track progress and thereby rest assured that efforts are being expended on aligned, priority challenges. This, in essence, is "doing the right things…right."

An overview of the steps to successfully "doing things right."

Step 1. The "Vital Few" are isolated… "There are too many balls to juggle…pick the important ones."

Step 2. The Job Ticket is issued… "Amazing! A single piece of paper eliminates ambiguity and ensures results will meet expectations."

Step 3. Team starts up... "By adhering to an understood team process, a group becomes a team."

Step 4. The Current State is determined. "You can't get from 'here' to 'there' unless you know where 'here' is and how things get done today."

Step 5. The Desired State is developed. "You can't get from 'here' to 'there' unless you know where 'there' is and how things must be done when you get 'there.'"

Step 6. The Transition Plan is developed. "It is a detailed route map that will ensure the safest and fastest journey to the desired state."

Step 7. Execution occurs. "With a road map in hand, the journey can be completed with confidence that the destination can be reached."

Step 8. Monitoring is on-going. "How is the project going and when it's completed, how did we do Vs. the expectations? Are we satisfied? Can we move on to the next 'Vital Few'? Do we need to recycle and try again or can we celebrate success?"

This powerful process is depicted graphically in Figure 8-1, <u>The Break Through Process™</u>.

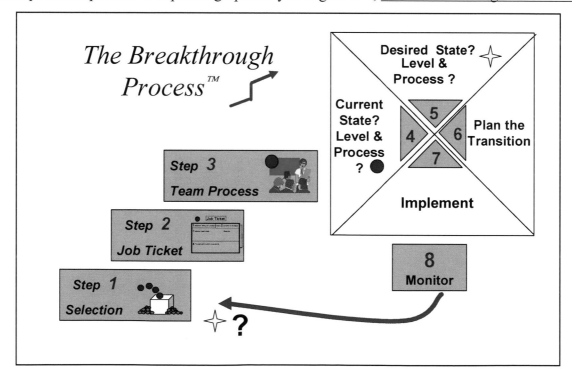

Figure 8-1, The Breakthrough Process™

The Breakthrough Process™ Steps, Summary and Detail

Step 1. Priority Selection

The deployment and assignment of priority issues and opportunities to individuals or teams by an organization's leadership are the critical starting points in breakthrough performance. The resources and talent of any organization are not infinite. They must be carefully deployed to the selected "Vital Few" challenges that are most meaningful to the success of the organization.

Detail. It is important to note that the tools in this selection step are extremely effective, and leaders can and should apply them to <u>any</u> issue of importance to the organization. This is especially true of those challenges that require substantial incremental resources and/or are expected to deliver substantially new levels of performance. Figure 8-2, <u>Mission/Vision/Values Alignment Check</u>, is a very useful matrix that enables an organization's leadership to consider the organization's mission, vision and values as priority decisions are made. Likewise, Figure 8-3, <u>Customer/ Employee/Financial Alignment Check</u> provides the same aid in judging whether decisions will measurably benefit the customer, employee and financial constituencies. Thus, the priority need of the work can be clearly established and documented before a team is engaged and resources are committed.

These two matrices can and should be utilized at <u>all</u> operational levels as group leaders and individuals make decisions.

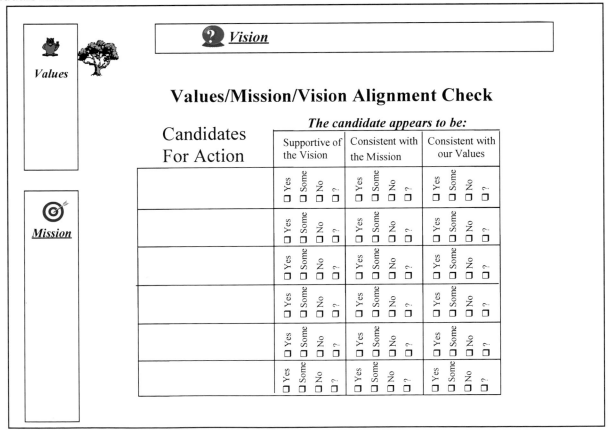

Figure 8-2, Mission/Vision/Values Alignment Check

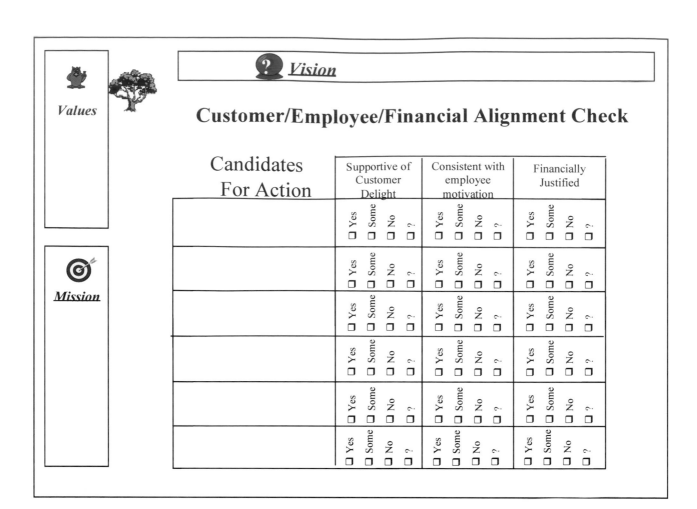

Figure 8-3, Customer/Employee/Financial Alignment Check

Step 2. The Job Ticket

Detail. Too often, an ambiguous assignment is passed on to teams who then wander inefficiently and ultimately are forced to assume their own direction. Each assignment should be made clear at the outset. The Job Ticket is marvelously effective in avoiding ambiguity and in ensuring that individual and/or team efforts will be both focused on the correct issue or challenge, and further, that their work will be performed in a manner that the requester or assignor will find most acceptable. The intent is to make the assignment completely clear to those who will work the task. The distinctive appearance of the ticket itself (paper color, icons, or both) is an important facet of this step. That is, when a distinctive form is employed, the project is readily identified to all as one of the "Vital Few." This can clear the way of what normally would be organizational road blocks.

There is a tendency for the author of a Job Ticket to expand its content to several pages of nitty-gritty instructions. To combat this tendency, the optimum Job Ticket confines its direction to a one-page, single-sided, 8 ½ x 11-inch page with 12 point or greater type font. This is a must! This set of format constraints has proven to be necessary and universally positive in countering the controlling individuals who have a tendency to over-direct and try to over-control work. It is a welcome example of simplicity that leaders and action teams find refreshing.

The Job Ticket, an effective action deployment tool, is depicted in Figure 8-4, The Job Ticket.

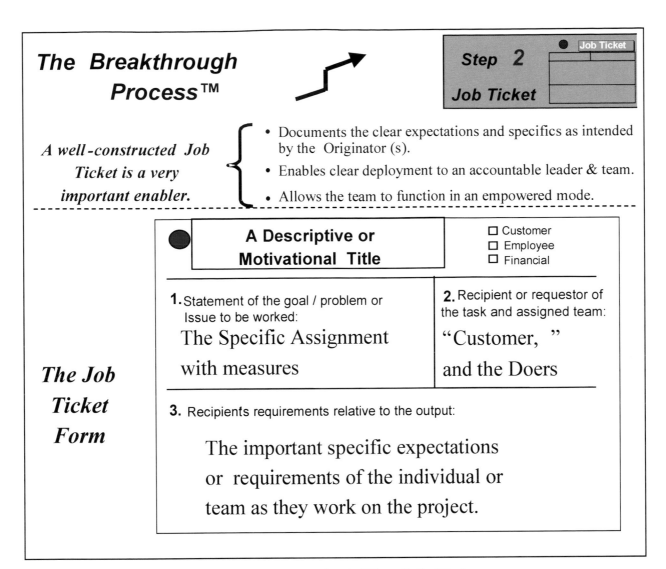

Figure 8-4, The Job Ticket

Step 3. The Team Process

Introduction. A quote from Casey Stengel, the legendary NY Yankee baseball manager provides a fitting introduction to this topic. *"It's easy to get good players. Getting them to play together, that's the hard part."*

A convenient definition of a team comes from The Wisdom Of Teams, a management book by Katzenbach and Smith. A team is defined as "A small number of people with complementary skills who are committed to a common purpose, performance goals, and who use a disciplined approach for which they hold themselves mutually accountable." This is a wonderfully clear definition of teams.

Detail. What follows is a simple check list that can be used to see if your teams conform to those of world class performers.

☐ A small number of people.
☐ With complementary skills.
☐ Committed to a common purpose.

☐ Having common performance goals.
☐ Using a disciplined approach.
☐ For which they hold themselves mutually accountable.

Well-structured teams are the way functional barriers that exist in a large organization can be overcome. The terms "functional foxholes" or "organizational silos" have been coined to describe this common change resistance phenomenon. The proper staffing and the clear working process of a team are vital to bashing the change barriers and producing measurable breakthrough results. The quality of the leader and the team members as well as the process that they follow will dictate the quantity and quality of the output as well as the speed of results production.

As such, the following are four critical elements of team formation shown in a checklist form.

a. Select a <u>Sponsor</u> (the leadership team's designee) who ideally:
- ❑ Can be the spokesperson for the senior management team.
- ❑ Has a passion for the specific challenge.
- ❑ Is results-oriented but also understands the importance of understanding the way things get done today.
- ❑ Will be available to answer key team questions and give needed direction.
- ❑ Will act to secure the time and resources needed by the team.

b. Select a <u>Team Leader</u> who ideally:
- ❑ Has a passion for the challenge.
- ❑ Has demonstrated skills in leading and coaching teams of diverse people.
- ❑ Is capable of subjugating parochial interests for the team effort.
- ❑ Is results oriented, but understands process improvement.

c. Select <u>team members</u> who ideally:
- ❑ Have needed talents and experience.
- ❑ Have a major involvement in or vested interest in the way things are done today.
- ❑ Are from functions or groups that are likely to be affected by the recommendations.
- ❑ Will be integrally involved in likely change implementation.
- ❑ Are judged to be respected members of their function or group.
- ❑ Are capable of working as a team and, if required, sacrificing personal, group, or functional interests for the sake of the common good.
- ❑ Are results-oriented and can understand the need for process change to get results.
- ❑ Will be given the time, resources and support necessary to work on the assignment.

d. Come to agreement on a <u>team meeting process</u> including:
- ❑ How often will it meet? Where will it meet?
- ❑ How long will meetings last?
- ❑ What work will be accomplished between meetings?
- ❑ Will agendas be published in advance of meetings with topics and times specified?
- ❑ Who will facilitate and record proceedings?
- ❑ How will we achieve consensus when needed?

The term "Consensus" is used throughout this text and is defined as "I agree to <u>support</u> the decision of the team, even though I may not agree that the selected option is best. I do so because my views were listened to and were given fair consideration." This is really an important difference from the more usual "majority rules" (which also means that the minority loses and gets to pout) or "unanimous agreement" (which almost never happens). Consensus has proven to be a major positive element in attaining support for a decision.

e. The adoption of a set of courteous behaviors is an important contributor to both the morale and success of a team. Successful teams come to agreement on a set of "Rules of the Road" to guide behavior. The following is a common set of team working rules:
- ❏ Start, stop, return, and end on time.
- ❏ Listen carefully and courteously.
- ❏ Express views briefly, openly and honestly.
- ❏ Do quality work, and yet do it quickly.
- ❏ No side conversations.
- ❏ No interruptions/no cell phones.
- ❏ Consensus, not majority decisions.

Step 4. The Current State

Detail. The first key team action step is to determine the fact-based current state. This covers both the current measured level <u>and</u> the processes or procedures that produce the current levels.

 When one decides to change a current process or approach in order to improve results, it is essential to know what you are changing from, so that the good can be preserved and the bad can be replaced. This understanding <u>must</u> be based on facts, not opinions.

Figure 8-5, <u>The Current State</u>, graphically portrays the required outputs.

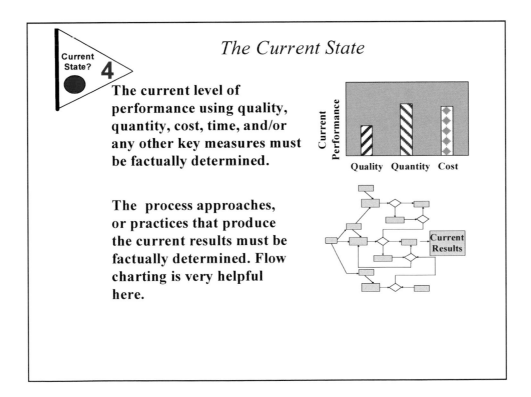

Figure 8-5, The Current State

Step 5. The Desired State

Detail. The development of Desired State levels of performance and the processes or approaches that will be necessary to deliver this desired level of performance are the next essential team steps. The team will have been given specific direction relative to the desired levels of performance from the Job Ticket or will be asked to develop same. This information can be augmented by discussions with the sponsor if needed.

In the unlikely event that the team was not given specific and measurable project goals in Step 1, the team should work to develop them by referring to and constantly checking to ensure alignment to the organization's mission, vision, values as well as the words of customers, employees, and/or the words of the financial cadre (if available). Agreement on such team-developed goals must be sought and gained from leadership early on in the process.

Figure 8-6, Step 5, The Desired State displays some key insights relative to this step.

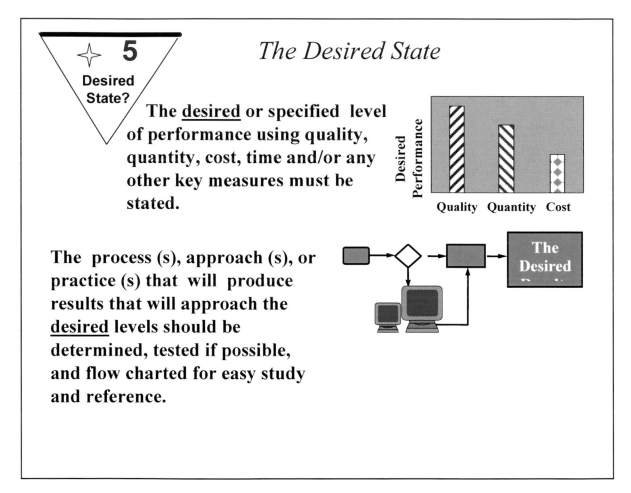

Figure 8-6, The Desired State

Step 6. The Transition Plan

Detail. The assigned individual or team must then develop a transition plan which, when executed with excellence, will move the organization from the current process and performance levels toward the desired process and its resulting improved levels of performance.

The team members are not only best positioned to fully understand the recommendations they developed in Step 5, but also should be the most passionate about seeing that the execution of their recommendations is carried out with excellence.

See Figure 8-7, <u>The Transition Plan</u>, for a depiction of the transition plan.

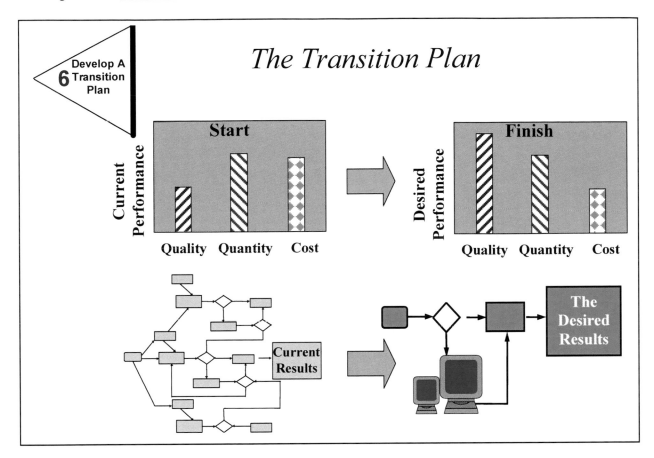

Figure 8-7, The Transition Plan

Proven effective steps to develop a Transtion Plan are as follows:

a. Brainstorm actions, which must be accomplished in order to move from the current processes to the desired state processes.

b. Eliminate redundancies and group "like" candidates.

c. Indicate which individual and/or organization should be accountable for each action.

d Develop approximate time schedules for each action and sequence them using the following steps:

- Write each of the actions on a "Post-It."
- Order the "Post-It" actions in chronological flow.
- Connect the "Post-Its" with arrows to produce a flow chart.
- Determine the "Critical Path," that is the path through the chart that will consume the longest time to the end point.

e. Develop a draft Implementation Job Ticket that delineates the transition execution requirements (talent, schedule, and resources, etc.) that are needed to bring the project to operational fruition. A Critical Path chart is extremely beneficial in this step. See Figure 8-8, The Critical Path for a simple schematic of the table of data (Activity/Description/Duration) and the Critical Path chart.

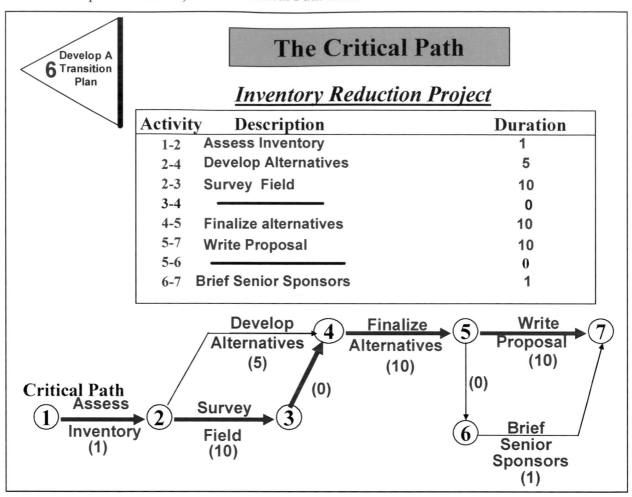

Activity	Description	Duration
1-2	Assess Inventory	1
2-4	Develop Alternatives	5
2-3	Survey Field	10
3-4	————————	0
4-5	Finalize alternatives	10
5-7	Write Proposal	10
5-6	————————	0
6-7	Brief Senior Sponsors	1

Figure 8-8, The Critical Path

Step 7. Implementation

Detail. The efficient and effective implementation of the Step 6 Transition Plan must be carried out with diligence. The team that initially worked the project through the development of the transition plan is not necessarily the best team to work the implementation. The selection of the implementation plan leader and the team members will depend on the specific elements of the transition plan and the details contained in the draft Implementation Job Ticket.

Simply put, the implementation phase team for this process follows the exact start up and organization steps outlined in Step 2 above. They are repeated here in summary form:

a. Select a sponsor who can represent and make decisions on behalf of the senior team relative to the implementation effort.
b. Select a qualified team leader.
c. Select qualified team members.
d. Come to agreement on a team meeting process.
e. Establish the team's project "Rules of the Road" for the project.

After reviewing, detailing, and, if needed, updating the Transition Plan, the implementation team is ready to commence work and execute the plan.

Step 8. Monitoring

Detail. The all-important and oft-neglected monitoring step wraps up the Breakthrough Process™. Upon completion of Step 7, the implementation team should produce a monitoring report. It would consist of three major sections:

1. A comparison of measured performance to the expectations delineated in the original Job Ticket (e.g., "Did we accomplish what we set out to do?").
2. A comparison to the quality, cost, and/or time expectations that were set in the Transition Plan.
3. An examination of the Transition Plan and the team process used, sharing positive and negative lessons learned.

The two key questions to be raised in this stage are:
- Did the team achieve the expectations indicated in the Job Ticket?
- Was the assigned "gap" sufficiently closed?

If either answer is negative, the leadership team needs to consider recycling of the project using the same or a different team.

See Figure 8-9, Monitoring, for a graphical depiction of this process.

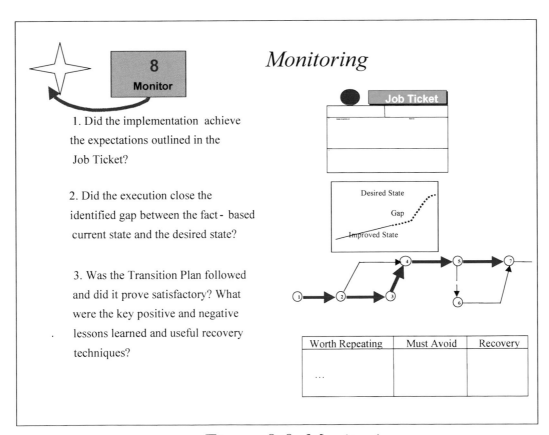

Figure 8-9, Monitoring

Bumps in the Road

The success journey is not without bumps in the road. First, the common questions that are indicative of a lack of faith or trust in the "doing things right" system are covered. Second, there are six common mistakes that are made as the system is executed. All are addressed in the following section using a question and answer format. The lack of faith or trust is addressed first.

Question: *"Aren't there some issues that are so hot that you really can't use the Breakthrough Process™? Can't we skip some steps and get on with it? For example, what if we face a sudden fire in the office?"*

Answer. There are no steps that can be safely omitted! It is obvious in the case of a dire emergency, each of the eight steps are best taken instinctively through extensive training. Let's consider that accidental office fire to make the point:

- If a life threatening office fire is discovered, it needs immediate action. **Step One**, selecting a priority issue that needs to be worked is easy. Contain and extinguish the fire!
- A call is placed to "911" and the situation and location are communicated as clearly as possible, answering the operator's questions and thus completing **Step Two**, delineating and deploying the issue to be worked. In effect, this is a verbal job ticket.
- The fire fighters form up the truck team, gather their equipment and head for the fire, thus completing **Step Three**, team formation. Their teamwork process has been established and practiced through prior training.
- The team arrives, sizes up the current situation, examines the location for hidden dangers, and checks for people in jeopardy. Thus they will have completed **Step Four**, the fact-based current state understanding.
- The fire fighters understand that the desired state is to save people first, and to then preserve and protect property. Thus **Step Five**, the desired state, is completed. Again, the desired state firefighting process has been practiced and is clearly defined.
- Even though team training has been intense, they will likely caucus to decide on a plan of attack that will allow them to approach the fire, thus completing **Step Six**, developing a transition plan.
- The plan is executed with excellence, rescuing people and putting out the fire, completing **Step Seven**, implementation.
- The team then checks to ensure that the fire is truly out and that all the people are safe. It is rare, but not impossible to have the fire rekindle, and then the fire personnel have to recycle to complete **Step Eight**. In most cases, a useful debriefing session is held to share lessons learned.

Question: *"What happens if, while in the midst of executing the Breakthrough Process™, a crisis arises that may or may not be integral to the project and is of such a magnitude that it will divert the team from working the project?"*

Answer: The answer is simple. The Breakthrough Process™ is applied to the interrupting crisis! The crisis, because it is a crisis, is ipso facto selected as a priority needing immediate attention. A Job Ticket is drafted detailing the "crisis project" and so on, continuing with the rest of the breakthrough steps. In this way, the crisis can be quickly settled and the team can get back to work on their assigned project.

Question: *"If the breakthrough model and team engagement are so logical and straight forward, why do leaders seem to have so much difficulty getting results that meet or exceed expectations from the efforts of their teams?"*

Answer: Here, let's employ the metaphor of a journey. The team embarks on a journey to move from an assigned current location to a desired destination. There are many bumps in the road ahead. These bumps can delay progress, cause unpleasant or expensive repairs, and, in some cases, can terminate the journey altogether. The most common barriers and counter measures are shown and discussed next.

Common Barriers and Counter-Measures

There are six common barriers that cause most team failures. Each cause is countered by elements of the Breakthrough Process™. Figure 8-10, <u>Bumps in the Road</u>, is a depiction of the obstacles that teams face, with indications of likely causes. Each is covered in detail in the paragraphs that follow this figure.

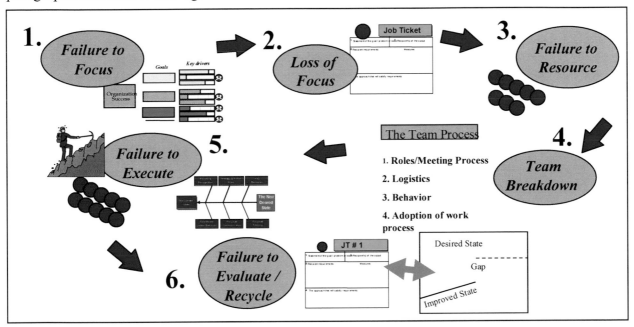

Figure 8-10, Bumps in the Road

Although the Breakthrough Process™ is logical and straightforward, there are many "bumps in the road" on the journey to world class performance.

There are six common obstacles in our breakthrough journey:

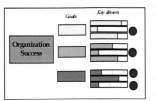

1. Failure to Focus. There are just too many issues and opportunities for a leader to juggle. There are never enough resources to accomplish it all. The work has to be prioritized before engaging the team.

The Success Tree® System takes care of this bump. Listen to the direction that comes from an organization's mission, vision, and values. Listen to the words of customers, employees, and the financial cadre. They can provide the criteria for prioritization. The identified "Vital Few" are, by definition, the breakthrough assignments that should have the full support and attention of the leadership team.

2. Loss of Focus. When teams are only given a verbal, or a very brief, written assignment, there is a strong likelihood that the team's subsequent expanded understanding of the assignment will differ from that of the leaders who assigned it. Over time, this discrepancy can grow. A good team will act to create direction that is missing. Further, there are many distractions and "fire drills" that can distract an individual, and/or team members from their assigned "Vital Few" project responsibilities.

The one-page, written job ticket (discussed in detail later in this chapter) provides the assigned individual and/or team, specific written direction from a leader or leadership team. It contains:

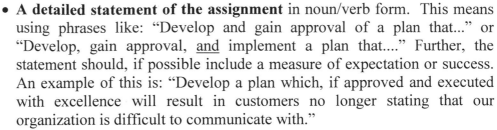

- **A descriptive and/or motivating project title**
- **A detailed statement of the assignment** in noun/verb form. This means using phrases like: "Develop and gain approval of a plan that..." or "Develop, gain approval, <u>and</u> implement a plan that...." Further, the statement should, if possible include a measure of expectation or success. An example of this is: "Develop a plan which, if approved and executed with excellence will result in customers no longer stating that our organization is difficult to communicate with."
- **A Listing** of the "approver(s)," the accountable project leader and team members, and the supportive project sponsor is needed.
- **The detailed requirements or expectations** of the requestor and/or approvers.

3. Failure to Resource Teams. Whether leaders agree or accept it, there is a <u>limited</u> amount of project management or team talent in any organization. Each talented player in an organization naturally has a limited amount of discretionary time for team efforts. They have a regular daytime job. This is a fact! One real-world experience is presented here to support the case:

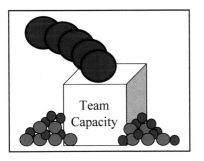

> A leader of a client company having 60,000 employees insisted that they had enough talent to resource nine "Vital Few" breakthrough teams. The firm had become accustomed to hip-shooting solutions for problems. Solutions thus produced never really resolved any issues. Over the objections of the consultant, all nine were staffed. After six months, progress on the nine projects was so poor that the leader called the group together, and announced that they would embrace a "vital one" until the group became comfortable with fact-based, disciplined, problem-solving. This produced very positive results that caused leadership to adopt a more disciplined selection process.

> We have to realize that the key players a leader would like to have on breakthrough teams are likely to be more than fully occupied with current work assignments. When the leader drops new major challenges on their plates, something has got to give. Lower priority work has to be displaced. A brute force approach just doesn't work over the long haul.

4. Team Start Up. This scenario will vividly describe the need for an organized team process:

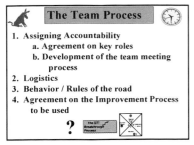

The Team Process
1. Assigning Accountability
a. Agreement on key roles
b. Development of the team meeting process
2. Logistics
3. Behavior / Rules of the road
4. Agreement on the Improvement Process to be used

A twenty-person group, with representatives from all involved functions and geographies, are asked to join in a team effort. This is 12 people too many! The optimum size for a breakthrough team is six to eight people. Nineteen members and one substitute attend the first meeting. Note that if someone is selected to be on a breakthrough team, it was for a reason. No substitutes should be accepted.

The first meeting is somewhat chaotic. Team members from one or more functions are defensive since it is likely that their home organization might be negatively impacted as a result of the team's recommendations. People with the loudest voices and most aggression seize the floor. There has to be an agreed meeting process with "rules of the road" clearly established, with assigned roles for a facilitator, a scribe, and an empowered timekeeper. There are discussions and debate during the team meeting on how the team's work will actually be conducted. One member is familiar with a six

step problem-solving process and lobbies for it. Another touts a nine-step process. Some indicate that they already know the "answer." After several chaotic hours, not much progress is evident. A hard agreement on a specific step-by-step process that the team will follow is absolutely essential.

After an hour of negotiation, a second meeting has been scheduled with only one member indicating an inability to attend. When the second meeting date arrives, only five people show up. They are the team leader and the defensive players. The rest, believing correctly that the effort is a waste of time, find excuses for absence.

Personal experiences with meetings and team efforts show that the above scenario is all too common. There is huge value to be gained by instituting and mandating the use of a common team process for breakthrough project work within an organization.

5. Failure to execute. An organization can plan many more initiatives than can actually be implemented. The resources for quality implementation are many times those required for planning. As such, it is the responsibility of the organization leader to be very critical in the acceptance of new or additional projects. A few years ago, a *Fortune* article appeared with the title "Why CEO's Fail" including a cover page with embarrassing photos of failed CEOs. The bottom line root cause for all the failures was attributed to a <u>failure to execute</u>.

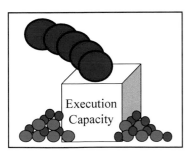

Execution Capacity

A real-world experience will give support to this conclusion. A major high-tech firm rapidly brought out new products with industry-leading features and capabilities. As time went by, the reliability of each product proved to be quite poor. A "lesson-learned" autopsy of the first four of these models showed that during development, environmental and operational testing had been either omitted or curtailed because of a shortage of test personnel and environmental chambers. The product-design capacity exceeded the testing capacity. The ultimate result was loss of market share and an earned reputation for poor performance.

6. Failure to anticipate resistance. Another important barrier to successful implementation is a failure to consider the magnitude of resistance that an organization will muster when facing change. The use of a change management model based on the fish bone cause and effect diagram has proven to be an effective guide for circumventing such resistance.

- The head of the fish represents the desired state, while the tail represents the current state.
- The false expectation is that once decided and announced, the organization will get behind the change. The reality is quite different. There are six organizational "systems" that will conspire to stymie change initiatives unless they are addressed in the project plan. These "resisters" are:

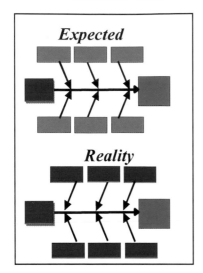

❑ **Reward and Recognition.** The word "reward" is used in this text to mean financial payment. The word "recognition" is used to connote non-monetary compensation. If we continue to reward and/or recognize current behavior, there will be reduced motivation to change. People must be recognized and/or rewarded for exhibiting behavior that is consistent with that which is expected in the desired state.

❑ **Measures.** If we continue to feature measures associated with the old way, we send a message that this is what is important to the leaders. New measures, including those that track progress in the adoption of the change, must replace or be added to the old.

❑ **Leader Role Modeling.** The leaders must take the lead in acting in a manner that is consistent with the desired state. This is the power of "do like I do."

❑ **Communication.** Under stress, the first thing to go is "hearing." There must be constant, clear communication of the change needed, why it is needed, how it will be wonderful when we arrive at the desired state, and why we cannot stay in the current state.

❑ **Training and Coaching.** The new way must rapidly become comfortable and become the accepted way. Training and coaching on the old way must be terminated and replaced by coaching on the new way.

❑ **Strategy and Plans.** A comprehensive game plan that includes all resistance countermeasures is a must.

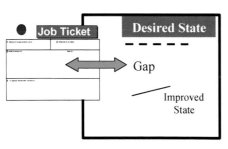

Failure to evaluate/recycle. Often this occurs with the statement: "There is little time or too few resources for such an evaluation." It is more comfortable, psychologically, to avoid facing poor performance. A real life example might help:

A leader wanted to improve the sales production of the organization's sales force. A team is asked to make it happen. The team decides, based on intuition and anecdotal evidence, that training is needed.

They develop a training program that is excellent by any measure. The training is delivered to all sales reps by certified instructors. The leaders are delighted and reward the training team with a bonus. Somewhere along the way, the task had been redefined to be "develop and deliver quality sales training" when the original assignment was to "improve sales." The actual result was no change in sales performance since the root cause of the sales productivity problem ultimately proved to be a lack of flexibility in pricing and terms and conditions, and not lack of sales training.

A One-Person Breakthrough Process™ Case Study

It would be useful to carefully examine a real world case study that demonstrates the use of the Breakthrough Process™. However, most cases contain sensitive organizational information. It would be inappropriate to use them in a text example. However, one client did agree to allow me to share a rather unique demonstration of the steps of a project. Some aspects were changed to preserve anonymity. The unique nature of this example is that this was carried out by a one-person team.

Step 1. Selection. The senior team of this organization was very unhappy with the conduct of senior staff meetings. It was decided that this was a worthy issue to pilot the Breakthrough Process™ before committing to organizational deployment.

Step 2. The Job Ticket. The senior team approved the Job Ticket shown in Figure 8-11, <u>Quality Staff Meetings</u>. Note especially that this assignment covers only the development and approval of a plan. It does not require this leader to implement approved recommendations. Thus, this person's responsibility ends with completion of Step 6, the Transition Plan.

● **Step 2** | **Quality Staff Meetings**

☐ Client/Customer
☒ Employee
☐ Financial

1. Statement of the goal / problem or issue:
Develop and gain approval of a plan which, when executed with excellence, will increase the number of Senior Staff members who indicate that the meeting is a valuable use of their time from the current 20% to 80% +

2. Recipient of the output:
Approvers: The senior staff
Sponsor: Jane Doe, COO
Project Manager: T. Smith
Team Members: None

3. Recipient's requirements relative to the output:

• Smith to self-facilitate the effort and use the assignment to role model the breakthrough process.

• Validate any estimates or assumptions in the assigned statement.

• Bring in outside expertise where appropriate.

• Ensure that behavioral change is considered.

• Provide one-page status reports each week.

• Plan to complete in time for presentation to the Senior Staff meeting next month.

• Solicit current state understanding from each of the Senior Staff meeting participants.

• Develop a graphic desired state.

• Test the desired state with the CEO and COO before it goes before the full Senior Staff.

• Benchmark other appropriate entities to examine how they achieve better results.

• Include meeting agenda, meeting conduct, and environmental improvements.

• Solicit input or solution advice from selected staff members as needed.

• Determine key measures of success for project in-process tracking.

Figure 8-11, Quality Staff Meetings

Step 3. Team Start Up. Since there was only one person on the team, there was less need for a formal team process. However, the assigned individual was required to rigorously follow the Breakthrough Process™ steps. Information from the staff would be gleaned through the use of a simple survey augmented by selected one-on-one interviews.

An additional unique facet of this project is that the task was to be regularly worked on each week for two hours on Friday mornings. As each step of the Breakthrough Process™ was completed, the work and the results were documented and shared with the sponsor via a matrix called the StopLight Report™.

See Figure 8-12, Team StopLight Report™, below. Note that the phases of the project are the steps of the Breakthrough Process™.

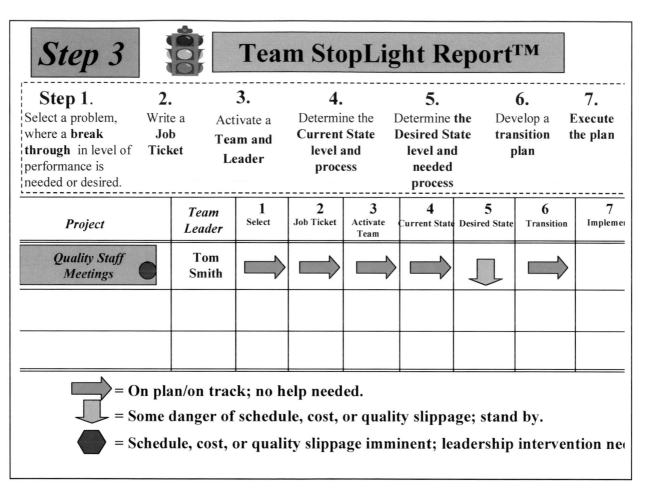

Figure 8-12, Team StopLight Report™

Step 4. The Current State. A simple written survey was sent to each staff member. Comments and suggestions for improvement were solicited. Results of the staff survey are summarized as shown in Figure 8-13, Current State Data, below.

Current State Data
Responses of Staff Participants

Respondents	Responded	Valuable
A	L	YES
B	X	NO
C	L	NO
D	X	NO
E	X	NO
F	X	NO
G	L	YES
H	NO	NO
I	X	NO
J	X	NO

Memo:

• 90 % response.

• The "yes and no" generally referred to: "yes," we need a meeting and "no," we aren't happy with it as conducted today.

• One respondent did not indicate specifically whether the meeting was a valuable use of time.

• L = late returns.

Figure 8-13, Current State Data

The comments and suggestions of the interviewed senior staff members, accompanied by the number of times mentioned, are summarized in Figure 8-14, Staff Interview/Comment Summary.

Step 4. Current State

Staff Interview/Comment Summary

Reasons to Maintain the Meetings   I, II, ...= # of respondents

• **Need a forum for sharing: IIIII IIII**

• Very useful source of info for new people.

• Need to build positive relationships.

• We need a more effective 4 hours.

Recommended Changes

• **Focus on Red/Yellow issues: IIIII II**

• Limit time of sharing to 10 minutes/person: IIII

• Spend time in meeting to set next agenda.

• Feature 1-2 departments per meeting.

• Reduce length to 2 hours: III

• Introduce some fun, variety, and recognition.

• Progress a.nd problem solving should be role modeled at the meeting.

• Limit length of presentations.

• **Stop presentations on any subject that is not necessary: IIIII III**

• Make it a decision-making forum.

• Insert a CEO Report of major events/issues.

• Agenda should have standard + contextual issues.

• **Hold meetings in a no-phone, off-site location: IIII**

Figure 8-14, Staff Interview/Comment Summary

Step 5. The Desired State. Next the individual examined the desires of the senior staff, and the changes that would counter the barriers uncovered during the current-state investigation. It was judged to be effective to use the format of a Mission, Vision, and set of Values for the meeting. A draft for each is shown in Figure 8-15, <u>Sample Senior Staff Meeting Mission, Vision, Values</u>.

| Step 5 Desired State | **Sr. Staff Mission, Vision, Values** |

What: The Senior Staff Meeting exists to provide an efficient forum for information sharing, discussion, and—when well prepared in advance—decision making.

For whom: Directly for the members of the senior staff and indirectly for their constituencies through subsequent communication.

How: By coming together once per month, for a well-planned, carefully orchestrated and managed, maximum four-hour meeting, that is judged to be an efficient and effective use of the participants' time, and by exercising excellent teamwork behavior.

Why: To ensure that the CEO and the members of the senior staff are generally informed about key organization issues, have their views understood on selected issues, and, where appropriate, participate in decisions that impact the organization and/or their own job functions.

Draft Senior Staff Meeting Vision

The members of the Operations Committee indicate when surveyed that the meetings are a valuable forum for sharing, discussing, and making decisions.

Draft Senior Staff Meeting Values

• Listening	• Respect	• Priorities	• Promptness
• Brevity	• Openness	• Focus	• Active Participation

Figure 8-15, Sample Senior Staff Mission, Vision, Values

Further, a structured meeting agenda was proposed. It included coded agenda items so participants know what is to be expected. The codes were:

I = One-way information only
E = Two-way Exchange
D = Decision Item
T = Staff Training
B = Burning Issue

Also, a simple staff meeting evaluation form to enable continuous improvement was proposed with the following statements to be applied to each section of the meeting:
"Rate each formal presentation, prepared communication or standard section of the agenda (1 poor to 10 excellent)." The statements were:
1. The subject matter was relevant and of importance to most of the members.
2. The subject could have been adequately covered in a written report.
3. The material and/or the verbal presentation was clear, concise, and brief.
4. The presenters were well-prepared.
5. This part of the agenda was a valuable use of our time.

Finally the recommendations included:

- Meeting roles and expected behaviors for the presenters, the participants, the meeting or topic manager, the scribe, and even for guests.
- A change in meeting location to a more suitable remote environment.

The work to this point was enthusiastically accepted by the senior staff.

Step 6. The Transition Plan. The plan summary was as follows:

"Commencing with the next Senior Staff Meeting, the transition of the meeting from its current state where 20% of respondents considered it to be of value to the participants, to the desired state, where 80%+ will indicate that it is of value as described in Step 5, will begin."

Resistance to change was expected. The Change Management Model™ was employed to guide development of elements of the plan that would counter the resistance. The key transition plan resistance countermeasures were:

- The COO will accept overall accountability for managing these meeting.
- One week prior to each meeting, a written agenda including topic codes will be sent to each member. Each agenda will include communication from the CEO and Financial reports from the CFO as standard agenda topics.
- The StopLight Report™ will be used to status programs, with one program manager presenting a status in person at each meeting.
- The requirement for decision topic preparation, and the management of allotted time shall be implemented
- A "free for all" sharing time shall be allocated on each meeting agenda.
- A quality presentation standard will be published for use by each meeting presenter.

Chapter Conclusions

At this point, the objectives of this chapter have been addressed:

The details of a logical, proven, efficient and effective approach to problem solving, working issues, and capitalizing on opportunities have been shared. A step-by-step barrier explanation is shown in the "Bumps in the Road" section. An abbreviated case study was presented to breathe life into the Breakthrough Process™.

Material has been provided that will help leaders gain comfort and assurance the issues and challenges can be uniformly addressed by each leader in the organization. The flexibility, and adaptability of the process was demonstrated.

A fitting quote to close this chapter emphasizes the value of prioritizing issues and opportunities and attacking them in an efficient, effective and rapid manner.

"Opportunities multiply as they are seized."

Sun-Tzu (500 BC), The Art of War

Do The **Right** Things ... Right!

It Is That Simple!

Chapter 9

The Organizational Report Card™

Chapter Objectives:

To share a proven, simple, effective approach for assessing an organization's performance against world-class standards and then isolate key areas for focused attention.

To help the leaders to commit to a continuous improvement effort in order to approach world -class performance levels.

© 2003 The Strategic Triangle Inc.

Do The <u>Right</u> Things ... Right!

It <u>Is</u> That Simple!

Chapter 9

The Organizational Report Card™

"Every manager wants to have their organization considered world class, but it takes a true leader and a process to make it so."   R.C. Palermo

The Organizational Report Card™ Positioning

The Organizational Report Card™ is the second of the two key elements of the "doing things right" part of the Success Tree® System, the first element being the Breakthrough Process™. It allows leaders to easily and quickly secure a high level assessment of the effectiveness of an organization's current processes, procedures and performance as compared to the processes and performance of a recognized standard of excellence. Its view is not from deep within "the forest" but rather above the trees thus providing leadership with a clear picture of the status of an organization.

The report card is a simple assessment tool that has been distilled from acknowledged world class organizational performance standards, including the U.S. National Quality Award. The resulting report card is comprised of eight categories containing five statements each. The contents are situationally sensitive and flexible. The eight categories are:

1. Leadership
2. Strategic Planning
3. Customer and Market Focus
4. Human Resources

5. Process Management
6. Information and Analyses
7. Business Results
8. Organization Specific Statements

See Figure 9-1, <u>The Organizational Report Card™ Form Derivation</u>, for a depiction of the derivation, content, and structure of this powerful tool.

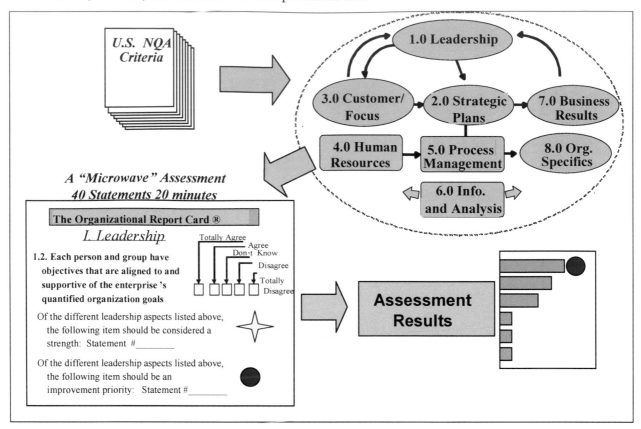

Figure 9-1, The Organizational Report Card™ Form Derivation

The Report Card Format

The report card format is a simple one. Fundamentally we are interested in determining:
- A judgment of the organization's position against each of the world class criteria (Do you agree or disagree with the organization's situation on each statement?)
- The prioritized reasons for disagreement (What do we need to fix to increase performance?)
- Areas considered notable strengths. (What should we be proud of?)

To secure this actionable information, the survey respondent indicates whether he or she: Totally Agrees, Agrees, Doesn't Know, Disagrees, or Totally Disagrees with each statement in the assessment. At the end of each of the eight categories, the respondent is asked to note by statement number, any areas of strength that the organization should rightfully feel proud of. A weakness that should immediately be addressed is also noted by statement number.

Figure 9-2, <u>Typical Report Card Category Content</u> is shown next.

Typical Report Card Category Content

<u>I. Leadership</u>

	Totally Agree	Agree	Don't Know/ Can't Say	Dis-agree	Totally Disagree
1.1. The leaders of the organization clearly and visibly demonstrate that commitment to clients begins at the top.	☐	☐	☐	☐	☐
1.2. The leaders of the organization ensure that each worker has objectives that are aligned to and supportive of the quantified goals of the organization.	☐	☐	☐	☐	☐
1.3. Each person in the organization is able to clearly describe how their personal and team results contribute to the success of the organization.	☐	☐	☐	☐	☐
1.4. The leaders encourage the open reflection on successes and failures withour finger pointing, helping them to profit from lessons learned.	☐	☐	☐	☐	☐
1.5. The leaders exhibit teamwork that is a model for other to follow.	☐	☐	☐	☐	☐

Of the different aspects listed above, I consider the following item to be a strength today: Statement #_____

Of the different aspects listed above, I consider the following item to be an improvement priority: Statement #_____

<u>Figure 9-2, Typical Report Card Category Content</u>

Report Card Process Steps

A successful report card process follows these steps:

Step 1. The leaders receive a short briefing about the derivation of the simple assessment tool. A starting point draft report card is provided and explained to the group. Past experiences are related to give the leaders understanding and a sense of comfort.

Step 2. An impartial facilitator is assigned to guide the team through this important step. A select group from the organization is assigned to customize the report card's first seven sections by adopting terminology that is most appropriate for the organization and proposing changes that will better fit the organization. A special section, specific to the organization, is populated by the team with five or so statements in an added Section VIII. Special care is taken to prevent biased language from being inserted in the assessment. This completes the transformation of the assessment vehicle from a <u>draft version</u> of a report card to the <u>organization's</u> report card. It is at this stage, after the organization's report card is accepted, that leadership "buy-in" has truly begun.

Step 3. The senior team and/or selected individuals are asked initially to fill out the assessment. While the on-line version of the report card is available and is a preferred response vehicle, a hard-copy version is available as an alternative.

Step 4. The results are tabulated and the comments logged. A +3 to -3 point scoring approach is applied to determine the average score, the median, and the range. A one-page management report is prepared and presented for comment and discussion.

Step 5. The senior team votes to choose which of the noted problem areas will be resourced and attacked first. Again, there are almost always insufficient resources to attack all of the challenges simultaneously, so prioritization and sequencing is a must.

Step 6. Job Tickets are prepared for each of the selected "vital few" issues for initial attack in order to ensure that the "doing it right" phase of the process will be executed with excellence.

It is important to note that the most efficient way to ensure that all of these steps are completed is to assign full accountability and power for them to a respected, qualified facilitator.

The report card process steps are graphically displayed in Figure 9-3, The Organizational Report Card™ Survey Process.

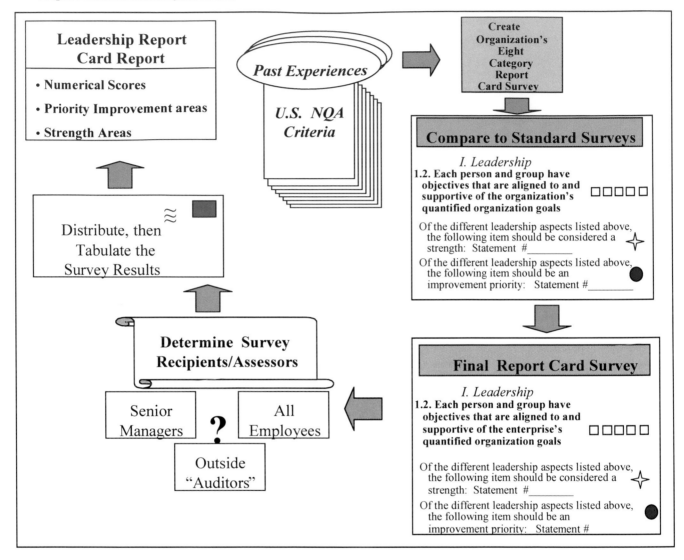

Figure 9-3, The Organizational Report Card™ Survey Process.

Report Card Forms and Process

Report card forms make clear the structure of an Organizational Report Card. A variety of examples are shown to demonstrate the versatility and universal applicability of the tool. The instructions that are used to lead the respondent or assessor through the process are also included.

Respondent Instructions

1. Read each of the statements provided in the report card. Note that the term "organization" refers to the enterprise of which you are a part. The term "leaders" refers to the CEO, direct reports, senior managers or the like.

2. Score each statement by placing an "X" in the appropriate box marked Strongly Agree, Agree, Don't Know, Disagree, or Totally Disagree. See the example below:

	Strongly Agree	Agree	Don't Know	Dis-Agree	Totally Disagree
7.1 We have a defined, effective process for determining the current and future requirements of those who will be served.	☐	☒	☐	☐	☐

3. At the end of each of the eight sections, if there is a statement that you feel is one that the organization should be most proud of; write the appropriate statement number in the blank space provided. Also, if there is a statement that you feel is one that the organization should work to improve, write the appropriate statement number in the space provided. See the example below:

Of the different statements listed above, the following are one or two items that:

I think we should be proud of: Statement #(s)   **1.2**   *(either choice may*

I think we need most to improve: Statement #(s)   **1.5**   *be left blank)*

4. Note in the comment sections any feedback relative to the usefulness of this assessment and how it might be improved. Also note any specific improvement suggestions relative to the organization and any relevant advice or message that you would like to send to leadership.

5. Sign your name if you wish, or you may choose to remain anonymous. Place your completed survey in the stamped, addressed envelope provided and place it in the mail.

Some Report Card Examples

Three different examples of real world report cards are offered in order to provide more insights, and, hopefully encourage readers to commit to the achievement of world-class performance via the use of a similar measurement tool. A few changes have been made to the material to respect the each organization's privacy. The essence of the report cards' contents has been maintained. The Category VIII Specific Organization Statements have been deleted for similar reasons.

The three examples of very different organizations follow:

Figures 9-4, 9-5, and 9-6 illustrate the categories of a <u>Public Business Report Card</u>. This refers to an organization listed on a major stock exchange.

Figures 9-7, 9-8, and 9-9 illustrate an <u>Internal Organization Report Card™</u>. This refers to a group within an enterprise that serves other internal groups as opposed to serving external customers.

Figures 9-10, 9-11, and 9-12 illustrate a <u>Non-Profit Report Card</u>. This refers to an organization that serves needy clients without a profit motive.

Public Business Report Card

Public Organization Performance Assessment

I. Leadership

	Totally Agree	Agree	Don't Know/ Can't Say	Dis- agree	Totally Disagree
1.1. The leaders of the organization clearly and visibly demonstrate that commitment to customers begins at the top.	☐	☐	☐	☐	☐
1.2. The leaders of the organization ensure that each each employee has objectives that are aligned to and supportive of the quantified goals of the organization.	☐	☐	☐	☐	☐
1.3. Each person in the organization is able to clearly describe how his/her personal and team results contribute to the success of the organization.	☐	☐	☐	☐	☐
1.4. The leaders encourage the open reflection on successes and failures without finger pointing in order to profit from lessons learned.	☐	☐	☐	☐	☐
1.5. The leaders exhibit teamwork that is a model for others to follow.	☐	☐	☐	☐	☐

Of the different aspects listed above, I consider the following item to be a strength today: Statement #_____

Of the different aspects listed above, I consider the following item to be an improvement priority: Statement #_____

II. Strategic Planning

	Totally Agree	Agree	Don't Know/ Can't Say	Dis- agree	Totally Disagree
2.1. The organization has an effective process for performing strategic planning.	☐	☐	☐	☐	☐
2.2. The organization's vision of where it wants to be in 3 years or so is clear and is understood by the employees.	☐	☐	☐	☐	☐
2.3. The organization's mission is effective in keeping the organization on track.	☐	☐	☐	☐	☐
2.4. Key performance measures—with comparisons to competitors and benchmark enterprises—are used in setting specific long-range expectations and goals.	☐	☐	☐	☐	☐
2.5. Contingency plans are developed for outcomes that would prove to be very damaging to customers, employees, or financial results. Specific countermeasures are ready, if needed.	☐	☐	☐	☐	☐

Of the different aspects listed above, I consider the following item to be a strength today: Statement #_____

Of the different aspects listed above, I consider the following item to be an improvement priority: Statement #_____

III. Customer Focus

	Totally Agree	Agree	Don't Know/ Can't Say	Dis- agree	Totally Disagree
3.1 A defined, effective process for determining the current and future requirements of customers has been developed and is regularly utilized.	☐	☐	☐	☐	☐
3.2 Customers seeking assistance or suggesting improvements find it easy to contact the right people.	☐	☐	☐	☐	☐
3.3 A defined, efficient process for handling and resolving customer complaints preventing recurrence has been developed and is effectively utilized.	☐	☐	☐	☐	☐
3.4 Customer retention is tracked and losses are identified and understood with process changes and/or countermeasures put in place to minimize repetition.	☐	☐	☐	☐	☐
3.5 Customer-focused leadership organizations are regularly benchmarked in order to identify quantum process improvements relative to the firm's performance for customers.	☐	☐	☐	☐	☐

Of the different aspects listed above, I consider the following item to be a strength today: Statement #_____

Of the different aspects listed above, I consider the following item to be an improvement priority: Statement #_____

Figure 9-4, Public Report Card Categories I, II, III

IV. Information & Analysis

	Totally Agree	Agree	Don't Know/ Can't Say	Dis- agree	Totally Disagree
4.1. Information and data needed to function effectively are collected, stored, and made readily available to all in the organization who have a need to know.	☐	☐	☐	☐	☐
4.2. Using a standard problem-solving format, facts are regularly used by individuals and teams to isolate root causes and then translate them into changes that improve results.	☐	☐	☐	☐	☐
4.3. Using a standard decision-making format, facts are regularly used to come to consensus decisions by all in the organization.	☐	☐	☐	☐	☐
4.4. External benchmarking is widely utilized to gain usable insights relative to how others perform information tasks with excellence.	☐	☐	☐	☐	☐
4.5. User assessments are in place to determine the efficiency, effectiveness, and the ease-of-use of information technology systems.	☐	☐	☐	☐	☐

Of the different aspects listed above, I consider the following item to be a strength today: Statement #_____

Of the different aspects listed above, I consider the following item to be an improvement priority: Statement #_____

V. Human Resource Focus

	Totally Agree	Agree	Don't Know/ Can't Say	Dis- agree	Totally Disagree
5.1. We have and use a system for regularly measuring employee motivation and making changes to improve results.	☐	☐	☐	☐	☐
5.2. Effective processes for recruiting, retaining, and growing talent are in place.	☐	☐	☐	☐	☐
5.3 Recognition (non-monetary) is regularly used to publicly acknowledge team and individual contributions.	☐	☐	☐	☐	☐
5.4. Succession planning in the organization is effective and efficiently managed.	☐	☐	☐	☐	☐
5.5. Diversity in the workplace is valued and it is demonstrated in recruiting and promotion results.	☐	☐	☐	☐	☐

Of the different aspects listed above, I consider the following item to be a strength today: Statement #_____

Of the different aspects listed above, I consider the following item to be an improvement priority: Statement #_____

VI. Process Management

	Totally Agree	Agree	Don't Know/ Can't Say	Dis- agree	Totally Disagree
6.1 A clear Mission (why the organization exists) and a Vision (a picture of the organization's desired future state) are visibly displayed and understood by all in the organization.	☐	☐	☐	☐	☐
6.2. Key business processes are carefully identified for evolutionary improvement or total reengineering efforts by considering the needed improvement that current performance dictates.	☐	☐	☐	☐	☐
6.3. Business process improvement is accomplished through teams that factually determine current performance levels and the process that generates them and then develop specific process changes that will produce desired or needed outputs.	☐	☐	☐	☐	☐
6.4. People are trained to understand our business processes and to continuously improve them to get better results.	☐	☐	☐	☐	☐
6.5. Processes are simplified, and inefficient and wasteful activities are reduced in a disciplined manner.	☐	☐	☐	☐	☐

Of the different aspects listed above, I consider the following item to be a strength today: Statement #_____

Of the different aspects listed above, I consider the following item to be an improvement priority: Statement #_____

Figure 9-5, Public Report Card Categories IV, V, VI

VII. Business Results

	Totally Agree	Agree	Don't Know/ Can't Say	Dis-agree	Totally Disagree

7.1. Key customer satisfaction, employee motivation, and financial performance levels are tracked, compared to plans, and , where appropriate,compared to those of appropriate benchmark institutions. ☐ ☐ ☐ ☐ ☐

7.2. Time is recognized as a valuable measure, and it is tracked and used to help deliver quality results faster, and at lower costs. ☐ ☐ ☐ ☐ ☐

7.3. We understand and track key measures/indicators of customer-perceived values and other aspects that help us build positive and lasting relationships with our customers. ☐ ☐ ☐ ☐ ☐

7.4. We track and appropriately react to a set of key measures that indicate the organization's performance in the area of public responsibility, legal and regulatory requirements, and community citizenship. ☐ ☐ ☐ ☐ ☐

7.5. Internal best practices within the organizaiton that have produced superior results are regularly shared and are emulated/adopted to improve performance. ☐ ☐ ☐ ☐ ☐

Of the different aspects listed above, I consider the following item to be a strength today: Statement #_____

Of the different aspects listed above, I consider the following item to be an improvement priority: Statement #_____

Summary Comments

Comments/ Suggestions about the key organization areas for major improvement:

Comments about the assessment:

General Comments/ Suggestions:

Figure 9-6, Public Report Card Category VII and Comments

Internal Organization Report Card™

Internal Organization Performance Assessment

I. Leadership

	Totally Agree	Agree	Don't Know/ Can't Say	Dis- agree	Totally Disagree

1.1. The leaders of the organization clearly and visibly demonstrate that commitment to internal customers begins at the top. ☐ ☐ ☐ ☐ ☐

1.2. The leaders of the organization ensure that each employee has objectives that are aligned to and supportive of the quantified goals of the organization. ☐ ☐ ☐ ☐ ☐

1.3. Each person in the organization is able to clearly describe how their personal and team results contribute to the success of the organization. ☐ ☐ ☐ ☐ ☐

1.4. The leaders encourage the open reflection on successes and failures without finger pointing in order to profit from lessons learned. ☐ ☐ ☐ ☐ ☐

1.5. The leaders exhibit teamwork that is a model for others to follow. ☐ ☐ ☐ ☐ ☐

Of the different aspects listed above, I consider the following item to be a strength today: Statement #_____

Of the different aspects listed above, I consider the following item to be an improvement priority: Statement #_____

II. Strategic Planning

	Totally Agree	Agree	Don't Know/ Can't Say	Dis- agree	Totally Disagree

2.1. The organization has an efficient process for performing strategic planning. ☐ ☐ ☐ ☐ ☐

2.2. The organization's vision of where it wants to be in three years or so is clear and is understood by the employees. ☐ ☐ ☐ ☐ ☐

2.3. The organization's mission is effective in keeping the organization on track. ☐ ☐ ☐ ☐ ☐

2.4. Key performance measures—with comparisons to those of other like-support organizations—are used in setting specific long range expectations and goals. ☐ ☐ ☐ ☐ ☐

2.5. Contingency plans are developed for outcomes that would prove to be very damaging to internal customers, employees, or to financial results. Specific countermeasures are ready, if needed. ☐ ☐ ☐ ☐ ☐

Of the different aspects listed above, I consider the following item to be a strength today: Statement #_____

Of the different aspects listed above, I consider the following item to be an improvement priority: Statement #_____

III. Internal Customer Focus

	Totally Agree	Agree	Don't Know/ Can't Say	Dis- agree	Totally Disagree

3.1 A defined, effective process for isolating enhanced internal customer-needed services has been developed and is diligently followed. ☐ ☐ ☐ ☐ ☐

3.2 Internal customers seeking assistance or suggesting improvements find it easy to contact the right people. ☐ ☐ ☐ ☐ ☐

3.3 A defined, efficient process for developing or acquiring, testing, and implementing new customer services is operational. ☐ ☐ ☐ ☐ ☐

3.4 Internal customer issues are tracked with causes identified, and with process changes made to prevent recurrence. ☐ ☐ ☐ ☐ ☐

3.5 Internal customers are regularly surveyed to determine their assessment of our performance. ☐ ☐ ☐ ☐ ☐

Of the different aspects listed above, I consider the following item to be a strength today: Statement #_____

Of the different aspects listed above, I consider the following item to be an improvement priority: Statement #_____

Figure 9-7, Internal Report Card Category I, II, III

IV. Information & Analysis

	Totally Agree	Agree	Don't Know/ Can't Say	Dis-agree	Totally Disagree
4.1. Information and data needed to function effectively are collected, stored, and are readily available to all in the organization who have a need to know.	☐	☐	☐	☐	☐
4.2. Using a standard problem solving format, facts are regularly used by individuals and teams to isolate root causes and then translate into changes that improve results.	☐	☐	☐	☐	☐
4.3. Using a standard decision making format, facts are regularly used to come to consensus decisions by all in the organization.	☐	☐	☐	☐	☐
4.4. External benchmarking is widely utilized to gain useable insights relative to how others produce and use information with excellence.	☐	☐	☐	☐	☐
4.5. User assessments are applied to determine the efficiency, effectiveness and ease-of-use of information technology systems.	☐	☐	☐	☐	☐

Of the different aspects listed above, I consider the following item to be a strength today: Statement #_____

Of the different aspects listed above, I consider the following item to be an improvement priority: Statement #_____

V. Human Resource Focus

	Totally Agree	Agree	Don't Know/ Can't Say	Dis-agree	Totally Disagree
5.1. We use a system for regularly measuring employee motivation and making changes to improve results.	☐	☐	☐	☐	☐
5.2. Effective processes for recruiting, retaining and growing volunteer talent are in place.	☐	☐	☐	☐	☐
5.3 Recognition (non-monetary) is regularly used to publicly acknowledge volunteer team and individual contributions.	☐	☐	☐	☐	☐
5.4. Succession planning in the organizaiton is effective and efficiently managed.	☐	☐	☐	☐	☐
5.5. Diversity in the workplace is valued, and it is demonstrated in recruiting employees.	☐	☐	☐	☐	☐

Of the different aspects listed above, I consider the following item to be a strength today: Statement #_____

Of the different aspects listed above, I consider the following item to be an improvement priority: Statement #_____

VI. Process Management

	Totally Agree	Agree	Don't Know/ Can't Say	Dis-agree	Totally Disagree
6.1 A clear mission (why the organization exists) and a Vision (a picture of the organization's desired future state) are visibly displayed and understood by all in the organization.	☐	☐	☐	☐	☐
6.2. Key work procedures are carefully identified for evolutionary improvement or total reengineering efforts by considering the needed improvement that current performance dictates.	☐	☐	☐	☐	☐
6.3. Selected work process improvements are accomplished through teams that factually determine current performance levels and the process that generates them and then developing specific process changes that will produce desired or needed outputs.	☐	☐	☐	☐	☐
6.4. Employees are trained to understand our procedures and to continuously improve them to get better results.	☐	☐	☐	☐	☐
6.5. Processes are simplified, and inefficient and wasteful activities are reduced in a disciplined manner.	☐	☐	☐	☐	☐

Of the different aspects listed above, I consider the following item to be a strength today: Statement #_____

Of the different aspects listed above, I consider the following item to be an improvement priority: Statement #_____

Figure 9-8, Internal Report Card Category IV, V, VI

VII. Business Results

	Totally Agree	Agree	Don't Know/ Can't Say	Dis-agree	Totally Disagree
7.1. Key internal customer satisfaction, employee motivation, and donation performance levels are tracked, compared to plans and , where appropriate, compared to those of appropriate benchmark institutions.	☐	☐	☐	☐	☐
7.2. Time is recognized as a valuable measure and is tracked and used to help deliver quality results faster and, at lower costs.	☐	☐	☐	☐	☐
7.3. We understand and track key measures/indicators of customer-perceived values and other aspects that help us build positive and lasting relationships with our internal customers.	☐	☐	☐	☐	☐
7.4. We track and appropriately react to a set of key measures that indicate the organization's performance in the area of public responsibility, legal and regulatory requirements, and community citizenship.	☐	☐	☐	☐	☐
7.5. Internal best practices within the organization that have produced superior results are regularly shared and are emulated/adopted to improve performance.	☐	☐	☐	☐	☐

Of the different aspects listed above, I consider the following item to be a strength today: Statement #_____

Of the different aspects listed above, I consider the following item to be an improvement priority: Statement #_____

Summary Comments

Comments/ Suggestions about the key organization areas for major improvement:

Comments about the assessment:

General Comments/ Suggestions:

Figure 9-9, Internal Report Card Category VII and Comments

A Non-Profit Report Card

I. Leadership

	Totally Agree	Agree	Don't Know/ Can't Say	Dis- agree	Totally Disagree

1.1. The leaders of the organization clearly and visibly demonstrate that commitment to clients begins at the top. ☐ ☐ ☐ ☐ ☐

1.2. The leaders of the organization ensure that each worker has objectives that are aligned to and supportive of the quantified goals of the organization. ☐ ☐ ☐ ☐ ☐

1.3. Each person in the organization is able to clearly describe how their personal and team results contribute to the success of the organization. ☐ ☐ ☐ ☐ ☐

1.4. The leaders encourage the open reflection on successes and failures without finger pointing, helping them to profit from lessons learned. ☐ ☐ ☐ ☐ ☐

1.5. The leaders exhibit teamwork that is a model for others to follow. ☐ ☐ ☐ ☐ ☐

Of the different aspects listed above, I consider the following item to be a strength today: Statement #_____

Of the different aspects listed above, I consider the following item to be an improvement priority: Statement #_____

II. Strategic Planning

	Totally Agree	Agree	Don't Know/ Can't Say	Dis- agree	Totally Disagree

2.1. The organization has an efficient process for performing strategic planning. ☐ ☐ ☐ ☐ ☐

2.2. The organization's vision of where it wants to be in 3 years or so is clear and is understood by the workers. ☐ ☐ ☐ ☐ ☐

2.3. The organization's mission is effective in keeping it on track. ☐ ☐ ☐ ☐ ☐

2.4. Key performance measures, with comparisons to those of like agencies are used in setting specific long range expectations and goals. ☐ ☐ ☐ ☐ ☐

2.5. Contingency plans are developed for outcomes that would prove to be very damaging to clients, employees, or to financial results. Specific countermeasures are ready if needed. ☐ ☐ ☐ ☐ ☐

Of the different aspects listed above, I consider the following item to be a strength today: Statement #_____

Of the different aspects listed above, I consider the following item to be an improvement priority: Statement #_____

III. Client & Environment Focus

	Totally Agree	Agree	Don't Know/ Can't Say	Dis- agree	Totally Disagree

3.1 A defined, effective process for isolating new client-needed services has been developed and is diligently followed. ☐ ☐ ☐ ☐ ☐

3.2 Clients seeking assistance or suggesting improvements find it easy to contact the right people. ☐ ☐ ☐ ☐ ☐

3.3 A defined, efficient process for developing or acquiring, testing, and implementing new client services is operational. ☐ ☐ ☐ ☐ ☐

3.4 Client issues are tracked with causes identified and with process changes made to prevent recurrence. ☐ ☐ ☐ ☐ ☐

3.5. Referral agencies are regularly surveyed to determine their assessment of our performance. ☐ ☐ ☐ ☐ ☐

Of the different aspects listed above, I consider the following item to be a strength today: Statement #_____

Of the different aspects listed above, I consider the following item to be an improvement priority: Statement #_____

Figure 9-10, Non-Profit Report Card Category I, II, III

IV. Information & Analysis

	Totally Agree	Agree	Don't Know/ Can't Say	Dis-agree	Totally Disagree

4.1. Information and data needed to function effectively are collected, stored, and are readily available to all in the organization who have a need to know. ☐ ☐ ☐ ☐ ☐

4.2. Using a standard problem-solving format, facts are regularly used by individuals and teams to isolate root causes and then translate them into changes that will improve results. ☐ ☐ ☐ ☐ ☐

4.3. Using a standard decision-making format, facts are regularly used to come to consensus decisions by all in the organization. ☐ ☐ ☐ ☐ ☐

4.4. External benchmarking is applied to gain usable insights relative to how others produce and use information with excellence. ☐ ☐ ☐ ☐ ☐

4.5. User assessments are gathered to determine the efficiency, effectiveness, and the ease-of-use of information technology systems. ☐ ☐ ☐ ☐ ☐

Of the different aspects listed above, I consider the following item to be a strength today: Statement #_____

Of the different aspects listed above, I consider the following item to be an improvement priority: Statement #_____

V. Human Resource Focus

	Totally Agree	Agree	Don't Know/ Can't Say	Dis-agree	Totally Disagree

5.1. We use a system for regularly measuring worker motivation and making changes to improve results. ☐ ☐ ☐ ☐ ☐

5.2. Effective processes for recruiting, retaining, and growing talent are in place. ☐ ☐ ☐ ☐ ☐

5.3 Recognition (non-monetary) is regularly used to publicly acknowledge team and individual contributions. ☐ ☐ ☐ ☐ ☐

5.4. Succession planning in the organization is effective and efficiently managed. ☐ ☐ ☐ ☐ ☐

5.5. Diversity in the workplace is valued and is demonstrated in recruiting workers. ☐ ☐ ☐ ☐ ☐

Of the different aspects listed above, I consider the following item to be a strength today: Statement #_____

Of the different aspects listed above, I consider the following item to be an improvement priority: Statement #_____

VI. Process Management

	Totally Agree	Agree	Don't Know/ Can't Say	Dis-agree	Totally Disagree

6.1 A clear Mission (why the organization exists) and a Vision (a picture of the organization's desired future state) are visibly displayed and understood by all in the organization. ☐ ☐ ☐ ☐ ☐

6.2. Key business processes are carefully identified for evolutionary improvement or total reengineering efforts by considering the needed improvement that current performance assessment indicates. ☐ ☐ ☐ ☐ ☐

6.3. Business process Improvement is accomplished through teams that factually determine current performance levels and the process that generates them; they then develop specific process changes that will produce desired or needed outputs. ☐ ☐ ☐ ☐ ☐

6.4. Workers are encouraged to continuously simplify and improve processes to get better results. ☐ ☐ ☐ ☐ ☐

6.5. Processes are simplified and inefficient/and wasteful activities are reduced in a disciplined manner. ☐ ☐ ☐ ☐ ☐

Of the different aspects listed above, I consider the following item to be a strength today: Statement #_____

Of the different aspects listed above, I consider the following item to be an improvement priority: Statement #_____

Figure 9-11, Non-Profit Report Card Category IV, V, VI

VII. Business Results

			Don't Know/ Can't Say	Dis-agree	Totally Disagree
	Totally Agree	Agree			

7.1. Key client satisfaction, worker motivation, and donation performance levels are tracked, compared to plans and, where appropriate,compared to those of appropriate benchmark institutions.

☐ ☐ ☐ ☐ ☐

7.2. Time is recognized as a valuable measure, is tracked, and used to help deliver quality results faster and at a lower cost.

☐ ☐ ☐ ☐ ☐

7.3. We understand and track key measures/indicators of client-perceived values and other aspects that help us build positive and lasting relationships with our clients.

☐ ☐ ☐ ☐ ☐

7.4. We track, and appropriately react to a set of key measures that indicate the organization's performance in the area of public responsibility, legal and regulatory requirements, and community citizenship.

☐ ☐ ☐ ☐ ☐

7.5. Internal best practices within the organization that have produced superior results are regularly shared and are emulated/adopted to improve performance.

☐ ☐ ☐ ☐ ☐

Of the different aspects listed above, I consider the following item to be a strength today: Statement #_____

Of the different aspects listed above, I consider the following item to be an improvement priority: Statement #_____

Summary Comments

Comments/ Suggestions about the key organization areas for major improvement:

Comments about the assessment:

General Comments/ Suggestions:

Figure 9-12, Non-Profit Report Card Category VIII and Comments

Report Card Scoring

When the Report Card assessments are completed and returned by mail— or completed using an on-line web-based option—the scoring for each respondent is completed using the following scoring system:

- + 3 points for each "Totally Agree"
- + 1 for each "Agree"
- 0 for each "Don't Know"
- -1 for each "Disagree"
- -3 for each "Totally Disagree"

This information is captured and the simple vote count system is applied. Regression analysis can yield the expected size of the impact on the current/desired gap for each. The respondents' suggestions for improvement and their assessments of strengths are tabulated, with the top "vote getters" being presented for leadership review. The resulting prioritized areas for action are labeled "key drivers." They will be the major candidates for ensuing gap-closing efforts.

A sample of the resulting single-page of actionable information is shown in Figure 9-13, Report Card Actionable Information. It is worth careful study.

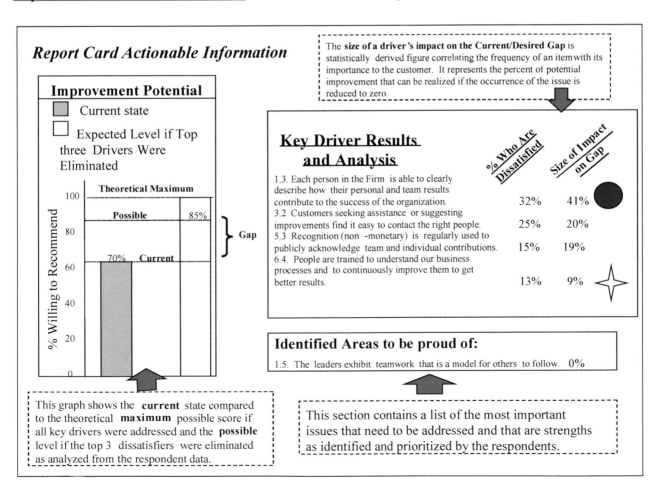

Figure 9-13, Report Card Actionable Information

The Quality Performance Branch Model

The tree diagram is a very effective tool for translating an amorphous concept like Organizational Performance into bite-sized actionable pieces. Action on the data provided by the report card results is enhanced by application of the tree diagram. Figure 9-14, <u>The Quality Performance Branch Model</u>, displays how the results of the survey will be positioned in tree format

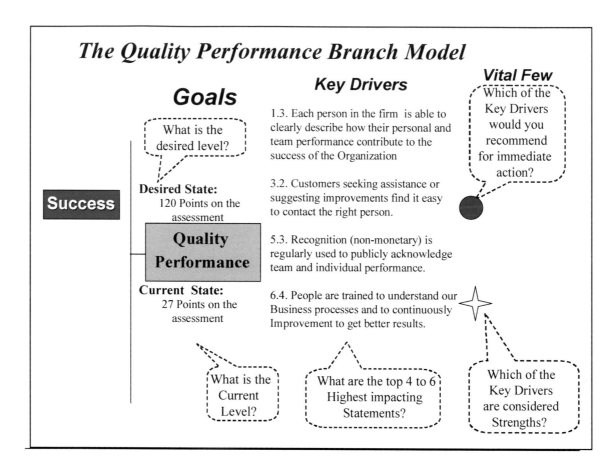

Figure 9-14, The Quality Performance Branch Model

Experiences with the Organizational Report Card™ Process

When the numerical score report is issued, it always evokes great interest. There is a natural desire on the part of some leaders to limit their interest in the report card results to a comparison of the organization's numerical score to other group scores. "Are we better or worse than others?" This leads to the following "business as usual" options:

- If yes, smile, make sure others know about it and go back to "business as usual."
- If no, demean the comparison by pointing out differences from the comparative organization and discard the report.

The actual numerical score really has little direct improvement relevance. It is merely the current score. The indicated, prioritized areas for improvement are the most important outputs. The value of these outputs lie in the "words" or "advice" of the respondents. For example, if 75 % of the respondents were to indicate that "Statement 1.2" is most in need of improvement, this would be the most salient feedback from the survey. The average score on that statement compared to that of other statements or Vs that of other organizations, while interesting, are of little value compared to the prioritization indication.

Some leaders understandably decide to hold off on the use of the report card until their organization's three-branch Success Tree® System is fully operational. A few leaders wish to start with the report card as the first endeavor on their organization's Success Tree® System journey because of a desire to rapidly gain a justifiable reputation as an organization having world-class processes and procedures.

Typical options for the exercise of the assessment phase of the report card process are noted as follows:

- **The Safe Approach.** In this approach, only top leadership completes the report card assessment. The value of this approach is two-fold: First, the leaders get a better understanding of the measures that really judge world class performance. Second, if the assessment by the top leaders is honest and accurate (unlikely), the bad news is limited to the executive suite. The downside is that this approach has very limited improvement impact because the "ivory tower" view rarely gives the true picture of the current perception by all the employees in an organization.

- **The Managers Only Approach.** Here, top leadership completes the report card assessment first, and then cascades the survey vehicle to only the managers in the organization. The added value of this approach is two-fold. First, the leaders get a comparison of their own perception of the organization's "World Class" performance status to that of their management team. Second, if the assessment is honest, the bad news is communicated to the full accountable management team, making appropriate improvement actions more likely. The downside to this approach is that truly achieving world class performance necessarily involves the ignition of the full employee "engine."

- **The Full Power Approach.** Here, the entire organization completes the assessment. This courageous approach is done from the top down, group by group, directed from the executive suite. Its value is that the assessment input includes the points of action in an organization, on the "firing line" if you will. Employees and first-line managers know how things actually work, and are best positioned to make effective improvement choices. Thus, the full power approach with the employee involvement can be brought to bear on improvement items. The down side is that employee expectations for involvement and leadership role model actions will be raised. Disappointment can occur if leadership waivers on the needed follow through.

- **The Inspector General Approach.** Finally, some leaders eventually engage an impartial external assessor for the report card assessment. This usually follows a few years of "self" assessment, and prior to application for a national quality award. The obvious value is that an <u>independent</u> <u>professional</u> assesses the organization. The downsides are that sometimes an "outsider" is resented sufficiently to devalue the results and, the results of a critical judge, if not temperate, can devastate the morale of an organization.

Many different factors affect which assessment route to follow. The organization leader is best positioned to make the decision relative to which assessment approach will be best. Which ever approach is adopted, the leader must be alert to the possibility that the improvement motives for adopting a report card approach may be very shallow. The following warrants consideration:

There is sometimes an attempt to "rig" the assessment system to get a good score on the Organizational Report Card™. It is easy to discern when this is happening. It is a sure bet that rigging is being attempted when:

- **During finalization of the contents of the report card, statements in the initial draft that are perceived to probe a weakness of an organization are argued for deletion or modification.**
- **Certain segments or groups in an organization may be excluded from doing the assessing because "their morale is poor" or "they have a bad attitude."**
- **Results of the resulting priority write-in areas for improvement are rationalized, "spun" and thus discarded or demoted to non-vital status.**

When this happens, it is a clear sign that the leaders have no intent to truly pursue world-class performance, and that the report card use as an instrument of positive change should be discontinued.

The Quality Performance Closed-Loop System

When the results of the Organizational Report Card™ are applied to the creation of the performance branch, and a problem-solving process is applied, the elements of a closed loop system are completed. Such a system is depicted in Figure 9-15, <u>A Quality Performance Closed-Loop System</u>. The effective, efficient corrective action step depicted in the system is detailed in Chapter 8, The Breakthrough Process™.

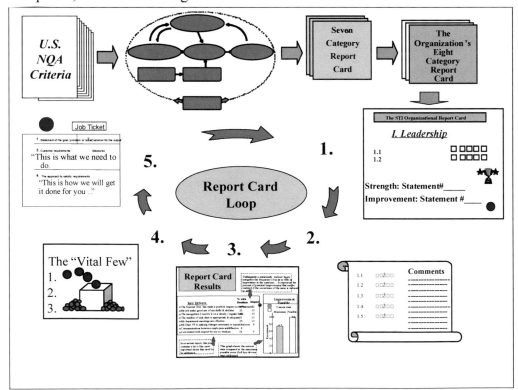

Figure 9-15, A Quality Performance Closed-Loop System

Chapter Conclusions

At this point, the objectives of this chapter have been addressed:

Share a proven, simple, effective approach for assessing an organization's performance against world-class standards, and then isolate key areas for focused attention.

Help the leaders to commit to a continuous improvement effort in order to approach world-class performance levels.

The approach to the development, distribution, and assessment of an efficient and effective "20 minute microwave" assessment was provided. The "how-to" details and real world examples make it easier to understand the road map for this journey to world class organizational performance.

 "Customers deserve world class treatment. Employees thrive on it. Leaders are energized by it. Stakeholders and supporters are rewarded by it. Time on this earth is too short to waste it on a mediocre journey."

R.C. Palermo

Assess, and go for it!

Do The **Right** Things ... Right!

It Is That Simple!

Chapter 10

The Change Management Model ™

Chapter Objectives:

To provide an effective model that will ensure that bold changes will come to fruition by anticipating resistance to change and then including plans that will counter such resistance.

To embolden leaders to accept aggressive levels for their organization's future state.

© 2003 The Strategic Triangle Inc.

Do The <u>Right</u> Things ... Right!

It Is That Simple!

Chapter 10

The Change Management Model

"If you think you are going to be successful running your business in the next 10 years the way you did in the last 10 years, you're out of your mind. To succeed, you have to disturb the present... and it will no doubt cause much disturbance."

Roberto Goizueta, CEO Coca-Cola

Positioning. Resistance to change is normal and is to be expected, even with evolutionary change. The status quo is generally comfortable and requires little, if any, conscious thought. There is also a hypocritical perception that is characterized by this actual client quote: "When I want to change you, it is progress. When you want me to change, it is disruption." The resistance to initiatives involving major change is massive.

Analyses of failed change initiatives are always instructive. Such analyses have led to the use of a *fishbone* or *Ishikawa* cause-and-effect chart as the basis for a powerful model that allows a leader to understand resistance, anticipate the reasons for change failure, and to then develop the means to neutralize or circumvent the change resistance.

When a discontinuous or breakthrough change is desired as opposed to an evolutionary, gradual one, the change is almost always contested by in-place resistant elements of an organizational "system." All work vigorously and in harmony to maintain the status quo.

If a leader attempts to move to a new state by merely communicating the details of the change–even in a passionate way–the change initiative will not take. This is because the in-place "resistance system" conspires to "kill the alien invader." Since the old behavior is still rewarded and recognized; since the old parameters are still featured; since people continue to be coached and trained to function in the old way; since the leaders' behaviors continue to role model the old way; and since old processes or tools die hard, the change doesn't stand a chance.

See Figure 10-1, <u>The Change Resistance Fishbone</u>, for a graphic expression of change resistance and its effect on solitary communication of the needed change.

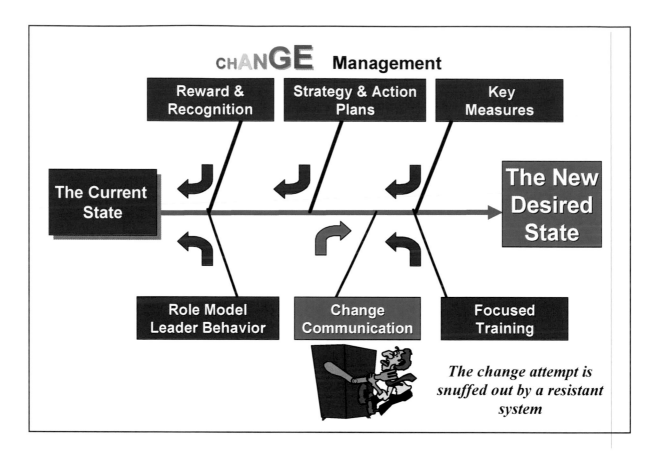

Figure 10-1, The Change Resistance Fishbone

A Proven Successful Change Approach

An effective approach to change implementation and adoption requires that each element of resistance be assessed and then countered. The following paragraphs provide insight to each of the resistance elements.

Current and Desired States. If a discontinuous or breakthrough change, or even evolutionary change is to be successful, the current state must be clearly portrayed as being undesirable (the uglier the better). The desired state after the change must be clearly portrayed as beautiful and the ideal place to be. Thus a driving force away from today and toward the future is initiated

Each of the organizational "resistance system" elements <u>must</u> be assessed, addressed and converted to elements that are fully supportive of the change. Specifically:

Reward and Recognition. Plans must be put in place to provide a positive reward and visible recognition for those who support the needed transition and who travel the change journey with enthusiasm. The intent is to incent others to do likewise. The leaders must provide positive answers to the common question, "What's in it for me?" If required, negative motivation may also be applied. That is, by highlighting that there is a level of pain associated with non-conformance to the desired state, leaders can reduce the level of comfort with the status quo.

Key Measures. The key measures of progress toward the desired state, and measures that reflect the successful achievement of desired performance must be developed and be monitored and regularly displayed in a manner visible to all. The change-tracking mechanism should include measures of progress and highlight any barrier issues. The intent is to move quickly with corrective actions when indicators have or are about to turn "red." There is a need to ensure that early indicators are available for the things that might go wrong and be damaging.

Focused Communication. A comprehensive communication plan that is designed to inform and encourage all to support the transition to the desired state must be developed and executed. Rumor-fighting flexibility and responsiveness must be included. Supportive changes in each of the fishbone elements should be highlighted. "Say it clearly and often" is the right rule.

Focused Training. Training for all affected personnel, especially those who will be key to the transition should be planned, resourced and executed as needed. "Fool-proof" training methodologies are the goal where, as always, "Simplicity trumps sophistication."

Strategy and Action Plans. A detailed schedule of chronological events and activities that will lead to the timely launch, execution, and completion of the change transition should be developed and implemented.

Role-Model Leader Behavior. Selected influential individuals and leaders should be impressed with the importance of visible support of the change. They should be given a clear understanding of "post change" behavior. Commitments to the desired-state behavior must be collected.

The Empowered Transition Manager. A key element of change success is the appointment of a respected and skilled transition manager who will be fully accountable for organizing the change effort and who will be empowered to make it happen. This is desirably the person who is among the first to "arrive" at the future change destination, and as such, should be considered a "high potential" individual for an important leadership assignment when the change is complete.

 A dedicated and driven Transition Manager is not to be confused with a change champion. The change champion's role rightfully belongs to an organization's leader. Day-to-day management of the development and implementation of the many elemental change strategies that will be necessary to convert the resisters to enablers requires the appointment of an impassioned change agent: the Transition Manager. In small organizations, the leader can handle both roles.

A graphic portrayal of the change plan objective where all are "green" is shown in fishbone format in Figure 10-2, The Change Enhancing Fishbone.

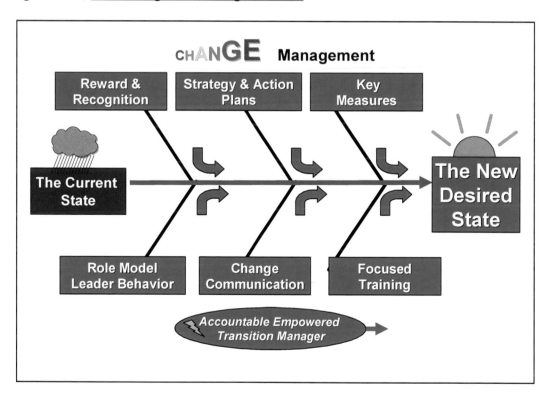

Figure 10-2, The Change Enhancing Fishbone

 Major change initiatives should be followed by a period of digestion and evolutionary change. Basically, the organization will need a breather. A repetitive cadence of breakthrough change followed by evolutionary change is most healthy. Change pressure must be continual.

See Figure 10-3, <u>Breakthrough and Evolutionary Change Cadence</u>, for a graphical portrayal of the comparison of an evolutionary change followed by a breakthrough change.

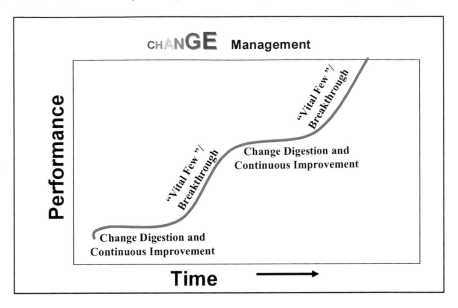

Figure 10-3, Breakthrough and Evolutionary Change Cadence

Experience shows that the ground has to be prepared for change to take root. The following six questions constitute a decent change checklist:

1. Are the critical people <u>convinced</u> that change is necessary?
2. Has the current state been clearly defined? Fact-based? With measures? Have we accentuated the negative?
3. Has the desired future state been clearly defined? Does it accentuate the positive? Is there a plausible rationale for the goal?
4. Have we appointed an accountable, empowered transition manager?
5. Have we considered an experienced, trusted external coach?
6. Has a comprehensive transition game plan been developed and approved? Does it include:
   - A communication plan.
   - Changes in reward and recognition.
   - Training plans.
   - Senior management behavioral definition and demonstration.
   - In-Process measures of progress.

Prioritizing the Change Elements

It is an interesting exercise to determine which of the six-fishbone elements is the most influential in either promoting the change or acting as a barrier a specific change. This study can be accomplished through the use of a quality tool classically called the Interrelationship Digraph. I prefer to use a more descriptive name that has been coined...the "Bubble Chart." This tool is wonderful for achieving priority judgments from a group of individuals.

The change bubble chart is constructed by drawing ovals and naming each of them with the six change resistance elements. The arrows indicate   Cause ⟶ Effect relationships.

A group of leaders are asked such questions as:
"Is a lack of change measures a cause of poor communication?" or "Is poor communication a cause of a lack of change measures?"
"Is a lack of change measures a cause of poor leadership role models?" or "Is a lack of leadership change role models a cause of a lack of change measures?"

Similar questions are asked of each pair of the six elements. The results of such an exercise are shown in Figure 10-4, <u>The Change-Priority Bubble Chart</u>, and are interpreted as follows:

- The bubble with the most arrows exiting the bubble is the most influential one, and as such should be given the most attention. I label this the "villain" to connote that it is a cause of many of the negative effects noted.
- The bubble with the most arrows entering it is affected by many of the factors and is the cause of few or none. It is rightfully called the "victim." Staying in this metaphor, the "victims" can be administered first aid, but unless the "villains" are addressed, more "victims" will result. Thus, the intense focus should be on removal of the "villains."

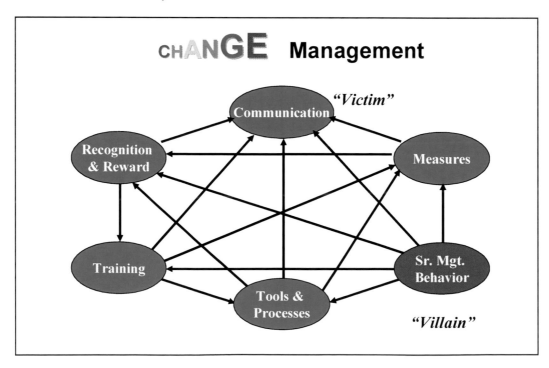

Figure 10-4, The Change-Priority Bubble Chart

A Successful Change Experience Analysis

It is interesting to examine a successful change action of an acknowledged world-class leader in the context of the fishbone model. Fortunately, a public case is available. In 1997, as reported in the *Wall Street Journal*, Jack Welch, then CEO of General Electric, outlined four key change strategies for the company:

- A shift to an aggressive quality focus.
- A shift to service from manufacturing.
- Profitable niche acquisitions.
- Worldwide expansion.

 These changes were not evolutionary but rather bold and discontinuous. It is also interesting to note that these were "opportunity-driven" as opposed to "crisis-driven" changes. It is clear and logical to expect that change is much easier when an organization is facing acknowledged disaster than when the organization is in a strong position. It is a great tribute to the leadership skills of Jack Welch that he promoted change and made it happen when his organization was riding a crest of success.

In 1997, GE was #1 in profitability among *Fortune 500 companies*. Thus, strong organizational resistance to change could rightfully be expected. These are the strategies that were outlined in the article:

- The creation and use of "black belt" transition managers.
- The change will be driven "top down."
- Everyone gets trained.
- 40 % of management bonuses will be applied to the changes.
- The change to quality, patterned after Motorola's approach, is critical to survival.

Note how the G.E. strategies line up to the elements of the change fishbone in Figure 10-5, A Change Fishbone Example.

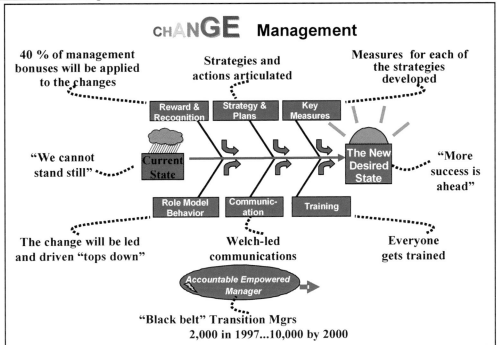

Figure 10-5, A Change Fishbone Example

Hence, whether consciously or not, G.E. successfully approached breakthrough changes by producing strategies that addressed each of the six fishbone elements. In addition, the current and desired states were also clearly articulated.

Change Management Preparation

When describing the current state, the negatives must be stressed, making it appear untenable for the organization to stay in place. Then, the desired state must be described, stressing the positives and making it the "place to be." The form shown in Figure 10-6, The Current and Desired Descriptions, is useful for documenting this part of the preparation.

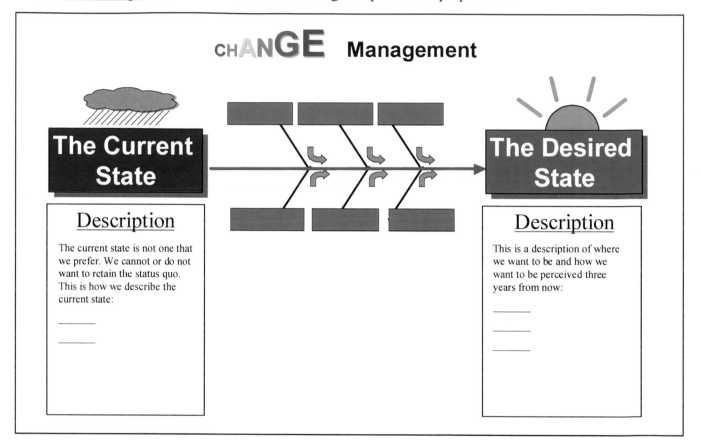

Figure 10-6, The Current and Desired Descriptions

The next critical step is to assess the current state of each of the six fishbone elements to determine which most need attention. Some of the elements will be found to be in pretty good shape and able to support the desired change. I have found that the use of colors emphasizes understanding and reinforces needed action and attention. Thus, these elements should be color-coded green. Some need modification, but are not in a change-adversary situation. They can be color-coded yellow. The elements that are judged to be in a most change-resistant state can be color-coded red and are thus ear-marked for intensive initial change strategies.

Figure 10-7, <u>Change-Element Current-State Assessements</u>, shows a convenient graphic for communicating the state of each of the six elements. Note the effective use of directional arrows and how colors can be used to communicate a great deal of information in a clear manner.

In this example:

- Communication, Processes, and Training are considered in good shape (green).
- Current policies for Recognition and Reward and currently tracked Performance Measures are considered to be "show-stopper" barriers for the desired change (red).
- Leadership behavior is judged to be neither supportive nor resistive (yellow).

The two reverse arrow bones are initially ear-marked for modifications that will convert them to become supportive of the change.

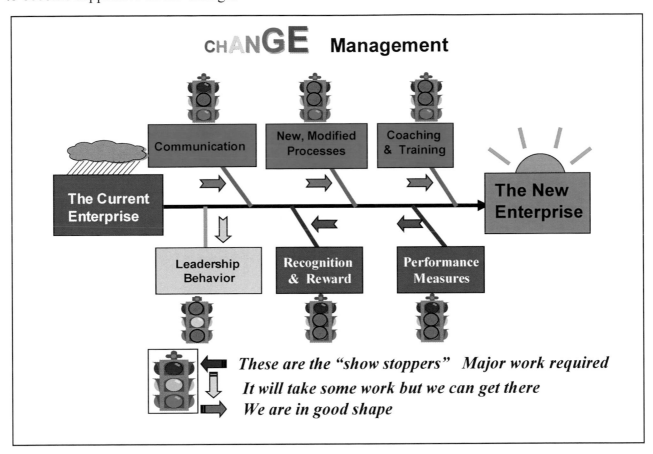

Figure 10-7, Change Element Current State Assessments

For the identified three fishbones needing attention, the usual current/desired/gap-closing approach is applied.That is, for each element, a measure or descriptor must be developed that describes their current states. Then, a picture or measure of the desired state for each element must be determined. Finally, strategies or actions that will close the gap between the current and desired levels must be determined and put into place. The Break Through Process™ described in Chapter 8 is best applied here.

Figure 10-8, <u>Change Management Plans</u>, shows an effective form for developing and recording the needed information and actions. Again, the intent is to use actions to convert the resistance elements to supportive ones.

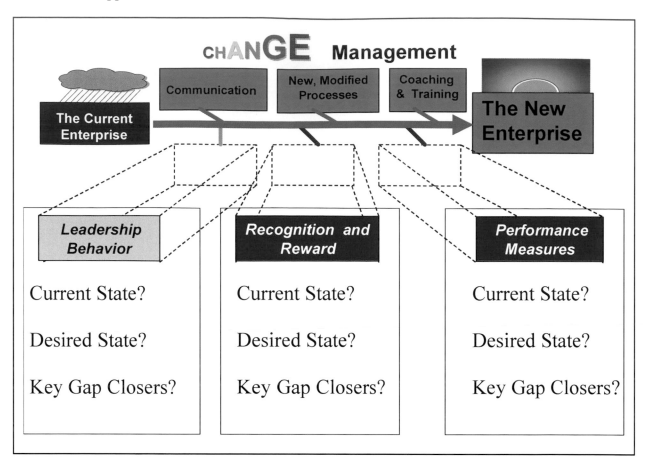

Figure 10-8 , Change Management Plans

Some discussion about qualitative or judgmental measures would be appropriate here. Recognition and Reward and Leadership Behavior are elements that have a soft quality. Some leaders find it difficult to imagine measures for them. Here, opinions are facts and the judgments of appropriate individual are helpful. A real-world sample of an approach for treating such qualitative measures for these elements is shown in Figure 10-9, <u>Change Management Progress Check</u>.

Note that when this change project commenced, the two elements shown were at the least-desired level of the selected measure. The chart indicates that past efforts have resulted in substantial improvement in Leadership Behavior to the "5" level from the original "1" level. More improvement is needed to approach the green, "10" change-supportive level.

Reward and Recognition have proven to be more obstinant and are currently at a level "2." Lots more is needed to be done to achieve the desired state and turn this important change element green.

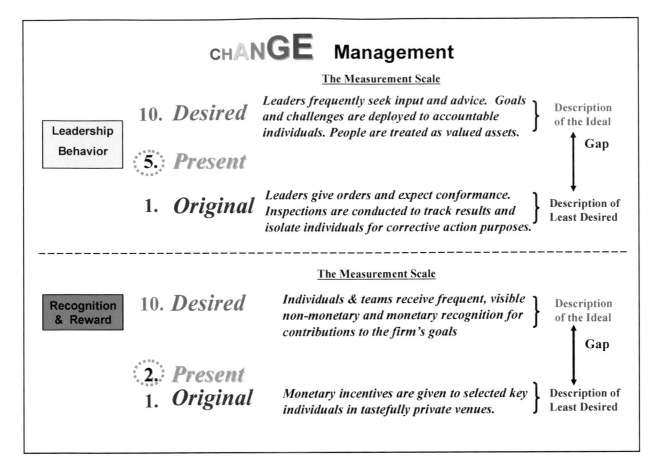

Figure 10-9, Change Management Progress Check.

A Real-World Example

A real-world example showing how a firm dealt with needed Reward and Recommendation changes is illustrative. The leaders in this case believed that profit growth was the sole reason for the firm's existence. Leaders often stated that it "went without saying" that customer satisfaction was vital and that compensation was the key to employee motivation. This was quickly followed by stating "profit is king."

Over time, the leadership team became aware that employee morale was suffering and customer satisfaction was declining. It had become apparent that actions taken to maximize revenues and cut costs had unintentionally taken their toll on customer satisfaction and employee morale. The organization was being outperformed by competitors who had embraced a balanced customer/employee/financial focus. Customer satisfaction and employee motivation could no longer "go without saying."

The leaders created an organizational desired state that evidenced a healthy, balanced focus on customer satisfaction, employee motivation and financial return. They recognized that financial health is needed to recruit, train, and retain great talent. Talent is necessary to develop and deliver world class services that delight customers. As a part of the comprehensive change strategy, the Reward and Recognition strategies had to undergo great changes in this organization:

- **Annual Performance Appraisals.** In the past, each individual was rated on a subjective 1 to 5 scale. In the desired state, each individual would be informed of their strengths and areas for improvement. Each would be asked to produce and gain approval of a Personal Development Action Plan that would grow their talent, performance, and value to the organization. Managers have their performance rated by their employees.

- **Management Bonus.** In the past, a management bonus was distributed based on a very complex return-on-asset, profit sharing formula. It was impossible to determine how to affect the bonus level. Recent results had averaged 2-5% of salary. It was hardly motivating. In the desired state, a simple per cent of organization profit would be used. However, a customer satisfaction gate was added. That is, if measured customer-satisfaction year-over-year decreased, there would be no financial bonus, regardless of profit levels!

- **Ownership.** In the past, managers granted stock options to managers for performance excellence as judged by the leadership committee. In the desired state, options would be granted both to managers and individual contributors in recognition of exceptional contributions to improvements in customer satisfaction, employee motivation, and/or financial return.

See Figure 10-10, <u>A Reward and Recognition Example</u>, for a summary of the changes noted.

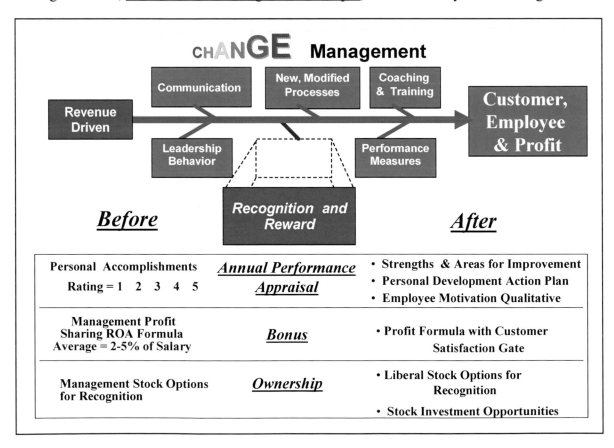

Figure 10-10, A Recognition and Reward Example

Chapter Conclusions

At this point, the objectives of this chapter have been addressed:

Provide the details of an effective model that can increase the likelihood that recommended changes will come to fruition through the anticipation of expected resistance to change and the inclusion of planned initiatives that will defuse such resistance.

Help leaders gain confidence that bold, desired states are worthy of embracing.

The fishbone change model has proved to be a very valuable leadership ally for facilitating change. Examples and forms were put forth in order to raise confidence in this proven approach to change management.

By understanding the change resistance "system" that awaits all bold ideas, and by including the means to identify and counter these resistance elements as they arise, major change success is assured.

"To improve is to change, so, to be perfect is to change often."

Sir Winston Churchill

Do The <u>Right</u> Things ... Right!

It <u>Is</u> That Simple!

Chapter 11
Lessons Learned

Chapter Objectives:

To review some key pitfalls that may be encountered on the journey to high performance and share useful preventative actions or effective countermeasures.

To examine a real world personal assessment that demonstrates the flexibility of the system.

To encourage the reader with a real life StopLight report that exhibits major progress in "closing the gap".

It is hoped that the material presented encourages the reader to put the system into practice.

© 2003 The Strategic Triangle Inc.

Chapter 11. Lessons Learned

Do The <u>Right</u> Things ... Right!

It Is That Simple!

Chapter 11

Lessons Learned

"The lessons that experiences have to offer have already been paid for by someone. Learning from them is free. What a deal!" R.C. Palermo

Positioning. Every organization has had successful and not-so-successful experiences. Often, the individuals and teams who actually had these experiences learn from them. In doing so, they grow in wisdom and skills. Of course, this learning is valuable, but it's usually limited to a small learning audience. If an individual can understand what worked well for many others and repeat it, and avoid what hasn't worked well for others, the organization's success rates in the future can be clearly enhanced.

 Experience has shown that an organizational commitment to continuous learning through the use of a formal organizational sharing process can yield remarkable benefits. Unfortunately, the use of well-structured sharing of experiences in organizations is rare indeed. This is especially true when the experience in question is negative. These valuable lessons, good and bad, have been fully paid for. Periodic, structured sharing events have proven to be a major asset in high-performing organizations. In fact, formal, structured sharing, combined with informal person-to-person sharing, represents an ideal combination.

In this chapter, key lessons learned during the coaching of client participants in prior Success Tree® System engagements are shared. The intent is to contribute to the future successful high performance journeys of the reader. The term "coach," as used in this section, is applied to the person who is using facilitation skills to support the team's efforts. With a coach's help, the teams can rapidly move forward toward recommendations and decisions with prudent speed. At the same time, the coach's efforts enhance the learning of the team.

These findings are organized into six sections in this chapter:

I.   *Coaching Experiences*
II. *Internal Sharing of Lessons Learned*
III. *External Benchmark Learning*
IV. *Personal One-on-One Coaching*
V. *A StopLight Example*
VI. *Words of Wisdom*

I. Coaching Experiences

As discussed in Chapter 8, <u>The Breakthrough Process</u>™, most of the challenges that an organization confronts or the opportunities that it decides to pursue will involve more than one group or function in an organization. This crossing of group lines occurs during both planning and execution. Such initiatives are difficult to deal with because of the fact that they naturally operate across functions. Functions become so entrenched and parochial that they have been appropriately dubbed "functional silos" or "functional fox-holes." Working across such barriers is indeed a challenge.

As such, the use of cross-functional or cross-group teams is an essential tool that can bridge the functional boundary barriers and, at the same time bring needed talent to bear on assigned critical tasks. This section of the book focuses on lessons learned that come from decades of coaching cross-functional teams to successful performance. The role of the team coach or facilitator is an essential one. This role may be performed by several types of individuals:

- The leader of the team can also perform the coaching role if he or she is a skilled facilitator.
- Facilitation can be provided by a team member who has the necessary respect and skills.
- Major benefits do come from the use of a skilled facilitator who will not be considered to have the bias that a team member may have.
- It is important to note that the most critical or most sensitive breakthrough tasks are best coached to success by an external facilitator who is known to have no vested interest in the issue or in the team's ultimate recommendations. The author has played this role on numerous occasions.

Lessons Learned About The Team Process

The next paragraphs expand on each of the team coaching findings with the hope that the reader will find benefits as they go on to lead or participate in teams. The information is posed as advice given to the team coach or facilitator.

The process steps that the team follows must be common and understood. Creativity can be brought to bear in working the challenges of each step of a team's process, but the steps themselves must be pre-set and followed. The alternative of "inventing process steps as we go" is to invite chaos. Specifically, we can be creative in <u>how</u> we determine the current-state performance and process, or <u>how</u> the desired-state is developed, or <u>how</u> the changes are to be implemented. There can be no vote applied as to whether a team should determine the current state, or whether or not a team should develop a transitions plan. Changing the steps of an already agreed, logical team process is just not needed, nor is it acceptable.

The following set of team steps is an example of those in an effective problem-solving process:

Step 1. Clarify the team charter.
Step 2. Agree on team member roles and expectations.
Step 3. Determine factually the current state and the processes that produce them.
Step 4. Develop the desired state, and the processes that will be needed to deliver them.
Step 5. Develop a transition plan that will move us from the current state to the desired state.
Step 6. Execute the recommendations.
Step 7. Monitor to assess success and recycle if necessary.

A team identity and agreed procedural and behavioral protocols are a clear help. In the initial team meeting, encourage the team to adopt a logo or nickname. Help the team agree on "rules of the road." Ask the team to consider and use the following terms as a common team shorthand language. Once agreed, no one takes offense when a team member uses one of these terms:

- *"Process Check:"* Indicates that a participant feels that the team may have gotten off course and wants them to get back to the appropriate topic or discussion subject.

- *"Time Check:"* Indicates that the team is on a course that will miss meeting its objectives. It tells the team that it needs to accelerate work efforts and minimize extraneous discussion.

- *"Seeking Understanding:"* Indicates that the participant needs someone to fully explain the topic or issue under discussion.

Agreement on good behaviors such as: starting on time, ending on time, seeking information, giving information, and proposing, will help the team work efficiently. Seek team agreement that they will avoid poor team behavior such as: attacking, defending, and shutting people out.

 The term "Consensus" has a specific meaning in this system. Seek team agreement on this specific definition of "consensus." Consensus is achieved when the even most strident dissenter will state: "I don't believe that this is the optimum approach but, because the team listened to my views and gave them suitable and fair consideration, I agree to support the team's position. I will not have to say it was my preferred position, but I will also not bad-mouth it."

Clarity at the end of each meeting is essential. Ensure that each team meeting ends with these activities:

- Summarizing agreements, decisions, and findings. Ensure that all are recorded.

- Coming to agreement on the next steps – actions to be completed before the next meeting and beyond. It is useful to develop "fill-in-the-blanks" forms for individual/sub-group reporting.

- Conducting a brief meeting evaluation for continuous improvement of meeting effectiveness.

Procedure Documentation. Someone in the team meeting must be "the scribe" and record key proceedings. It is best to do this with real-time visual recording, using a PC and projector. Recorded materials can be e-mailed to participants immediately at the end of each meeting session.

Start writing the final team report on the first day that the team meets. The coach should help the team package the output of each process step as they are completed. For example:
- Capture the initial Job Ticket or assignment sheet, and note any subsequent negotiated changes.
- Document the "how-to" approaches that the team uses for each of the task requirements.
- Retain the improvement process briefing materials for use in the final report.
- Note the agreed measures, current level, and current process understandings.
- Save all of this in final PowerPoint presentation form Use an icon for each of the improvement processes to keep the material organized.

In essence, after each team meeting, needed materials for the leadership presentation would have been created. The workload at the completion of the project will thereby be minimized. Finally, sharing at a subsequent lessons learned session is facilitated.

Lessons Learned About The Team's Work

Focus, focus, and focus. A key contribution of a coach is to keep the team focused on the specifically assigned problem or issue, on the measures of progress, and on the current step of the improvement process (e.g. the current state, the desired state, transition planning, etc.).

Actionable information is in short supply. Though there is a great deal of data available, actionable information is hard to come by. Almost without exception, the coach will have to encourage the team to develop or acquire needed information through rapid research. Time pressures may push the team to rely on opinion with supportive studies to follow.

The coach has to carefully examine the output to make sure that the team has exhausted efforts to acquire facts before defaulting to opinion.

The "Cliff Notes" Version. The coach must encourage the team to emphasize simplicity in every aspect of the team effort. Reports from outside sources, feedback from benchmarking work, literature searches, etc. all should be distilled down to only that which is absolutely relevant to the team's mission. All must be summarized in useful formats. The team's recommendations should likewise stress easy-to-do, burden-free, user-friendly actions. Recognition must be given to the fact that leaders and workers are very busy and have little free time to peruse and ponder complex reports and recommendations. Complicated recommendations will not likely be given the attention intended and, thus, leadership adoption may be jeopardized.

Lessons Learned About Team Meetings

Saw-toothed team progress. There is a temptation to hold a few two-day meetings rather than more frequent half-day or one-hour team meetings. In two-day sessions, the team's energy and attention fade by 2 PM on each day (if not sooner).

A team's work is paced to team meetings. The work immediately after a meeting seems to fall to zero and then increases geometrically as the next meeting date approaches. The longer the time between meetings, the slower is the team progress.

See Figure 11-1, <u>Team Progress,</u> for a graphic picture of this proven phenomenon. Better to push for more frequent, shorter, crisp team meetings.

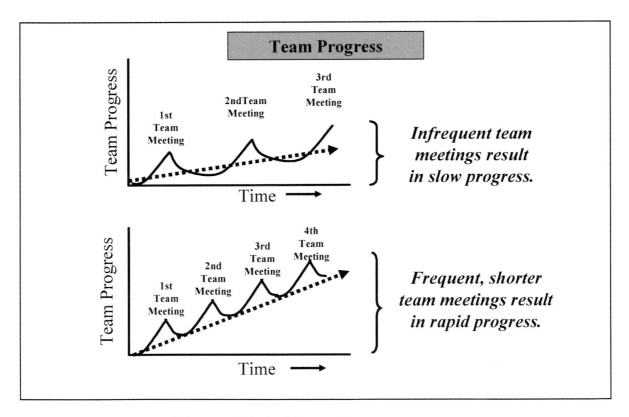

Figure 11-1, Team Progress

There is no such thing as a short break. A 10-minute break takes 20 minutes. A 20-minute break takes 30 minutes and so on. Best is 20 minutes and ring a bell to reassemble.

Set very aggressive time goals. For example, it is wise to include a statement that is something like: "Complete step four by the next session." Then drive the group to meet or exceed these goals. Reflect on failures and celebrate successes at each appropriate time.

Other Lessons about Coaching

Measures, Measures, Measures. Coaches instinctively understand that "If it doesn't get measured, it doesn't get done." Vital areas that are essential to the success of the organization <u>must</u> be measured. Two types of measures are essential:

- Measures related to the levels of the issues in question.
- Process measures that indicate the effectiveness and efficiency of the <u>way</u> things are done.

Thus, a team's findings and recommendations must be accompanied with both results and process measures.

Do what's needed when it's necessary and useful. Coaches should feel free to accept team-related work assignments where their skills and experiences permit. This is especially welcome when the team workload is high. As an example, the team may be hard-pressed to do quality benchmarking or conduct a detailed literature search. These are good candidates for the team's coach to personally handle. However, one has to take care that the coach doesn't wind up doing all the team's work.

Help the leader lead. While working with a team, the coach should consciously try to position the leader as a skilled, respected, resourceful, decisive individual who is worth following. Working behind the scenes and between meetings with the leader can help accomplish this. Give advice, suggest use of tools, and prepare materials for the leader to use.

Teach by coaching. A coach will often encounter resistance to the use of quality team tools, especially those tools that may be new to the team members. This client quote is a good example: "The heck with quality tools, let's just argue it out." The coach may find it useful to walk the team through each step of a quality tool, such as brainstorming, or the priority matrix (see the explanation below) or the bubble chart (see Chapter 8 for details) in a "just-in-time mode" without labeling it a quality tool. Only after the tool has produced excellent team results should the coach divulge that a team tool was used. The coach should try to create team interest in learning/trying more such tools, since that can help them in future projects.

The priority matrix is a powerful team tool. When people vote for/or against an option chosen from a list of candidates, there is often a strong disagreement about the voting outcome. The disagreement likely arises from the fact that the voters used different criteria when deciding where to cast their votes. The Priority Matrix is a powerful tool that has produced excellent consensus team agreements where very complex and sometimes contentious decisions are required. It is best applied when the list of options or decision candidates has been reduced to a manageable number (ten or less). To use this tool, the team first decides on the criteria that will be used <u>before</u> a vote is taken by answering the question: "When we vote, what are the criteria that affect our votes? Cost? Location? Size? Time?"

After agreeing on four to eight criteria, the criteria are then weighted, again before voting commences. The team is asked: "Which of these criteria is the most important relative to our decision? Which is the least important? Where on this scale of 'most important' to 'least important' do the remaining criteria fall?"

The use of a PC with a spread sheet projected on a screen during the decision process has proven to be a wonderful aide to an expedited, quality decision. Using this tool, any of the ratings or weightings can be changed to see if, and how they affect the results. The team can apply this decision process to prioritize a list of key drivers. It is so powerful that I share an example in this section of the book. Using this tool, a team can not only vote and examine the outcomes, but can also examine the reasons for the outcomes. In this way, a solid consensus is often readily achieved.

The Priority Matrix Procedure

1. Write the list of candidates on a matrix form such as that shown in Figure 11-2, <u>The Priority Matrix</u>, below.

2. Have the decision-makers brainstorm a list of evaluation criteria that can be used to best judge the relative worth of the candidates. State the criteria so that a high score is positive. That is, "Ease of doing" and "Low risk" are stated as positives.

3. Have the team agree on the most appropriate criteria (eight or fewer) from the brainstormed candidate list and write them on the matrix form.

4. Come to an agreement on a weight for each of the criteria. This represents the relative strength of each of the selected criteria. Use "10" for a very strong positive factor, "5" for modest strength, and "1" for a weak factor. Note the weightings on the matrix. An easy way to complete this step is to ask the group to come to agreement on the strongest positive and give it a "10." Determine which is the next strongest and come to agreement on its numerical value. Continue this process to completion.

5. Rate each of the selected options in question against each of the criteria in order. For example, when considering "Low Cost," how would you rate the first option? The second? Others? Consider using these ratings which have been found to be very discerning and effective

> **9 = High, quick, easy, inexpensive, clear**
> **3 = Middle ground**
> **1 = Small, difficult, costly, bothersome, vague are some useful measures.**

6. Multiply each candidate's rating by its weighting, and note the product on the form. Add the points across the rows to arrive at each candidate's score.

7. Discuss the results and come to consensus on the selected candidate. If a team member is uncomfortable with the indicated answer, the spreadsheet's power can be used to vary any weighting or rating to examine its impact on the outcomes. This often helps settle an issue.

8. Use the Priority Matrix Form and the process used to report results of the exercise.

An example matrix is shown below in Figure 11-2, The Priority Matrix. In this example, the challenge was for a new church committee to select a location from a number of available real estate options. There was the possibility of contention in this decision.

The Priority Matrix

Criteria / Candidates	A. Location Good = 3 miles or less from Center OK = 3-6 miles Poor = 6+ miles	B. Anticipated cost Good = Donated OK = <$100K Poor => $100K	C. Cost of site preparation. Good =< $30K OK =< $60 K Poor =>$ 60K	D. Road Frontage Good = 300 ft.+ OK = 200 to 300 Poor = < 200	
Knock Out Levels	KO = 8+ miles	KO = $ 100K+	KO = $ 100K	KO = < 200'	
Weights	0.9	1	1	0.8	
Jones Lot Score Score X Weight	Good 10 9	OK 5 5	Good 10 10	KO 1 0.8	24.8
Smith Lot Score Score X Weight	Ok 5 4.5	Good 10 10	Poor 1 1	OK 5 4	18.5
Brown Lot Score Score X Weight	Good 10 9	OK 5 5	OK 5 10	OK 10 8	32

Figure 11-2, The Priority Matrix

Establish a team understanding of work apportionment. Come to an understanding that most of the work of the team will be done in the time <u>between</u> the team meetings. The minority of work will be done by the participants <u>in</u> team meetings. A great deal of work can be out-sourced to external talent as well. See Figure 11-3, <u>Teamwork Allocation</u>, for a graphic portrayal of the normal successful team time allocation.

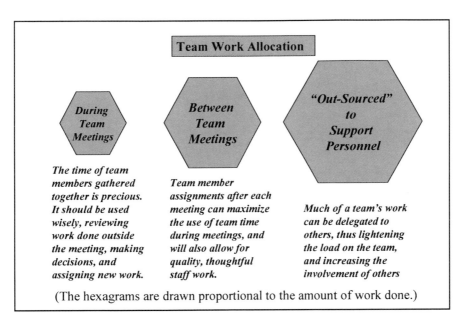

Figure 11-3, Teamwork Allocation

Pay me now or pay a lot more later. Diligently drive the work during Step 4, the Current State. It is essential that the team clearly understand <u>factually</u> both the level of performance, <u>and</u> the process, procedures, practices or approaches that currently deliver today's undesirable outcomes. Fight the tendency to accept "we all understand the way it is today, why study it?" When the team is ready to move to Step 5, the Desired State, do an Improvement Process Check by asking the team, "Are you all comfortable that you fully understand the current state? Are the ways we do things that produce the poor outcomes clear as well?"

Role-playing has a value. Use questioning and role-play methods to evoke insights, understanding and agreements from the team. For example, sequentially ask "Why? Why? and Why?" (It will be truly remarkable if you get fact-based answers by the third "why"). Indicate that "I will play the role of the person or group who will question your output. Specifically how does your team know that the recommendations will minimize the gap that you have been given to reduce?"

Clearly establish the coach's commitment to the team. Strive to be the "improvement process guru," not a problem subject-matter expert. Continually assure the team that the improvement process is working and that they are "on-track." Make it clear that the coach's success is measured by the team's success, not by well-facilitated. A good coach will not let the team fail!

Lessons Learned About Team Members

Every project, team, leader, sponsor is different: There are no "cookie cutter" courses of action for dealing with them. A coach's skills are wonderfully challenged by each situation. Consider the following oft-encountered team characters/behavior, and suggested approaches for dealing with them:

- **The quiet, silent type:** Use "bringing in" techniques. Never ask a question that can be answered "yes or no." Use these types of questions: "Jane, what is your opinion on this?" "What have been your experiences?"

- **Johnny One Note:** This is the person on the team who has a specific position in mind that is raised at every possible opportunity. It doesn't matter whether the situation warrants it or not. Try recording the person's opinion or position and visibly posting it. When the position is raised again, point to the chart.

- **Anti-process people:** "I am against form over function." Try stating "As a coach, I am for results! Sticking to this simple approach always produces results. Stay with us on this."

- **"This will take forever, I know the answer."** Even though the team is in the discovery phase of Step 4 (current-state information gathering), these persons are ready to propose a solution now. Try recording their opinion or suggestion in a visible location, and note that the team will get back to it when the team is in Step 5, the Desired State.

- **Worse late than never.** There are persons who join the team late or miss the team meetings. They will continually ask questions that can cause the team to ratchet back and revisit ground that's already been covered. Here, the coach can try to ensure that this person is briefed on the team's past accomplishments and assignments before the next team meeting. Privately indicate and remind them that they have a responsibility to take questions off-line until they have caught up with the team.

- **Guest Speakers.** Subject-matter experts should be given to understand that they are invited to the session to deliver their insights, field questions, give advice, and then leave. If they stay for the full session, they tend to become participants without the understanding the team process, past discussions, and current status. In doing so, they also can ratchet the team backwards, at best, or take the team totally off course, at worst.

- **Disrupters.** Some team members will occasionally get "out-of-sorts." Some team members will be "out-of-sorts" most of the time. Encourage the leader to call a "time out" to address this person's attitude. It is often important for the leader to hold a "shaping session" with the person off-line. Offer sympathy and understanding, if appropriate, and stress the need to "cool it" and get back to a team effort.

- **Conservatives.** Team members will often exhibit a strong reluctance to "break glass." Open or implied criticism of leadership, one's boss, one's group, or organization should be suppressed. The coach should focus the criticism on the process, procedures, practices, or approaches that are used, not on an individual or group that employs the approach. Try asking, "What was there in the approach used that caused the issue?" as opposed to "What did that manager do that caused the problem?"

The 80/20 or the Pareto rule applies to people. Twenty percent of the team members will do 80% of the work. The rest will have to be constantly asked for input and critique, and subsequently be convinced that they should "buy in" to the outcomes. The 80% cannot be ignored and yet, they cannot be allowed to pace the team's progress.

Coaching Lessons Summary

 The efficient and effective performance of cross-group teams is absolutely an essential element of a high performing organization. Leaders should focus substantial attention on the make-up of the team and the processes it will use to produce the breakthrough performance results that are so vital to the success of an organization.

A summary listing of the 24 lessons that have been gleaned during work with a broad variety of teams over the years is shown below in Figure 11-4, Team Lessons Learned.

Team Lessons Learned

The Team Process

Common team process steps
Consensus has a specific meaning
A team identity and protocols help
Clarity at the end of each meeting
An on-line scribe is a great help
The final team report starts on day one

Coaching

Accountability/responsibility
Teach by coaching
Work Apportionment
Pay now or pay a lot more later
Role playing has great value
The coach's commitment to the team

Focus

Focus, focus, focus
Actionable information is in short supply
The "Cliff notes" version
Measures, measures, measures

Meetings

More, shorter team meetings
There is no such thing as a short break
Saw-toothed progress
Set very aggressive goals

People
Every project, team, leader, recipient, and
sponsor is different. The 80/20 Pareto
rule applies to people.

Figure 11-4, Team Lessons Learned

II. Internal Sharing of Lessons Learned

Over time, every organization experiences successes and failures. Each experience offers valuable lessons that can provide great benefits to the organization. Regular sharing at group staff meetings is invaluable. Simply ensuring that there is time allocated on each staff meeting agenda for such sharing will be useful.

Sharing Forum Process

Lessons learned from the performance of major organizational projects can be of significant value to the full organization and any sister organization that may exist in an enterprise. Here, a formal Sharing Forum can prove to be very effective. A formal sharing process need not be overly bureaucratic to be effective. Rather, a simple approach for securing the open sharing of people on the firing line is desirable.

The outputs of such a process are summarized in the following six statements:

- The results that were achieved, and the processes/procedures that produced them.
- Insights re the issues that were encountered, the counter-measures that were brought to bear and their effect on the issue.
- Recommendations for future avoidance, and for additional or changed practices that should be adopted as standards.
- Dispassionately displayed facts and reasoned opinions.
- Proposed new, more effective organization processes.
- The growth of people through learning.

The intent of the Sharing Forum is to gather all of the organization employees who would benefit from listening to a project's successes and failures onto a suitable site. The structure, meeting flow, and a typical agenda of a successful forum follow:

Structure.

1. The presenters are the members of the project team and selected key participants.
2. The audience is made up of key players in the firm who are most likely to benefit from hearing the sharing of experiences and advice of a completed project's team members.
3. A select review panel is constituted. It should consist of two or three respected senior representatives of key groups or functions within the organization, and one or two external experienced participants. These panelists are expected to:
   - Listen.
   - Ask questions of clarification.
   - Probe for root causes.
   - Ultimately, formulate observations and recommendations to the organization leaders, and the audience.
4. The division leader attends, introduces the meeting, and sums up findings at the end.
5. A scribe is appointed to record key findings and action items. The session may be videotaped for further dissemination throughout an organization.
6. Throughout, there is no finger pointing and no "witch hunts."

The Flow of a Successful Sharing Meeting

A typical agenda is shown in Figure 11-5, <u>A Sample Sharing Forum Agenda</u>.

<u>Sample Sharing Forum Agenda</u>

8:00 -8:30	Introductions/expectations/meeting process
8:30-10:00	Project description, history, and chronology • Processes followed • Practices used
10:00-10:15	Break
10:15-12:00	Key successes shared: what, how, impact • Recommendations • Q and A
12:00 -1:00	Lunch
1:00 -4:00	Key opportunities shared • What happened, when, where, how, who? • Causal Analysis techniques and findings • Counter measures adopted and impacts • Suggestions and recommendations • Q and A
4:00-4:45	Panel observations and recommendations
4:45 -5:00	Leadership observations/meeting evaluation and wrap-up

---

<u>Figure 11-5, A Sample Sharing Forum Agenda</u>

Presentation Topics.

The following topics are presented to the panel and audience during a forum:

1. Project description. A summary of the challenge that was assigned to the team.
2. The team leader introduces the team members, gives a summary of each person's background and experience. The team structure, processes, and practices followed are shared.
3. Chronology/cycle times/schedules are shared.
4. Key successes. Outcomes that the team is pleased with or proud of, including possibly results achieved and the processes utilized are discussed.
5. Key opportunity areas. Things the team would do differently are shared:
    - Description/scenarios.
    - Causes, root causes, and methods used to determine them.
    - Countermeasures adopted and their effectiveness.
    - Process change recommendations for future avoidance.
6. Major lessons learned and recommendations to colleagues.

Panel Questioning.

Some suggestions for the panel questioning of the team are:
- Introduce the panel members, and indicate the panel's intentions. Take pains to assure the team that we are trying to learn so we can change the processes or pressures that caused issues. We are not trying to affix blame! We are trying to fix the process.
- Ask questions in a non-intimidating fashion. (E.g., "What was the process used that caused...?" vs. " Why did you...?")
- Try to balance criticisms with commendations.
- Ask questions of clarification during the session. Keep questions clear and brief. "Why?" followed by another "Why?" are terrific questions that help drill to the root causes.
- Avoid giving opinions until the final feedback. Be prepared to summarize panel conclusions and process change recommendations. Write notes as the forum proceeds. It will keep the panel from getting absorbed in the detail, and the audience will know that the panel is interested. Keep feedback brief and on the subject of improvement.

Some typical questions that can be posed to the team members by the panel are:

- Was the necessary talent or resources assigned to the effort? If no, why not? When did you realize this? What corrective actions were entertained? Why weren't they effective?
- When did you first know that there was a major project problem or obstacle? Did you proceed anyway? Why? What were the forces that pushed you to do so?
- If you could have anticipated the difficulty coming, what preventative countermeasures would have been effective?
- Once seeing the obstacles or issues, what were the team's possible options? Which did the team adopt? Why were other options discounted?
- What new, different, or additional processes or procedures should be standardized in order to avoid a repeat of the specific issues or shortcomings in the future?

To conclude this section, the formal and informal sharing of positive and negative lessons learned pays big dividends to the organization.

III. External Benchmark Learning

Benchmarking is probably the most underutilized beneficial business tool available to leaders. The basic reason for this oversight is attributed to a lack of benchmark understanding and experience. Like many other leadership tools, creeping elegance has made benchmarking very complex when simplicity will suffice. This section presents an easy-to-use overview of an effective benchmarking approach.

There are six simple steps which, when followed, will produce useful benchmarking enlightenment:

Step 1. What specifically is to be benchmarked? For example: Where do we need a break-through? Where will continuous improvement not be enough?

Step 2. Describe the current relevant process, procedure, or approach that is used today. What exactly is it that we do that delivers the current undesirable level of performance?

Step 3. Locate comparative entities for study. E.g. Who produces similar types of outputs and is reputed to do it better? Check the Internet. Check local business schools for suggested benchmarking targets.

Step 4. Plan the interview by detailing the information-collection approach.

- Determine and record the questions that will be asked of the benchmark.
- List the additional questions that initial answers may prompt.

Step 5. Compare the current-state to the benchmark state.
- How does our performance compare? What are the process steps we use?
- What are the process steps that the model organization used to achieve its results?

Step 6. Determine the desired state and propose the changes.
- What of the benchmark's process elements can/should be transplanted to our organization?
- Where must additional improvements be initiated?
- Share benchmark work, get buy-in, and develop a change action plan.

See Figure 11- 6, <u>Benchmarking Steps</u>, for a graphic summary.

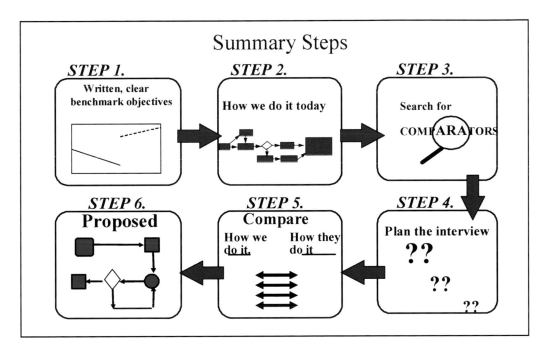

Figure 11-6, Benchmarking Steps

Summary words of advice relative to benchmarking follow:

- **Practice, practice, and practice. With practice, benchmarking can become second nature.**
- **The first one to try it learns and teaches others.**
  The amount of information and the value of the information available through carefully orchestrated benchmarking are truly awesome.

IV. Personal One-on-One Coaching

The Success Tree® tools and approaches are very flexible and can be readily adapted to any situation. To demonstrate this, an informative example is presented below. Here, the Success Tree® assessment approach is applied to personal one-on-one coaching. Specifically these steps were utilized when asked to coach a leader to who wanted to achieve world class performance:

1. Select a measure...*develop execute a personal assessment survey.*
2. Determine the current state...circulate *the survey to those who are in a position to judge the individual.*
3. Identify the gap... *compare the results of the survey to a perfect score.*
4. Select priority improvement areas... *the statements with the most improvement write-ins.*
5. Prepare for action...*write job tickets for the top two most important areas.*
6. Execute and repeat.

A personal assessment form, a summary of the results, and the set up for two job tickets are provided in Figure 11-7, <u>An Assessment of Jon Sample</u>, and Figure 11-8, <u>Assessment Scoring and Action.</u> Careful perusal will provide the reader with many important insights.

Figure 11-7, An Assessment of Jon Sample

Figure 11-8, <u>Assessment Scoring and Action</u>, shows the summary results of Jon Sample's survey with an indication of the work that needs to be done in the form of Job Ticket assignment statements. All signals indicate a need for work on verbal communications skills, especially brevity, and on developing new business for the firm.

**_The Assessment Results Indicate that Jon Sample_
has two areas to concentrate on for improvement**

Problem Solving

⊙ **1.1 He is considered to be
an efficient problem solver**

Job Ticket Project: Develop and gain approval of a plan, which when executed with excellence will cause Jon 's colleagues to judge that he is an efficient problem solver.

Communications

⊙ **2.5 He gives clear and specific
directions to subordinates**

Job Ticket Project: Develop and gain approval of a plan, which when executed with excellence will cause his colleagues to judge that Jon Sample gives clear and specific directions to subordinates.

Figure 11-8, Assessment Scoring and Action

With this information in hand, the "student" and the mentor/coach can come to agreement on the specific actions that will be taken to "close the gap" and create positive momentum toward successful processes for delivering concise verbal speech, and for developing business for the Firm. Again, the steps of the Breakthrough Process™ as detailed in Chapter 8 will be followed religiously.

V. A StopLight Report™ Example

The StopLight Report has not only proven to be successful in keeping leadership fully apprised of the status on "Vital Few" efforts, but it has become a clear measure of the major progress that teams can make for an organization. To demonstrate this, StopLight Report forms are presented for consideration. The first, shown in Figure 11-9, <u>Start Point Team StopLight Form</u>, is a blank form that represents the start of the team efforts. The second is Figure 11-10, <u>12 Months of StopLight Progress</u>. This shows the status after one year of team efforts. The last is Figure 11-11, <u>18 Months of StopLight Progress</u>.

Even the most skeptical of individuals will find this to be an impressive performance.

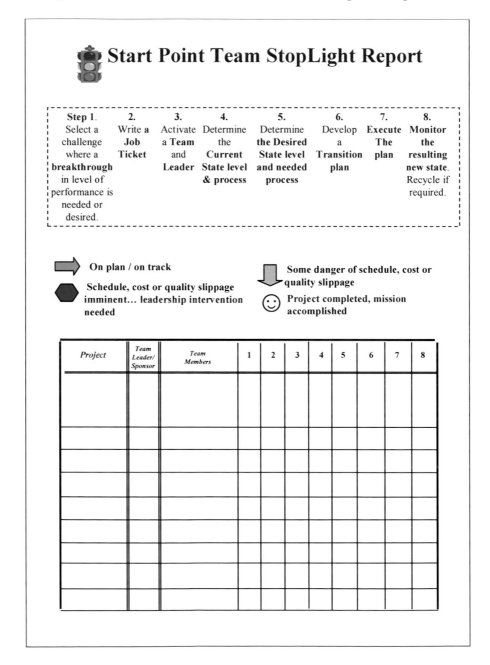

Figure 11-9, Start Point Team StopLight Form

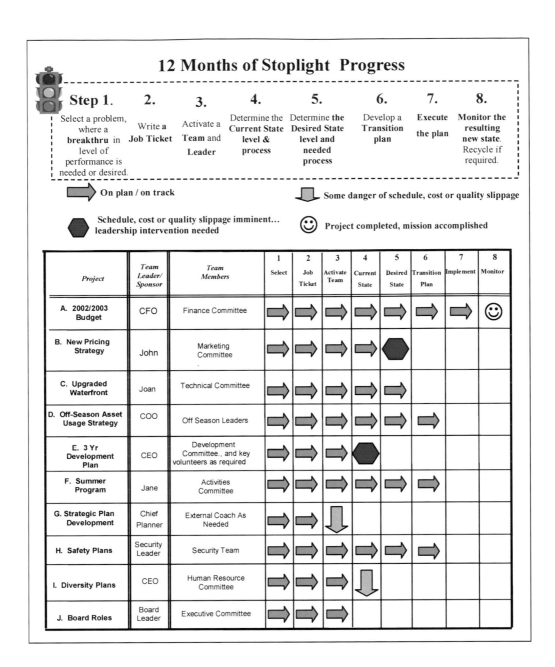

Figure 11-10, 12 Months of StopLight Progress

The reader will note several important facets of the work reported in this StopLight report:

1. As indicated by the 10 projects and the assigned leaders and teams, the organization has been able to resource the projects by deploying the work to different groups.
2. As indicated by the left-to-right arrows, the steps of the Breakthrough Process™ are being followed in a much disciplined manner.
3. The two down arrows indicate that two teams are encountering some difficulties, but none that they feel that they can't handle.
4. The octagons indicate that two teams are stymied and need leadership intervention.
5. Finally, the smiley face indicates that one project have been brought to successful conclusion and have achieved the challenges outlined in their job tickets.

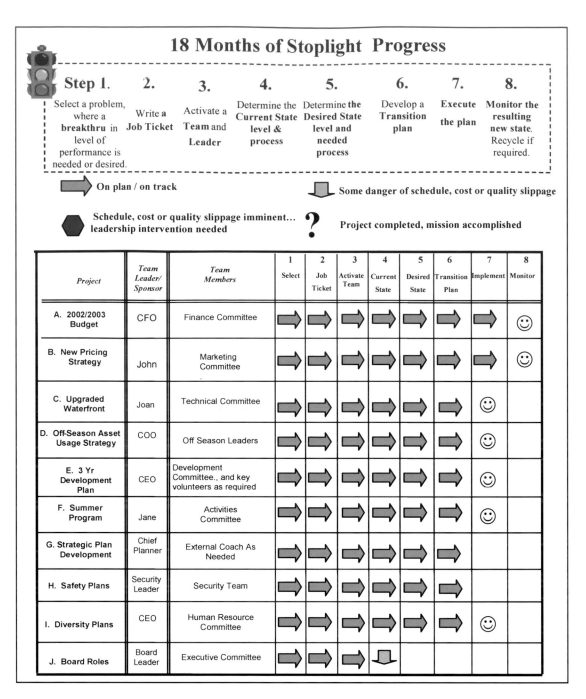

18 Months of Stoplight Progress

Step 1. Select a problem, where a **breakthru** in level of performance is needed or desired.

2. Write a Job Ticket

3. Activate a Team and Leader

4. Determine the Current State level & process

5. Determine the Desired State level and needed process

6. Develop a Transition plan

7. Execute the plan

8. Monitor the resulting new state. Recycle if required.

➡ On plan / on track

⬇ Some danger of schedule, cost or quality slippage

⬡ Schedule, cost or quality slippage imminent... leadership intervention needed

? Project completed, mission accomplished

Project	Team Leader/ Sponsor	Team Members	1 Select	2 Job Ticket	3 Activate Team	4 Current State	5 Desired State	6 Transition Plan	7 Implement	8 Monitor
A. 2002/2003 Budget	CFO	Finance Committee	➡	➡	➡	➡	➡	➡	➡	☺
B. New Pricing Strategy	John	Marketing Committee	➡	➡	➡	➡	➡	➡	➡	☺
C. Upgraded Waterfront	Joan	Technical Committee	➡	➡	➡	➡	➡	➡	☺	
D. Off-Season Asset Usage Strategy	COO	Off Season Leaders	➡	➡	➡	➡	➡	➡	☺	
E. 3 Yr Development Plan	CEO	Development Committee., and key volunteers as required	➡	➡	➡	➡	➡	➡	☺	
F. Summer Program	Jane	Activities Committee	➡	➡	➡	➡	➡	➡	☺	
G. Strategic Plan Development	Chief Planner	External Coach As Needed	➡	➡	➡	➡	➡	➡		
H. Safety Plans	Security Leader	Security Team	➡	➡	➡	➡	➡	➡		
I. Diversity Plans	CEO	Human Resource Committee	➡	➡	➡	➡	➡	➡	☺	
J. Board Roles	Board Leader	Executive Committee	➡	➡	➡	⬇				

Figure 11-11, 18 Months of StopLight Progress

The smiley faces connote the progress of several marvelous team effort reported in this StopLight report:

1. As indicated by the right pointing arrows, the steps of the Breakthrough Process™ are still being followed in a much disciplined manner.
2. The one down arrow indicates that only one team is encountering some difficulties, but none that they feel that they can't handle.
3. The red octagons are gone, indicating that there are no stymied teams after the requested intervention of leadership six months ago.
4. Finally, the smiley faces indicate that seven projects have been brought to successful conclusion and have achieved the challenges outlined in their job tickets.

It is hoped that this real world example serves as an inspiration to the readers and that a belief that similar success awaits the adoption of the Success Tree® system.

VI. Words of Wisdom

The words of several successful leaders and teachers conclude this chapter. In each case, the contents represent words of wisdom and lessons of value that can inspire and guide current and prospective leaders who aspire to world class performance.

The Wisdom of Dr. Noriaki Kano

Dr. Kano, a consultant and a professor at Tokyo University was hired in the 1980's to coach Xerox executives. His observations and wisdom about business were always worth pondering. Some of his most provocative personal counsel is summarized here:

1. There are two types of change motivation:

   • The first is change that is induced by crisis. With <u>good</u> leaders, this kind of change can be accomplished with some ease. It will allow the organization to survive and thrive again. Imminent demise provides enough incentive for all in an organization to cooperate. This type of change is relatively easy.

   • The second type of change is that which is prompted by significant opportunity. This type of change takes <u>great</u> leadership to accomplish. Even so, it will be met with resistance since the current success will cause the organization to want to adhere to the current state.

2. Change must be championed by a senior executive committed to the desired change. Significant change cannot come from the bottom up.

3. The barriers between functions in an organization are substantial. Cross-functional teams are an effective way to surmount the obstructions. However, teamwork does not come naturally to organizations, so team process and coaching are mandatory.

4. Only a small percentage of training dollars spent actually produce change. The rest of the "resistance system" snuffs out the training.

5. U.S. entities are strong in strategic planning, but they are exceptionally weak in the implementation of strategies. In particular, Americans tend not to fully grasp that it takes time and focus to realize bold dreams.

6. "You chase too many rabbits." By this, Dr. Kano meant that we fail to set priorities and fail to focus on the "vital few." Note the revealing quote below from a former Kodak CEO. It came in 1997 after Kodak had suffered three sluggish quarters in a row. The company had experienced a nine-month loss of $300 Million in digital imaging alone, and had suffered significant management departures. It had to layoff 10,000 people. After all this, the CEO captured the root cause of his difficulties with this simple quote:

   "The big mistake we at Kodak have made is that we've tried to do it all. I think what we're finding is that opportunities are just too many, too diverse, that we just can't afford it all."

8. Americans operate on opinions and apparently have little time or temperament for gathering facts.

9. You don't take the time to reflect on lessons learned. How foolish.

10. Success can make one "fat." As such, competitive cats know that a fat cat is easy to catch.

Each of these ten gems has great meaning to a leader committed to high performance.

The Words of Fredrich F. Reichheld, in his 1996 book, *The Loyalty Effect.*
Reichheld point out these important facts:
- "U.S. companies now lose half their employees every four years, half their customers in five years and half their investors in less than twelve months."
- "Companies create value by understanding that they can only retain loyal customers with a base of loyal employees."
- "By decreasing the defection rates of customers, employees, and investors, companies can achieve prodigious growth."
- "Our accounting systems fail to measure the value of loyal customers, employees, and stockholders."

The use of the Success Tree® System approach (see Chapter 1, The Success Tree® System Overview) to manage an organization prevents these losses and frees leaders to grow the enterprise.

Market Research of U.S. National Quality Award Winners. In the opinion of these award-winning business leaders, the following are the skills that are needed in the new millennium:
- Interpersonal skills.
- Team process and team member effectiveness.
- Listening to the voice of the customer.
- Cross-functional teamwork.
- Customer-supplier relationships.
- Team-building skills.
- Process understanding.
- Meeting dynamics.

Note that each of these needed skills can be enhanced by putting into practice elements that are covered in the chapters of this book

Jack Welch, former CEO of General Electric stated in a 1997 article in *USA Today,* that to be a leader at G.E. a person has to:

- Have a passion for excellence.
- Hate bureaucracy.
- Be open to ideas from anywhere.
- Live quality...and drive cost and speed for competitive advantage.
- Have the self-confidence to involve everyone.
- Behave in a boundaryless fashion.
- Create a clear, simple, reality-based vision.
- Have enormous energy and an ability to energize others.
- Stretch...set aggressive goals...reward progress...yet understand accountability and commitment.
- See change as an opportunity, not a threat.

In fact, the elements of the Success Tree® System address each of the G.E. CEO's beliefs.
Note especially the items covering the need for a clear vision in Chapter 3, The Three-Year Vision, and the need to see change as an opportunity in Chapter 10, The Change Model.

Chapter Conclusions

The objectives of this chapter have been addressed:

Review some key pitfalls that may be encountered on the journey to high performance and share useful preventative actions or effective countermeasures.

Examine a real world personal assessment that demonstrates the flexibility of the system.

Encourage the reader with a real life StopLight report that exhibits major progress in "closing the gap."

It is hoped that the material presented encouraged the reader to put the full system into practice.

> **"There is just not enough time to make all the mistakes ourselves.**
> **We have to learn from others."**   Humor from Harriet Hall

Chapter 11. Lessons Learned

Do The **Right** Things ... Right!

It Is That Simple!

Chapter 12
High Performance Assessment

Chapter Objectives:

To share with the reader a one-page High Performance Management assessment tool that covers all the elements required for success.

To help the reader self-assess or have others assess their organization.

With the assessment results in hand, guide the selection of areas for immediate attack through the use of the materials found in the chapters of this book.

© 2003 The Strategic Triangle Inc.

Chapter 12. The High Performance Assessment™

Do The <u>Right</u> Things ... Right!

It <u>Is</u> That Simple!

Chapter 12

The High Performance Assessment™

"The critical steps for a leader on a world class journey are to embrace a measure of greatness, to determine the current state, and then to select the priority areas for improvement that will most efficiently close the gap to greatness ."

R.C. Palermo

Using the juggler metaphor first put forward in the introduction to this guide book, the right way to address the constant trials and tribulations of a leader in any active organization is simply to determine the "<u>right</u> things to do," and then "do them <u>right</u>."

To accomplish this, a simple and yet effective one-page assessment vehicle has been developed. It has been applied successfully over the past ten years in a wide variety of organizations by their leaders. All seven critical elements of the Success Tree® System are itemized and summarized on a one-page questionnaire that follows. The assessment elements are as follows:

1. **A set of Guiding Values.** This set describes the behavior that is expected of all employees as they conduct the work of the organization.
2. **A Directive Mission.** This describes (1) what the organization does or provides (2) who are served or benefit from the organization's work and (3) how the services are provided.
3. **A Prescriptive Vision.** This outlines specifically where the organization expects to be, or needs to be, three years from now. It also covers how the organization wants to be perceived by those it serves, by its employees, and by financial judges at that future time.
4. **Customer Satisfaction Measures.** These customer-provided measures describe: (1) the level of satisfaction, (2) areas that the organization should be proud of and (3) the key drivers that should be best worked to move toward the ideal level of performance.

5. **Employee Motivation Measures.** These employee-provided measures describe (1) the level of current employee motivation, (2) the employee elements that the organization should be most proud of, and (3), the key drivers that should be worked to move employee motivation toward the ideal state.

6. **Financial Performance Measures.** These measures: (1) provide the one or two most important key measures of financial success for the organization, (2) define both the current and the desired or needed levels for each measure, and (3) isolate the key, prioritized financial drivers that most effectively will close the gap to improve performance.

7. **An Effective Improvement Process.** This is a system that is commonly used to address organizational challenges and opportunities. It provides the means for: (1) documenting challenges, (2) delineating management expectations and requirements, (3) recognizing change resistance issues, (4) producing identified solutions, and (5) serving as a road map for the step- by-step management of projects that will produce excellence in execution.

The Assessment Approach

Using the form in Figure 12-1, The High Performance Assessment™, an individual or team assessors provide the requested demographic information at the top of the assessment form.

Each assessment statement is then read carefully. A respondent's judgment about the importance of each element is provided by checking off one of the following choices after each statement:

❑ **Vital**   ❑ **Important**   ❑ **Some**   ❑ **No Value**

Then the respondent indicates his or her assessment of the current state of each of the seven elements by checking off one of the following choices:

❑ **In Place**   ❑ **So-So**   ❑ **None**

The Success Tree® System
Finding the Right things...

Name: _____ Organization: _____

Responsibility/Area _____ Title _____

e-mail _____ Date: _____ Feedback Desired? Yes _____ No _____

	Importance to me:	Vital	Important	Some	No Value
1. A set of shared values. This set describes the behavior that is expected of all our people as they conduct the work of the organization.	Importance to me:	O	O	O	O
	Our Current State:	In Place O	So-So O	None O	

	Importance to me:	Vital	Important	Some	No Value
2. A Directive Mission. This describes what the organization does or provides; who are served or benefit from the organizations work; and how the services provided and the skills applied are acquired and delivered.	Importance to me:	O	O	O	O
	Our Current State:	In Place O	So-So O	None O	

	Importance to me:	Vital	Important	Some	No Value
3. A Vision. This outlines specifically where the organization expects to be, or needs to be three years from now, and how it wants to be perceived by those it serves, its employees and financial judges at that time.	Importance to me:	O	O	O	O
	Our Current State:	In Place O	So-So O	None O	

	Importance to me:	Vital	Important	Some	No Value
4. Customer Satisfaction Measures. These measures describe:(1) the level of satisfaction (2) the areas that the organization should be proud of, (3) The key drivers that should be best worked to move toward the specified desired level of perfection.	Importance to me:	O	O	O	O
	Our Current State:	In Place O	So-So O	None O	

	Importance to me:	Vital	Important	Some	No Value
5. Employee Motivation Measures. These measures describe: (1) the level of current staff motivation (2) the elements that the organization should be proud of (3) the key drivers that should be worked to improve employee motivation.	Importance to me:	O	O	O	O
	Our Current State:	In Place O	So-So O	None O	

	Importance to me:	Vital	Important	Some	No Value
6. Financial Performance Measures. These measures describe: (1) the important few key measures of financial success for the organization (2) the current & desired or needed levels for each measure (3) the key, prioritized drivers that can close the gap to improve performance.	Importance to me:	O	O	O	O
	Our Current State:	In Place O	So-So O	None O	

	Importance to me:	Vital	Important	Some	No Value
7. An Effective Improvement System. This system is used to address problems and opportunities. It provides: (1) the documented challenges (2) delineated management expectations and requirements (3) recognized change resistance issues with solutions (4) a road map for the step by-step monitoring of projects to ensure excellence in execution.	Importance to me:	O	O	O	O
	Our Current State:	In Place O	So-So O	None O	

Figure 12-1, The High Performance Assessment™

The evaluation of the interpretation of the assessment results is quite simple and is shown in Figure 12-2, The High Performance Assessment™ Evaluation.

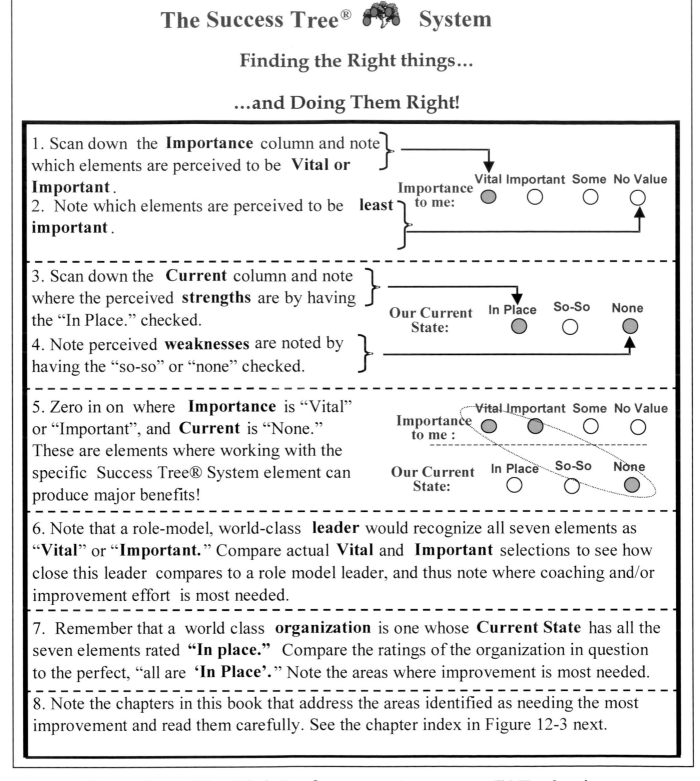

The Success Tree® System

Finding the Right things...

...and Doing Them Right!

1. Scan down the **Importance** column and note which elements are perceived to be **Vital or Important**.
2. Note which elements are perceived to be **least important**.

3. Scan down the **Current** column and note where the perceived **strengths** are by having the "In Place." checked.

4. Note perceived **weaknesses** are noted by having the "so-so" or "none" checked.

5. Zero in on where **Importance** is "Vital" or "Important", and **Current** is "None." These are elements where working with the specific Success Tree® System element can produce major benefits!

6. Note that a role-model, world-class **leader** would recognize all seven elements as **"Vital"** or **"Important."** Compare actual **Vital** and **Important** selections to see how close this leader compares to a role model leader, and thus note where coaching and/or improvement effort is most needed.

7. Remember that a world class **organization** is one whose **Current State** has all the seven elements rated **"In place."** Compare the ratings of the organization in question to the perfect, "all are **'In Place'.**" Note the areas where improvement is most needed.

8. Note the chapters in this book that address the areas identified as needing the most improvement and read them carefully. See the chapter index in Figure 12-3 next.

Figure 12-2, The High Performance Assessment™ Evaluation

The correlation of the elements of the High performance Management Assessment™ to the chapters of this book is shown in Figure 12-3, <u>Assessment Help</u>.

The Success Tree® System
Finding the Right things...

Name: _____ Organization: _____
Responsibility/Area_____ Title _____
e-mail _____ Date: _____ Feedback Desired? Yes ____ No ____

1. A set of shared values. This set describes the behavior that is expected of all our people as they conduct the work of the organization.	**See Chapter 4, Organizational Shared Values, for help**
2. A Directive Mission. This describes what the organization does or provides; who are served or benefit from the organization's work; and how the services provided and the skills applied are acquired and delivered.	**See Chapter 2, The Directive Mission, for help**
3. A Vision. This outlines specifically where the organization expects to be, or needs to be three years from now, and how it wants to be perceived by those it serves, its employees and financial judges at that time.	**See Chapter 3, The Three-Year Vision, for help**
4. Customer Satisfaction Measures. These measures describe: (1) the level of satisfaction (2) the areas that the organization should be proud of, (3) The key drivers that should be best worked to move toward the specified desired level of perfection.	**See Chapter 5, Customer Satisfaction, for help**
5. Employee Motivation Measures. These measures describe: (1) the level of current staff motivation (2) the elements that the organization should be proud of (3) the key drivers that should be worked to improve employee motivation.	**See Chapter 6, Employee Motivation, for help**
6. Financial Performance Measures. These measures describe: (1) the important few key measures of financial success for the organization (2) the current & desired or needed levels for each measure (3) the key, prioritized, drivers that can close the gap to improve performance.	**See Chapter 7, The Financial Performance Branch, for help**
7. An Effective Improvement System. This system is used to address problems and opportunities. It provides: (1) the documented challenges (2) delineated management expectations and requirements (3) recognized change resistance issues with solutions (4) a road map for the step-by-step monitoring of projects to ensure excellence in execution.	**See Chapter 8, The Breakthrough Process™, for help**

Figure 12-3, Assessment Help.

Throughout each of the chapters in this guide book, the focus has been on the organization and the leaders that guide it. As a "bonus," a personal assessment form is provided in the Figure 12-4, <u>A Personal Assessment</u>. The message is that this assessment and <u>all</u> of the Success Tree® System elements can and have been applied to an individual, by the individual or with the help of a coach. It works for a person in a non-profit group, a private firm, or a public company. In 10 years of coaching, I have yet to find an organization or individual where it cannot be magnificently effective. It's worth a personal try.

The Personal Success Tree® System
Finding the Right things…

Name: _____ Date: _____

1. My set of personal values. This describes the behavior that I should be exhibiting as I go through each day..

	Vital	Important	Some	No Value
Importance to me :	○	○	○	○

	In Place	So-So	None
My Current State:	○	○	○

2. My Directive Mission. This describes what I do or want to do; who are served or benefit from my efforts; and how I go about getting it done, and how needed skills are acquired.

	Vital	Important	Some	No Value
Importance to me :	○	○	○	○

	In Place	So-So	None
Our Current State:	○	○	○

3. A Vision. This outlines specifically where I want or expect to be, or need to be three years from now, and how I want to be perceived by those I serve or interact with at that time.

	Vital	Important	Some	No Value
Importance to me:	○	○	○	○

	In Place	So-So	None
Our Current State;	○	○	○

4. "Customer" Satisfaction Measures. These measures describe: (1) the level of satisfaction (2) the areas that the I should be proud of (3) the key drivers that should be best worked to move toward my specified desired level of perfection in serving others.

	Vital	Important	Some	No Value
Importance to me:	○	○	○	○

	In Place	So-So	None
Our Current State:	○	○	○

5. Personal Motivation Measures. These measures describe: (1) the level of my current motivation (2) the elements that the I should be proud of (3) the key drivers that should be worked to improve my own motivation.

	Vital	Important	Some	No Value
Importance to me:	○	○	○	○

	In Place	So-So	None
Our Current State:	○	○	○

6. Financial Performance Measures. These measures Describe: (1) the important few key measures of my financial success or comfort (2) the current desired or needed levels for each measure (3) The key prioritized drivers that best close the gap to improve my financial situation.

	Vital	Important	Some	No Value
Importance to me:	○	○	○	○

	In Place	So-So	None
Our Current State:	○	○	○

7. An Effective Improvement System. I have a system used to address my problems and opportunities. It covers: (1) the key challenges that I face (2) my expectations or needs (3) the recognized change resistance that will likely get in my way as I continually work to improve (4) a road map for the step-by-step plan to ensure that I move toward defined goals

	Vital	Important	Some	No Value
Importance to me:	○	○	○	○

	In Place	So-So	None
Our Current State:	○	○	○

Figure 12-4, A Personal Assessment

Chapter Conclusions

At this point, the objectives of this chapter have been addressed:

Share with the reader a High performance Management Assessment™ that covers all elements that are required for success.

Allow the reader to self-assess or have others assess their organization.

With the assessment results in hand, facilitate the selection of areas for immediate attack using the materials in this book.

The assessment material presented can be effectively used to gain an understanding of the current-state of the organization as judged by an individual or group. By focusing on the elements that are judged to be important or vital by the assessor and at the same time, are judged to need work, the organization can move toward world-class performance in the most efficient and effective manner.

"It's really this simple. Find out both what's truly important and that needs work. Then fix it and go back for the next challenge."
R.C. Palermo

Final Comment

Best wishes on your journey to the level of world class leadership of organizations that serve delighted customers with motivated employees and thereby generate healthy financial performance for investors. Can there be anything sweeter?
R.C. Palermo

Chapter 12. The High Performance Assessment™

Do The **R<u>igh</u>t** Things ... Right!

It <u>Is</u> That Simple!

Appendix A
The Gem Collection

Appendix Objectives:

To share with the reader the gems that are shown throughout this guide book.

To encourage the reader to periodically select a gem or a set of gems and ponder them.

© 2003 The Strategic Triangle, Inc.

Do The <u>Right</u> Things ... Right!

It <u>Is</u> That Simple!

This appendix is a type of executive summary of the key points and messages contained in this guidebook. Throughout the guidebook, there are quotes and gemstones highlighting an earned piece of wisdom that is worth pondering and internalizing. Periodically returning to this section and reviewing the chapter by chapter gems that have been mined from the guide book will pay big dividends

Introduction Gems

If you are comfortable being a manager who does not have an effective, defined high performance management system in place, and you are satisfied with the status quo, put this guide down, but keep it handy. When unacceptable performance surfaces and it inevitably will, you will hopefully come to realize that you and your organization need such a system.

All within an organization, and all constituencies served by the organization, will benefit from the application of a system that ensures that <u>everyone</u> in the organization can comfortably and regularly select the "right things to do" and then "do them right."

The three constituencies (customers, employees, financials) are as the legs of a three-legged stool. If you are standing on it, and the three legs are supporting you, which leg is the most important? If one is damaged, do you not have to fix it? Do you not ensure that the other two are not damaged by your fix? No! All are <u>equally</u> vital to the success of an operation!

Ultimately, "doing the right things" must include checking an organization's overall performance by measuring it against agreed standards that define "world-classness." This must be accomplished by utilizing an easy-to-use "organizational report card" that assesses the state of the organization and identifies areas that are most in need of improvement. This must include an assessment of customer, employee and financial performance. With this assessment in hand, selected "vital few" issue areas can be isolated for outstanding performance improvement.

"Anyone can manage with a bag of gold. It takes a good leader to manage with limited resources. Remember that <u>doing the wrong things right is as bad as doing the right things wrong</u>." History shows, over and over again, that without leaders who employ and deploy a system for "finding the right things and then doing them right," the long term future–and even survival–of any organization is continually in jeopardy.

Over time, an organization that is managed in a haphazard way will find itself in an organizational death spiral characterized by:

- Customers who are not delighted go elsewhere and readily share their negative perceptions and experiences with all who will listen.
- Sooner or later, financial results suffer greatly.
- Then, employees lose heart as they have to endure compensation constraints and or downsizing. The most talented employees seek and find more satisfying work environments elsewhere.

Think of an organization that you believe delights its customers, has motivated employees, and that has very healthy financial returns. What is the name of that organization? – Notice how few readily come to mind. – Did you name your own organization? – Why not? If you adopt, execute, and internalize the Success Tree® System, it will be <u>your</u> organization that is so honored, by you, your employees, your customers, your alliance partners, and the marketplace.

Further, given the pressures that leaders are under today, a leadership system also has to be capable of dynamic adoption (changing the wheel on a moving car comes to mind). It must be easy-to-monitor, readily deployable throughout an organization, and one that will require only low on-going maintenance. The Success Tree® System is exactly such a system!

The rewards for developing and exhibiting good juggling skills are more balls to juggle. As an individual moves up the career ladder, heavier and bigger balls are added to the challenge.

- It seems that few, if any, balls are ever taken away. Eventually, even the best jugglers drop a ball or two. When a major ball is fumbled, the juggler reaches for it, and thus drops a few more.
- When this stage is reached, the leader goes from directing to reacting and from initiating to merely coping. Serenity, security, and the comfort of a job well-done become distant memories. A good day is a day that is merely survived.

A salient and underlying feature of the system is its simplicity. This enables the elements of the system to be understood, adopted and executed with remarkable speed. It is especially rewarding to note that many of the time-pressed leaders who had been exposed to the Success Tree® System elements in prior companies, have continued to apply the Success® System approach when they moved on to new, very different companies with new, very different challenges. This is an especially rewarding testimonial to the flexibility and value of the system.

With this simple system in place, control will be regained and retained, allowing a leader to appropriately serve customers, motivate employees, and achieve needed financial performance, all in a most efficient and effective manner! This, after all, can be the only true definition of success no matter what the endeavor!

Chapter 1. The Success Tree® System Overview Gems

The gap-closing concept basically involves these steps:

Step 1.   Factually determine the current state (as things are today), both the measured level of results, and the processes that delivers them.

Step 2.   Determine the desired state levels (how we want or need things to be) including the processes that will be needed to put in place to deliver the desired state.

Step 3. Assess which drivers makes up this gap between the current and desired states.

Step 4. Determine which of the many gap drivers are best attacked first.

Step 5. Judge how much of the gap closed.

Step 6. Repeat until satisfied with the amount of gap closed, and go on to the next gap.

There is a profound and unique benefit that is gleaned from the Success Tree® System. We know of no other approach other than the Success Tree® System that actually displays the strategic foundation (mission/vision/values), the goals, key drivers and selected "vital few" needed actions, on a single sheet of 8 ½ X 11 inch sheet of paper. This feature facilitates important communication and deployment throughout an organization.

A Directive Mission gives specific guidance and sets organizational boundaries by delineating:

<u>What</u> the organization produces or provides.

<u>For Whom</u> the goods and/or services are provided.

<u>How</u> the goods or services are acquired or developed and delivered by the organizations.

<u>Why</u> the "business" of the organization is fundamentally conducted.

For simple logical reasons, a three-year time frame for the Prescriptive Vision is favored. Major advances and breakthrough improvements cannot generally be achieved in less than three years. Focused leadership for more than three years has proven to be quite unlikely. In fact, promotions, changes and turnover of key players combine to make sustained very long term efforts impossible.

The years 2000-2002 have given us painful examples of unethical and even illegal behavior by once-respected leaders of major organizations. It is not enough to agree on, and profess adherence to organizational values. It is <u>essential</u> to constantly assess the levels of actual conformance in practice. "Trust but verify" is the right thinking.

What leaders really should want to know about Customer Satisfaction are the answers to these simple questions:

- What percent of the people we serve are delighted as characterized by such measures as: "Would willingly recommend the organization to others?"
- Of those who respond in the negative, we need to know what the prioritized reasons are for dissatisfaction. In essence we need to know, "If the organization could just improve one or two things, what would the customers recommend? In your opinion what should we be working on?"
- Finally, we need to know what the things these customers perceive to be that the organization is doing very well? We can publicize and brag about these.

What the leaders really should want to know about employee motivation is simply the answers to these questions:

- What per cent of the employees are positively motivated, as characterized by such measures as: "Would you willingly recommend working for the organization to qualified others?"
- Of those who respond in the negative, we need to know what the prioritized reasons for their reticence to recommend are. "If the organization could improve one or two things, what would you recommend they be?"
- Finally, we need to know what the exceptional people-related things that the organization is doing are. "What are the things our people say that we should be touting?"

Answers to the following simple questions are all that are needed to cull out key drivers from the trivial many and get down to critical financial gap-closing actions:

Step 1.   What are the <u>one or two</u> key, overall, all encompassing measures of the financial contribution of a group, or the performance of an organization? (E.g. Is it earnings per share, profit, market share, cost, revenue, donations, <u>etc?</u>)

Step 2.   For each of the one or two such selected measures, what are the current levels and processes? Where are we now and how is it we get here?) and what are the desired levels and processes? What is it that defines financial success and what processes are needed to get us there?

Step 3.   What are the four to six key drivers which if improved, will have the greatest impact on the gaps between the desired financial performance and the current levels of performance for the selected measures?

Step 4.   If the organization were to attack one or two of these drivers first, which ones should they be? Where should we best apply out resources to positively impact our financial performance?

Step 5.   Finally, we can also answer these questions: What are the key areas of positive financial performance that the organization should be most proud of?" What is it that we should be touting and using for rewards and recognition of employees?

The Job Ticket is basically a communications vehicle and an enabler that defines clearly, and in sufficient detail, the specific requirements and expectations that leadership places on a vital task assigned to an accountable team leader and team. With a job ticket in place, can the team be fully empowered with confidence to carry out the task, but they can do so with a sense of comfort that their efforts and outputs will gain rightful respect from those who are to judge the quality of the team's work.

It is always wise to pause and reflect on both successes <u>and</u> failures to extract the maximum in increased knowledge from each experience. Informal sharing of experiences combined with periodic, structured, formal sharing sessions can be a major asset for the organization. Basically we seek to understand what the results were, and what the processes were that produced these results. Experience has shown that a true personal and organizational commitment to learning and a formal lessons learned sharing process can yield remarkable benefits. Even so, the evidence of actual well-structured, organized sharing in practice is sparse indeed.

A world class leader knows that <u>all</u> <u>eight</u> system elements are important. A world class organization has <u>all</u> <u>eight</u> systems in place and operational. Think about it. Rate yourself and your organization. If you disagree that all eight are vital to the success of an organization, try to rationalize why anyone of them (the Directive Mission, a Prescriptive Vision, a set of Organizational Shared Values, or the fact-based advice of customers, employees and/or financial advisors) are not important to have in place. It cannot be done rationally. Leaders must commit to having each Success Tree® System element at an operational state and at a high level of performance.

Finally, I am absolutely convinced that adoption of all eight elements of the Success Tree® System, followed by diligent, continuously improved operational execution, will produce exceptional advances in all facets of an organization's performance. This will prove to be rewarding for all your constituencies, and intriguing to analysts, assessors, academics, and pundits.

As the system is embraced, a calm serenity falls over the leadership. Control of one's organizational destiny is a bonus that no doubt will prove to be personally rewarding to the leaders involved.

"Bottom line, each of you current and aspiring "jugglers," will be able to efficiently and effectively find the right things, and then do them right, thereby achieving the ultimate in efficiency and effectiveness in carrying out the mission and achieving the vision of an organization."
R.C. Palermo

Chapter 2. The Directive Mission Gems

The <u>Directive Mission Statement</u> describes <u>what</u> is done or provided...<u>who</u> is served, taught, treated, or supplied...<u>how</u> it all gets done...and <u>why</u> it is done. Its intent is to communicate a clear understanding of the "business" of the organization in order to give some guidance as daily and long term decisions are made. It enables great questions be asked, such as: "Is this decision consistent with our directive mission?"

The <u>Prescriptive Vision Statement</u> is the description of the organization's <u>destination</u>. It depicts how we want the organization to be perceived, positioned, performing, and described three or more years from now. It gives guidance as questions are asked, such as: "Does this decision move us positively toward our Prescriptive Vision?"

Some managers state that there isn't time for a mission session or that the world is too fast moving and dynamic to stop and try to formulate a detailed mission. Real world experiences dispute this. Even in the most contentious situations, leadership consensus can be reached on a Directive Mission in four hours or less. Surely the benefits of having the leadership team come to a common understanding of why an organization exists and the benefits of having the entire workforce share the same understanding is worth four hours or less!

The value of offering <u>fewer</u> products or services that meet or exceed customer-defined requirements, far exceeds the value of offering a broad or full line of products or services having mediocre or poor quality and/or questionable reliability in order to claim a "full product line." Bottom line:

Do only what you will do well!

Whether some leaders like it or not, every person in an organization will be called upon to make organization-related decisions almost every day. It is not enough to hope that they make the "right" decisions that are best for the organization. It is true that leaders sometimes go to extraordinary means to restrict a worker's power to act independently, and that "empowerment" is then just a catch phrase. It is also true that such dictatorial organizations develop and seem to succeed...at least for a while. An underlying reason for this control behavior is a belief that people cannot be trusted to make the "right" decisions. Experience shows us that there is much unused and unchallenged brainpower in all organizations. What a shame! If and when this talent is unleashed by enlightened leadership, the results are truly astounding.

Chapter 3. The Prescriptive Vision Gems

This is a good point to address some common questions about the vision time frame. "Why three years?" "Why not five years?" "Why not one year?" Simply put, one year is too short to investigate, plan, and execute initiatives that are intended to produce breakthrough results. Five years is often too long for people to retain focus and momentum. Further, the rapid pace of the competitive world may not tolerate a five year period between plans. Finally, people can lose interest and intensity after just a few months on a project. Leadership support can wane. Thus, longer term plans often fail to come to fruition. Experience has shown, and logic supports a three-year vision horizon.

Vision statements are often misunderstood. They are sometimes confused with mission statements. A vision statement is profoundly different from a mission statement. Think of it in this way: the mission describes an organization's <u>mode</u> of transportation, while the vision describes its <u>destination</u>. Both are equally important to "finding the <u>right</u> things."

For whichever reasoning led to it, the "a specific vision is not needed" position is unsupported by insights gleaned from customer, employee and financial surveys. These insights are supported by discussions with selected constituencies of a variety of organizations. All these constituencies consistently express a <u>strong</u> desire to understand the intended destination of an organization in which they have a vested interest. The numbers of organizations that have crashed because they failed to have developed and/or articulated and disseminated a longer-term destination are legion. Failure to develop and drive a game plan that is consistently supportive of a stated vision is often fatal.

Does this mean that once the journey starts that you can't change the destination? No, of course not. A vision is never carved in stone! In fact, it should be revisited at least annually to see if an update or course correction is needed. All that has to be done is to take the time to re-examine the vision, gain consensus on any needed changes, share the new vision with constituencies, and then redirect resources as may be appropriate to the updated vision. Your customers, alliance partners, suppliers, and financial backers have a vital interest in any substantive vision change.

A distinction must be made between a motivational sound bite that is intended to be used for inspiration and to shape public sentiment, and that of a Prescriptive Vision that gives specific guidance to the organization's citizens as they journey forward as a unit. The vision needs to be clear and explicit and should unambiguously describe the intended destiny of the organization.

This is a good point to address some common questions about the vision time frame. "Why three years?" "Why not five years?" "Why not one year?" Simply put, one year is too short to investigate, plan, and execute initiatives that are intended to produce breakthrough results. Five years is often too long for people to retain focus and momentum. Further, the rapid pace of the competitive world may not tolerate a five year period between plans. Finally, people can lose interest and intensity after just a few months on a project. Leadership support can wane. Thus, longer term plans often fail to come to fruition. Experience has shown, and logic supports a three-year vision horizon.

Vision statements are often misunderstood. They are sometimes confused with mission statements. A vision statement is profoundly different from a mission statement. Think of it in this way: the mission describes an organization's <u>mode</u> of transportation, while the vision describes its <u>destination</u>. Both are equally important to "finding the <u>right</u> things."

For whichever reasoning led to it, the "a specific vision is not needed" position is unsupported by insights gleaned from customer, employee and financial surveys. These insights are supported by discussions with selected constituencies of a variety of organizations. All these constituencies consistently express a <u>strong</u> desire to understand the intended destination of an organization in which they have a vested interest. The numbers of organizations that have crashed because they failed to have developed and/or articulated and disseminated a longer-term destination are legion. Failure to develop and drive a game plan that is consistently supportive of a stated vision is often fatal.

Does this mean that once the journey starts that you can't change the destination? No, of course not. A vision is never carved in stone! In fact, it should be revisited at least annually to see if an update or course correction is needed. All that has to be done is to take the time to re-examine the vision, gain consensus on any needed changes, share the new vision with constituencies, and then redirect resources as may be appropriate to the updated vision. Your customers, alliance partners, suppliers, and financial backers have a vital interest in any substantive vision change.

A distinction must be made between a motivational sound bite that is intended to be used for inspiration and to shape public sentiment, and that of a Prescriptive Vision that gives specific guidance to the organization's citizens as they journey forward as a unit. The vision needs to be clear and explicit and should unambiguously describe the intended destiny of the organization.

Chapter 4. Guiding Values Gems

Thoughtfully developed and carefully communicated values can provide a true guiding light that enables the employees of an organization to actually behave in much the same way as the founders or leaders expect. This is not to say that having and communicating values is sufficient. Unless the leaders "role model" the values through their every day behavior and decision-making, published values are worthless. Unless the leaders also monitor to ensure that all leaders and employees are actually putting these values into practice, the values can too easily be ignored or forgotten.

An organization must continually reinforce its values. It is wise to regularly survey employees to see if they perceive that the organization's values are being put into practice by their co-workers, managers and leaders. Customers can also be queried to see if the organization is perceived to be modeling published values. Without these assessment actions, the leaders are either behaving as if the values are merely words on paper or are operating on faith that the values will be embraced. Both are dangerous paths. It is interesting to note that the challenge: "Don't act like that!" has little meaning if expectations of behavior are not well understood in an organization.

Finally, I believe that an organization's values should be limited to eight or less in number. Committees who work to produce a set of values tend to reach consensus by including everyone's desired value in the organizational set. This can lead to sets containing 10 to 20 or more values. The more values there are, the more devalued is the currency of each one.

"It is not enough to say that the organization has shared values. It is not enough to write them down and communicate them. The leaders need to role model behaviors that are consistent with the organization's values every single day? R.C. Palermo.

Chapter 5. Customer Satisfaction Gems

The basic premise, supported by numerous examples and experiences and consistent with the words of the late Dr. Deming, is that customer obsession is the most appropriate principle for a world class leader. Customer obsession is defined here as accepting no less than <u>delighted</u> customers as the ultimate desired state, and then continuously driving toward that goal with a single-minded passion.

What customer obsessed leaders really should want to know are the simple answers to these three customer questions:

1. What percent of those people who are served are delighted? E.g., "Would willingly recommend the organization to others?"
2. If the serving organization could improve one or two things, which would the customers recommend? E.g. "If you're going to fix something, fix these."
3. Finally, "What are the things that the organization is perceived to be doing exceptionally well?"

When leaders listen to customers, they often don't really <u>hear</u> the words of the customer. Rather, they consciously or unconsciously "translate" customer words (which are often quite clear and even brutal) to "organization speak." "It's awful" becomes "There are still some challenges." The lesson: Do not translate customer words! Listen and react to the actual <u>words</u> of the customer.

What leaders really should want to know from customers is simply conveyed by the answers to four questions:

- What per cent of those served are delighted (e.g., would willingly recommend the organization to qualified others)?
- Of those who respond in the negative, what are the prioritized reasons for dissatisfaction?
- If the organization could improve one or two things, what would the customers recommend as a change priority?
- Finally, what are the things that the customers perceive that the others do very well today?

Chapter 6. Employee Motivation Gems

The fundamental performance of any organization will dramatically improve if the management team puts honest effort and heart into ensuring that employee-related issues are identified, prioritized, and sequentially attacked. Improved employee motivation has to begin at the top. Any lower level initiative can either suffer from neglect or quickly be snuffed out by unsupportive management.

Typical research study outputs sorely disappoint action-oriented leaders who really want to know if the organization is doing a good job in the eyes of its employees. It will frustrate leaders who want to understand the largest, most frequently encountered issues that its employees want addressed. The usual outcomes of common employee research are:

- High cost
- Lots of pages
- Lots of tables and graphs
- Little actionable information
- Cynicism from the employees
- Low ultimate return on investment.
- Frustrated Leaders

What leaders really should want to know from employees is simply portrayed by the answers to four questions:

1. What percent of those who serve are delighted (e.g., would willingly recommend the organization to qualified others?).
2. Of those who respond in the negative, what are the prioritized reasons for dissatisfaction?
3. If the organization could improve one or two things, which would the employees recommend?
4. Finally, what are the things that the employees perceive are done very well?

Chapter 7. Financial Performance Gems

The financial bottom line of every organization will improve if the management team puts both effort and heart into ensuring that <u>prioritized</u> financially related issues and opportunities are identified, shared throughout the organization and sequentially attacked with a passion. This is as opposed to the shotgun approach of trying to influence or act on all elements of a financial picture.

This "Important Multitude" approach is just plain foolish. No one has the resources to adequately address all the financial issues, challenges, or opportunities that an organization faces. Communicating them and exhorting staffs to manage all of them or worse criticizing and berating staff because of a failure to improve the "important multitude" won't cut it over the long run. Using a focused, sequential attack on a selected "vital few" is a powerful, effective approach to increased financial performance results.

Some leaders question the desirability of having 100% of their employees informed about the financial <u>key</u> drivers of their organization. They lack confidence that making each person aware of the numbers, will lead to dramatic financial improvement of their organization or group. One leader encountered was proud to state that he uses the "Orange Theory of Financial Management." That is, "You just keep squeezing your employees, suppliers, and customers. It's the way to get the most juice," in his words. It is sad to note that the "Orange Theory" did not keep his firm from Chapter 11.

Simply put, organizations adopting this squeezing approach can not hope to compete with organizations that have fully engaged all of their employee assets in an attack on the financial "vital few."

Chapter 8. The Breakthrough Process™ Gems

The Breakthrough Process is a simple, logical, proven, versatile, and effective approach to working challenges and resolving issues that have been highlighted in any organization. The process is readily applied to the selected "right things" that have been derived from the organization's mission, vision, values, customer words, employee words, and/or the selected financial drivers. It lets accountable individuals and teams attack assigned issues and challenges with confidence that the challenges are vital to the success of the organization. It also allows leaders to effortlessly track progress and thereby rest assured that efforts are being expended on aligned, priority challenges. This, in essence, is "doing the right things…right."

The deployment and assignment of priority issues and opportunities to individuals or teams by an organization's leadership are the critical starting points in breakthrough performance. The resources and talent of any organization are not infinite. They must be carefully deployed to the selected "Vital Few" challenges that are most meaningful to the success of the organization.

Well-structured teams are the way functional barriers that exist in a large organization can be overcome. The terms "functional foxholes" or "organizational silos" have been coined to describe this common change resistance phenomenon. The proper staffing and the clear working process of a team are vital to bashing the change barriers and producing measurable breakthrough results. The quality of the leader and the team members as well as the process that they follow will dictate the quantity and quality of the output as well as the speed of results production.

The term "Consensus" is used throughout this text and is defined as "I agree to <u>support</u> the decision of the team, even though I may not agree that the selected option is best. I do so because my views were listened to and were given fair consideration." This is really an important difference from the more usual "majority rules" (which also means that the minority loses and gets to pout) or "unanimous agreement" (which almost never happens). Consensus has proven to be a major positive element in attaining support for a decision.

Chapter 9. The Organizational Report Card™ Gems

There is sometimes an attempt to "rig" the assessment system to get a good score on the Organizational Report Card™. It is easy to discern when this is happening. It is a sure bet that rigging is being attempted when:

- During finalization of the contents of the report card, statements in the initial draft that are perceived to probe a weakness of an organization are argued for deletion or modification.
- Certain segments or groups in an organization may be excluded from doing the assessing because "their morale is poor" or "they have a bad attitude."
- Results of the resulting priority write-in areas for improvement are rationalized, "spun" and thus discarded or demoted to non-vital status. When this happens, it is a clear sign that the leaders have no intent to truly pursue world-class performance, and that the report card use as an instrument of positive change should be discontinued.

"Customers deserve world class treatment. Employees thrive on it. Leaders are energized by it. Stakeholders and supporters are rewarded by it. Time on this earth is too short to waste it on a mediocre journey."
R.C. Palermo

Analyses of failed change initiatives are always instructive. Such analyses have led to the use of a *fishbone* or *Ishikawa* cause-and-effect chart as the basis for a powerful model that allows a leader to understand resistance, anticipate the reasons for change failure, and to then develop the means to neutralize or circumvent the change resistance.

When a discontinuous or breakthrough change is desired as opposed to an evolutionary, gradual one, the change is almost always contested by in-place resistant elements of an organizational "system." All work vigorously and in harmony to maintain the status quo.

A dedicated and driven Transition Manager is not to be confused with a change champion. The change champion's role rightfully belongs to an organization's leader. Day-to-day management of the development and implementation of the many elemental change strategies that will be necessary to convert the resisters to enablers requires the appointment of an impassioned change agent: the Transition Manager. In small organizations, the leader can handle both roles.

These changes were not evolutionary but rather bold and discontinuous. It is also interesting to note that these were "opportunity-driven" as opposed to "crisis-driven" changes. It is clear and logical to expect that change is much easier when an organization is facing acknowledged disaster than when the organization is in a strong position. It is a great tribute to the leadership skills of Jack Welch that he promoted change and made it happen when his organization was riding a crest of success.

Chapter 11. Lessons Learned Gems

Experience has shown that an organizational commitment to continuous learning through the use of a formal organizational sharing process can yield remarkable benefits. Unfortunately, the use of well-structured sharing of experiences in organizations is rare indeed. This is especially true when the experience in question is negative. These valuable lessons, good and bad, have been fully paid for. Periodic, structured sharing events have proven to be a major asset in high-performing organizations. In fact, formal, structured sharing, combined with informal person-to-person sharing, represents an ideal combination.

The term "Consensus" has a specific meaning in this system. Seek team agreement on this specific definition of "consensus." Consensus is achieved when the even most strident dissenter will state: "I don't believe that this is the optimum approach but, because the team listened to my views and gave them suitable and fair consideration, I agree to support the team's position. I will not have to say it was my preferred position, but I will also not bad-mouth it."

The use of a PC with a spread sheet projected on a screen during the decision process has proven to be a wonderful aide to an expedited, quality decision. Using this tool, any of the ratings or weightings can be changed to see if, and how they affect the results. The team can apply this decision process to prioritize a list of key drivers. It is so powerful that I share an example in this section of the book. Using this tool, a team can not only vote and examine the outcomes, but can also examine the reasons for the outcomes. In this way, a solid consensus is often readily achieved.

The 80/20 or the Pareto rule applies to people. Twenty percent of the team members will do 80% of the work. The rest will have to be constantly asked for input and critique, and subsequently be convinced that they should "buy in" to the outcomes. The 80% cannot be ignored and yet, they cannot be allowed to pace the team's progress.

The efficient and effective performance of cross-group teams is absolutely an essential element of a high performing organization. Leaders should focus substantial attention on the make-up of the team and the processes it will use to produce the breakthrough performance results that are so vital to the success of an organization.

Summary words of advice relative to benchmarking follow:
- Practice, practice, and practice. With practice, benchmarking can become second nature.
- The first one to try it learns and teaches others.
The amount of information and the value of the information available through carefully orchestrated benchmarking are truly awesome.

Chapter 12. High Performance Assessment™ Gem

Throughout each of the chapters in this guide book, the focus has been on the organization and the leaders that guide it. As a "bonus," a personal assessment form is provided in the Figure 12-4, <u>Personal Assessment</u>. The message is that this assessment and <u>all</u> of the Success Tree® System elements can and have been applied to an individual, by the individual or with the help of a coach. It works for a person in a non-profit group, a private firm, or a public company. In 10 years of coaching, I have yet to find an organization or individual where it cannot be magnificently effective. It's worth a personal try.

Do The **Right** Things ... Right!

It Is That Simple!

Appendix B
A List of Exhibits

Appendix Objectives:

To provide easy reader access to the exhibits in this guide book.

© 2003 The Strategic Triangle, Inc.

Appendix B.   A Listing of Exhibits

Appendix B. Listing of Exhibits

Chapter 1. The Success Tree®

Chapter 2. The Directive Mission

Chapter 3. Vision

Chapter 4. Values

Chapter 5. Customer Satisfaction

Chapter 6. Employee Motivation

Chapter 7. Financial Performance

Continued on next page

Appendix B. Listing of Exhibits